SECONDARY SCHOOL CURRICULUM

SECONDARY SCHOOL CURRICULUM

Edited by

S.R. VASHIST

ANMOL PUBLICATIONS PVT. LTD.
NEW DELHI - 110 002 (INDIA)

ANMOL PUBLICATIONS PVT. LTD.
4374/4B, Ansari Road, Daryaganj
New Delhi - 110 002
Ph.: 23261597, 23278000
Visit us at: www.anmolpublications.com

Secondary School Curriculum

ISBN 81-7041-757-0

PRINTED IN INDIA

Published by J.L. Kumar for Anmol Publications Pvt. Ltd., New Delhi - 110 002 and Printed at Mehra Offset Press, Delhi.

Preface

The programme for curriculum making begins with a survey of educational needs. This survey leads, by way of observation, analysis, and interpretation of life to the discovery of educational values. When these values are integrated with subject matter and pupil activities, they form the basis for educational objectives. Each subject of programme of studies must be developed upon this pattern. Obviously, then, present day curriculum planning must be limited by the incomplete results of present-day observation, analysis, and interpretation of life and by available subject.

Editor

Contents

1

Introduction

When curriculum development is considered a means which the school should employ to discharge more effiectively its fundamental social responsibilities, a different source of orientation is required than has generally been made the basis for changes in the curriculum. There are four important influences which have conditioned the development of the curriculum. They are the influence of logically organized subject matter, secondly the influence of the textbook, thirdly the influence of organized minority groups and fourthly the influence of quantitative standards.

The theory of curriculum development is woven around these four themes and in this volume, the theory of curriculum development has been discussed on these mainlines.

2

Curriculum Development

The primitive secondary school. Imagine, if you will, a glorious day and all members of the tribe gaily advancing in groups to the soft grass of the open plain, and you will see primitive adolescents tripping their way to their secondary school. For the school of these primitive boys —girls are often given equally formal training for their duties—begins by tribal marching, dancing, and singing. The women take the boys to their place of acceptance by the men. When the open plain is reached the dancing begins—the women arrayed in line begin their dance forward and backward with the boys, while the men in a line facing the women dance in and out of the openings in the women's line. In and out, back and forth, sally the two lines until at the last advance the women fall to the ground and are carefully concealed, while the boys are frisked away by the men amid the shrieks of bull-roarers. No longer need the boys dance with their sisters and their mothers : with the onset of puberty, nature has marked the members of their bold sex for deeds of valor, for exploits too strenuous for women, for schemes too daring and subtle for their timid, heavy-headed sisters. If these boys succeed in their educational tasks, they will thereby be intiated into the life of stalwart sex and may thereafter have quarters in the men's house.

Prior to this ceremony of recognized manhood, the boy *s* have already received certain elementary training. They have learned from their fathers and mothers, and from each other, according to the tribal arts of life, how to swim, how to make certain rude implements, how to make fire, how to hunt, how to fish, how to hurl weapons, how to weave, or how to make pottery. While that elementary training was in progress for the boys, their sisters received such fundamental preparation as fitted the feminine sex in the particular tribe ; this training might include, as among the girls of the Homeric Age, carding, spinning, weaving, embroidering, and bread-making, or, among other peoples, the girls' training might include pottery, flaking stones for implements and weapons, stripping bark for clothing and other, purposes beadwork, and cookery.

Before the boys may fully share life with the male adults of their tribe and live in the men's house, it is fitting that certain civic and vocational training be added to the incidental elementary schooling which they have already received. This subsequent training is often referred to as a series of initiatory rites, because it marks the end of childhood and abiding with children and women and the beginning of manhood and living with men. These rites are of varying duration, according to the wealth of tribal lore. Soon after the picturesque opening of adolescent training, the boys are, in many tribes, assigned individually to the old men of the tribe, who instruct them thoroughly in tribal knowledge, superstition, charms, the ways of the gods, the rites and duties pertaining thereto ; the ways of men, the customs, regulations, and other civic arrangements : the secrets of animism, including much that women could never know—and remain in a proper state of subjection ; and the standards and ideals of men of the past and the present in both peace and war.

Although much of the boy's training is undertaken to enforce group solidarity rather than to present a formal body of subject matter, no modern student of Latin has a more formal task than those lessons of the primitive boy: no modern teacher undertakes with greater earnestness the solemn duty of making citizens than does the ancient elder who accepts his zealous lad ; no modern school plant provides a more auspicious setting for serious mental activity than that within which the youth of young tribes is set to work. In short, the primitive youth is trained as is the youth of other levels according to the culture of his tribe in from four to seven branches of the curriculum. These branches we should call by the following terms : literature, mathematics, science, social studies, religion, fine and applied arts, and physical education. The content of each of these branches of training will be described in subsequent paragraphs. The descriptions of this content are based upon source materials and as far as possible give illustrations of content actually used or still in use by primitive peoples. Had the records of ancient primitive peoples been available, such records would, of course, have been utillized.

What primitive boys study

1. *Literature*. All tribes possess traditions or folklore. The quality and variety of these literary elements vary with the tribal plane of culture. A review of thousands of pages of this folklore convinces one that much of it will never develop and branch into the fulness of a beautiful tree. Many specimens excel Boccaccio in frankness, a few of them even approach his gift for story-telling, while thousands of them reek with the primitive filth from which they spring. The samples which follow indicate a few of the poetic fights and something of the commonplace which one finds among the collected lore of primitive man. Many other similar samples can be found in the school readers of our own day.

The tale of the Maiden who was sacrificed by her kin, and whom her lover brought back from below

Told by Na-Ga-Tu-U, Mother of one of the Herds of the Chief N'Du-I-Ni.

The sun was very hot and there was no rain, so the crops died, and hunger was great ; and this happened one year, and again it happened a second, and yet a third year the rain failed ; so the people all gathered together on the great open space on the hill-top, where they were wont to dance, and said each to the other, "Why does the rain delay in coming ?" And they went to the Medicine-Man, and they said to him, "Tell us why there is no rain, for our crops have died, and we shall die of hunger ?" And he took his gourd and poured out the lot, and this he did many times ; and at last he said, "There is a maiden here who must be bought if rain is to fall, and the maided is Wanjiru. The day after tomorrow let all of you return to this place, and every one of you from the eldest to the youngest bring with you a goat for the purchase of the maiden."

So the day after the morrow, old men and young men all gathered together, and each brought in his hand a goat. Now they all stood in a circle, and the relations of Wanjiru stood together, and she herself stood in the middle ; and as they stood the feet of Wanjiru began to sink into the ground; and she sank to her knees and cried aloud, "I am lost," and her father and mother also cried and said, "We are lost" ; but those who looked on pressed close, and placed goats in the keeping of Wanjiru's father and mother. And Wanjiru went lower to her waist, and she cried aloud, "I am lost, but much rain will come" ; and she sank to her breast : but the rain did not come, and she said again. "Much rain will come" ; then she sank to her neck, and the rain came in great drops, and her people would have rushed forward to save her, but those who stood around pressed into their hands more goats, and they desisted.

So she said, "My people have undone me," and sank to her eyes, and as one after another of her family stepped forward to save her, one of the crowd would give to him or her a goat, and he fell back. And Wanjiru cried aloud for the last time, "I am undone, and my own people have done this thing." And she vanished from sight, and the earth closed over her, and the rain poured down, not, as you sometimes see it, in showers, but in a great deluge, and every one hastened to their own homes.

Now there was a young warrior who loved Wanjiru, and he lamented continually, saying, "Wanjiru is lost, and her own people have done this thing." And he said, "Where has Wanjiru gone ? I will go to the same place." So he took his shield, and put in his sword and spear. And he wandered over the country day and night ; and at last, as the dusk fell, he came to the spot where Wanjiru had vanished, and he stood where she had stood, and, as he stood, his feet began to sink as hers had sunk; and he sank lower and lower till the ground closed over him, and he went by a long road under the earth as Wanjiru had gone, and at length he saw the maiden. But, Indeed, he pitied her sorely, for her state was miserable, and her raiment had perished. He said to her, "You were sacrificed to bring the rain ; now the raln has come, I wlll take you back." So he took her on his back like a child, and brought her to the road he had traversed, and they rose together to the open air, and their feet stood once more on the ground, and he said, "You shall not return to the house of your people, for they have treated you shamefully." And he bade her wait till nightfall ; and when it was dark he took her to the house of his mother, and he asked his mother to leave, and said he had business, and he allowed no one to enter. But his mother said, "Why do you hide this thing from me, seeing I am your mother who bore you?" So he suffered his mother, but he said, "Tell no one that Wanjiru is returned."

So she abode in the house of his mother ; and then she and his mother slew goats, and Wanjiru ate the fat and grew strong ; and of the skins they made garments for her, so that she was attired most beautifully.

It came to pass that the next day there was a great dance, and her lover went with the throng ; but his mother and the girl waited till every one had assembled at the dance, and all the road was empty, and they came out of house and mingled with the crowd; and the relations saw Wanjiru, and said, "Surely that is Wanjiru whom we had lost" ; and they pressed to greet her, but her lover beat them off, for he said, "You sold Wanjiru shamefully." And she returned to his mother's house. But on the fourth day her family again came, and the warrior repented, for he said, "Surely they are her father and her mother and her brothers." So he paid them the purchase price. and he wedded Wanjiru who had been lost.

STORIES FROM BORNEO

We'll Make it Tomorrow

One wet night Kra, the monkey, and Raong, the toad, sat under a log complaining of the cold. "Kr-r-r-h," went Kra, and "Hoot-toot-toot" went the toad. They agreed that next day they would cut down a *kumut* tree and make themselves a coat of its bark. In the morning the sun shone bright and warm, and Kra gambolled in the tree-tops, while Raong climbed on the log and basked in the sunlight. Presently down comes Kra and sings out, "Hello, mate ! How are you getting on ?" "Oh ! nicely," says Raong. "Well, how about that coat we were going to make ?" says Kra. "Oh ! bother the coat," says Raong. "We'll make it tomorrow ; I'm jolly warm now." So they enjoyed the sunshine all day long. But, when night fell, it began to rain again, and again they sat under the log complaining of the cold. "Kr-r-r-h," went Kra, and "Hoot-toot-toot" went Raong. And again they agreed that they must cut down the *kumut* tree and make themselves a coat of its bark. But in the morning the sun was shining again warm and bright ; and again Kra gambolled in the tree tops and Raong sat basking in the sunshine ; and again Raong said, "Oh ! bother the coat, we'll make it tomorrow." And every day it was the same, and so to this day Kra and Raong sit out in the rain complaining of the cold, and crying "Kr-r-r-h" and "Hoot-toot-toot."

STUPID SALEH

One day Saleh and his father set out in their boat for their farm, "Look out for logs" (*i.e.*, floating timber), said Saleh's father. They had not gone very far when Saleh sings out, "I see some timber." "Where ?" says his father. "Why, there on the bank," says Saleh, pointing to the jungle. "Oh ! you silly," says his father, "go on." So they went on and landed, and the father. leaving Saleh to cook some rich in the large pot, began to cut down some trees. Presently he came back and found Saleh with the pot upside down over the fire, and nothing cooked. "What are you at ?" cries the father. "Well," says Saleh, "I put the pot over the fire as you told me to do, but when I poured the water on it, it all ran into the fire and put it out." "You stupid boy, you should have put the pot on the other way up." "But you didn't tell me so," says Saleh.

The father had chipped his axe, so he sends Saleh home to fetch another. Saleh sets out gaily singing, the blade of the axe lying in the bow of the boat. Soon the boat strikes a snag and overboard goes the axe-blade. "Oh, bother !" says Saleh, "but never mind, I'll mark the place," and he whips out his knife and cuts a notch in the gunwale of the boat at the spot where the axe fell in. Arriving at the landing stage before his father's house. he begins to dive into the water to find the lost axe-head, and continues vainly seeking it till his mother comes out to ask what he is doing. "I'm looking for the axe that fell into water just at this notch, as I was coming down river," says Saleh. "Oh ! you are a stupid," says his mother, and fetches him a new axe. Saleh goes back to his father, who has found a fruit tree. He tells Saleh to gather the fruit in his basket while he goes on felling trees. Presently the father comes back and finds Saleh fastened with his back to the tree by the shoulder-basket, which he has put right round its stem, and his legs going up and down. "Hello ! what are you up to now ?" says the father. "Why, I'm carrying away the whole tree to save trouble," says Saleh, "and I'm watching the clouds up there to see how fast I'm walking with this tree on my back."

2. *Mathematics.* Among primitive as among cultured peoples, the conditions of life—physical and economic—determine largely the curricular activities. The following descriptions portray a highly complicated system (that of the Borloki) and a very simple system (that found at Alice Springs, Australia). As the Borloki of Congo are keen traders, the boys of the tribe must know the first cost of the articles which they sell, the time spent in hawking them, and the payment and keep of those who help to paddle the trader from place to place in search of a buyer. For this mercantile activity, the boys are thoroughly trained in an elaborate system of counting, which Weeks describes as follows :

> The numerals from 1 to 5 are declinable. The letter in brackets is the particle that changes according to the class of the noun used, *e.g.*, two persons would be *batu* (*ba*) *bale* = persons two, but two cloths would be *bilamba* (*bi*) *bale* = cloths two.
>
> The numerals are :
>
> 1, (*y*) awi ; 2, (*i*) bale ; 3, (*i*) atu ; 4, (*i*) ne ; 5, (*i*) tanu ; 6, motoba ; 7, nsambu ; 8, mwambi ; 9, libwa ; 10, jumu or mokangu mwawi = one tying ; 11, jumu na (*y*) awi ; 12, jumu na (*i*) bale ; 20, mikangu mibale ; 30, mikangu miatu ; 40, mikangu mine ; 50, mikangu mitanu ; 60, mikangu motoba ; 70, mikangu nsambu ; 80, mikangu nwambi ; 90, mikangu libwa ; 100, nkama or munkama ; 200, minkama mibale ; 1000, nkutu yawi ; 2000, nkutu ibale ; 10,000, mokoko ; 20.000, mikoko mibale.

The meaning of *mikangu mibale* (20) is, two tyings, 10 is often called *mokangu mwawi* = one tying, fiom *kanga* = to tie. It is the custom of the natives to roll their 15-inch brass rods (the currency) into a series of rings about 1½ inches in diameter, and these they run one on another, like split rings, until there are ten linked together, and they call that *mokangu mwawi*=one tying=10. The ordinal numerals are :

Motu wa bo=The person who is first, or the first person.				
,, *bane*	,,	four	,,	fourth ,,
,, *motoba*	,,	six	,,	sixth ,,
,, *libwa*	,,	nine	,,	ninth ,,
,, *mikangu mibale na wawi*=twenty-first person.				

To use a word of another class we will take *elamba*= cloth.

Elamba ya bo=the cloth that is one, or the first cloth				
,, *bine*	,,	four,		fourth ,,
,, *motoba*	,,	six	,,	sixth ,,
Elamba ya mikangu miatu na bibale=the cloth that is thirty and two, or the 32nd cloth.				

The fingers are constantly used in counting. If a man wants to say thirty-four he will say *mikangu* (=tying=tens) and hold up three fingers for those to whom he is speaking to say *miatu* (=three), *na*=and, hold up four fingers for them to say (*i*) *ne* (=four). The letter in brackets changes according to the class of the noun understood. By this means they ensure their hearers following and understanding them, and no one can afterwards plead that they did not hear the price properly, as any discrepancy between the number mentioned by the hearers and the number of fingers held up would be corrected at the time.

The way in which the Boloki folk use their fingers is somewhat irregular, and for the sake of clearness I draw two hands and number the fingers 1 to 10—1 to 5 left hand, and 6 to 10 right hand. 1 and 10 are the thumbs. The right hand is used more than the left.

One is expressed by doubling 6, 7, 8 and putting 10 over them, thus leaving 9, the index finger, standing alone.

Two, by doubling down 6 and 7 and putting 10 over them, thus leaving 8 and 9 standing.

Three, by doubling down 9 and putting 10 over it, leaving 6, 7, and 8 standing.

Four, by putting 10 at the bottom of the division between 7 and 8, that causes 6 and 7 to come forward a little, so the hand is turned about so that the two sets of two fingers may be clearly seen.

Five, the whole of the fingers of the right hand are left standing with the palm turned towards the person to whom you are speaking.

Six, by doubling down 2 on the left hand and putting 1 over it, so leaving 3, 4, and 5 standing, and doubling down 9 on the right hand and putting 10 over it, so leaving 6, 7, and 8 standing, thus making two sets of three fingers.

Seven, the same as 4 with the right hand and doubling down 2 on the left hand and putting 1 over it, thus making a 4 and a 3.

Eight, by working the right hand as under 4 and putting 1 at the bottom of the division between 3 and 4, and twisting the hands about so that the four sets of two fingers may be clearly seen.

Nine, by holding up the fingers of the right hand as under 5 and putting 1 at the division between 3 and 4, and twisting the left hand about to show the two sets of two fingers.

Ten, by holding all the fingers of the two hands with the palms towards the auditors, and every folding down of the fingers and re-spreading of them means another 10. *Second way* - by clapping the hands together, and every clap stands for 10. *Third*, and more frequent method—by holding out the first of the right hand, and every decided shake of the fist stands for ten.

Eleven, by shaking the right fist and holding up one finger as described under one.

Twelve, by shaking the right fist and holding up two fingers as described under two ; and so on.

The toes are very rarely used in counting. I have only seen them used when counting 20,000, and then the man stretched down and put the fingers of both hands on the toes of both of his feet and said : *mikoko mibale*=20,000. Sometimes, when trying to give me an idea of vast numbers, they would say : "It will take all our fingers and toes to tell you," *i.e*,, tens of thousands.

For addition and subtraction under 10 they use their fingers, but for higher numbers they use palm nuts, or anything suitable to hand. This is not because they are incapable of adding and subtracting mentally, but because they are so suspicious of each other that they want an ocular proof that the sum is right, and that neither one is getting the better of the other. Those who know figures and ean run through their arithmetical tables accept each other's sums, but in transactions with the untaught they resort to the fingers and palm nuts for counting.

They always count by five and tens, *e.g*., if a person wants to make up 26 brass rods he will take 3 rods and then put 2 with the 3 and push that 5 on one side, he will make another 5 in the same way, and then put the two fives together, making 10, and then make two more fives and put those together, keeping, however, the tens separate, then another 5 is made by the 3 and 2 process, and at last 1 put down. Then the two tens are counted, and the 5, and lastly the 1.

In contrast with the mathematics of the Borloki, is that of the natives of Central Australia, whose simple life requires only rudimentary forms of computation :

> At Alice Springs (Central Australia) they (the natives) occasionally count, sometimes using their fingers in doing

so, up to five, but frequently anything beyond four is indicated by the word *oknira*, meaning much or great... Time is counted by "sleeps" or "moons," or phases of the moon, for which they have definite terms : longer periods they reckon by means of seasons, having names for summer and winter.

3. *Science*. The science possessed by primitive man covers as wide a range and is nearly as voluminous as his "literature." An Agassize would, perhaps, see little worthy of the name of science in these primeval gropings. Here are found, however, types of the first explanations – the first guesses of how the world was started, of how man learned his own humanity, and of how animals got their spots, their stripes, or their tails. Unfortunately, these early guesses became established as facts and satisfied all save the foolhardy questioner who was summarily executed, while his parents in shame took their own lives. Such as it is, this lore has to be learned—some of it incidentally, some of it aimed the rigorous strictures and intoxicating frenzy of the initiation. These mixtures of childish fancy and adult grotesqueness are exemplified by the following passages.

HOW HUMAN BEINGS GOT KNEECAPS

Once, long ago, a woman named Nka Yenge went fishing in the river. When her were many other women. They all went into the water, some down stream and some up. Now deep down in one of the pools a smooth white stone was lying something like a Nimm stone. As the women went by, several of them said, "What a beautiful stone !" but when Nka Yenge came, she stood looking at it for a long time and said, "I wish I could get that stone !" When she came back she said the same thing, and as she passed a third time she said :

"I must have that stone."

Suddenly the stone sprang out of the water and struck against her knee. There it stayed and she could not loosen it;

so she went home weeping with pain. On the way thither, she met a man, who asked, "Why do you weep ?"

The woman could not speak for tears, but the stone answered, "I was lying in the water. When the woman passed up and down, she said that she wished to have me. Her wish was so strong that it drew me up out of the water. Now I have joined myself to her, and shall never leave her again."

The man was very sorry, and called to the woman, "Come here. We will go to my house, and I will try what I can do." When they reached his house, he got a strong knife and tried to chop off the stone, but it was no use. The stone had gone inside.

That is the reason why we have kneecaps. Formerly we did not have any.

The science offered to the boys of the Boloki of Darkest Africa is summarized by Weeks, who spent thirty years (1881—1911) among these people. Some Korean customs and notions as collected by Waters will be presented after Week's summary.

They picked up a little astronomy from their elders. Venus was called "wife of the moon"; a shooting star was "fetish fire"; a cluster of stars (Pleiades) was a "crowd of young woman"; the "Milky Way" was "the road of floods and drought." Both on the Lower and Upper River the natives connect the "Milky Way" with the abundance and scarcity of rains; they say that when the "Milky Way" is bright, clear, and well seen there will be plenty of rain. Three bright stars in Orion's belt were named the "three paddlers"; and the five stars near each other in Orion were regarded as the "bundle of thunder or lightning." In the constellation Lepus there is a set of five stars thus* * * * *, and these were said to resemble a man—the top star being the head, the two lower stars the hands, and the two bottom stars the feet. When this set of stars, called *kole,* reached the meridian the natives did more planting than at any other season. This *kole* was so well recognized by the natives that we used the word as an equivalent for our word year.

There is a legend that the moon was once a python and made a road for itself on the earth. Some adventurous trappers, however, shared it, but on noticing there was no more moonlight, they let it go, whereupon it sprang into the sky and never again returned to earth. When there is no moon, some say that the python has gone on a long journey, and others that it dies every month. There is much shouting and gesticulating on the appearance of a new moon; and those who have enjoyed good health ask that it may be continued, and those who have been sick ascribe their complaint to the coming of the new moon, and ask it to take away bad health and give them good health in its place.

Here, as on the Lower Congo, many believe that the sun returns from the west to the east during the night to be ready to rise in the morning. They were taught that the stars were a species of large fire-flies that formerly existed on the earth, but have now gone into space, and that the comets are signs that a great chief has recently died.

Another thing necessary to the young Congo boy was to teach him, not the movements of the clock's hands, but the crowing of the cocks, the notes of the *nkuku-mpembe* (name of a bird), and the movements of the sun : 2 A.M. was "the lying fowl"; 3 A.M., "the lying bird" – because they falsely heralded the dawn which was not due until later; 4 A.M., was "the first fowl"; 4 to 5 A.M., "the sun is near"; 5 : 30 to 6 A.M., "the dawning"; 6 A.M., "the sun is come"; 6 : 15 to 7 A.M., "the first sun"; 12 noon, "the meridian"; 6 P.M., "when the fowls go in", or "the sun enters"; 11 to 12 P.M., "one set of ribs", or "one side of a person", and means that about that time a person turns from lying on one side over on to the other. For all these and many other divisions of the day there were special names or phrases.

SOME KOREAN CUSTOMS AND NOTIONS

On the 14th and 15th days of the first month of each year, every man and boy in Soul, the capital, walks over three particular bridges in succession. By doing so, exemption from pains in the legs and feet is procured for one year.

There is another curious custom in Corea in connection with the above-mentioned days. All men and women born under the Jen or "Man" star make certain straw images on these days, especially on the 14th. These images are sometimes dressed with cloths, and each one contains a number of the copper "cash" constituting the currency of the country. There ought to be as many "cash" in an image as the person making it is years old, but the rule is not strictly followed. When the images are complete they are placed on the path outside of the house, and the poor people seize them and tear them up in order to get the "cash" which they contain. The destruction of the image, or figure, saves the person represented from death for ten years. It is, accordingly. only once in ten years that the ceremony must be performed, but it seems to be observed every year, at least by some.

Smallpox is supposed by the Coreans to be the work of a malevolent demon, and hence its name among them, *viz.*, Ok-Sin or Plague-God. When a child dies of smallpox its body is not buried. but is tied up in straw and hung on the city wall in Soul or from a tree. The body is thus hung up because it is believed that there is a chance of the spirit which had left it returning to it again. But some say that the deceased child is thus hung up in order to secure a longer life for the next-born. It is chiefly daughters, I believe, whose dead bodies are treated in the manner here indicated. The custom is explained as having arisen from an actual occurrence. One occasion a young girl died in Soul and her parents were unable to bury her. They wrapped her up in paper and left her hanging from the city wall above the reach of beasts of prey. During the night a poor man, who had taken shelter near the spot where the corpse was hanging, heard it utter sounds. He found the body reanimated, took the girl down, and made her his wife.

If a younger brother dies of smallpox in a family in which there is an elder brother. the deceased may not be interred until after the lapse of thirteen days from the date of death.

The moon of the 15th of the first month is carefully and anxiously observed by the Coreans in order to obtain prognostics for the year. If the moon is what is called "thin", that is, dull and pale, the year will be a bad one. The crops will fail, trade will be bad, there will be much sickness, and things generally will go wrong. If the "thinness" is only partial, the misfortunes will be confined to the districts lying in the direction of the "thin" part.

The 15th day of the first month is also the day specially set apart in Corea for the worship of ancestors with much sole--mnity and formality. On the morning of this day also all the members of the family meet together for a wine-drinking ceremony. On this one occasion the youngest member of the household, whether boy or girl, takes precedence in drinking. By doing so, it is believed, the child is secured against ear-ache for a year.

4. *Social studies.* Primitive boys, like the youth of America. have to learn by precept and example the simple art of living together. Much that America regards as amenable to ethical principles rather than to statutory laws has to be enforced among primitive peoples by stern regulations with bitter penalties. Much that seems too trivial to teach in a formal manner to accidental boys is, therefore, given all the pomp and circumstance of elaborate tribal ceremony. One's notions of primitive life may lead one to suspect that the social studies of primitive boys are simple. and, consequently, one may scoff at the possibility of primitive peoples' having as definite civics materials as modern man has; in that case let the scoffer turn to the accounts written by witnesses of the rites of "simple" tribes and find the discipline he craves for manhood in the making.

The passages which follow show by implication some of the civic problems which primitive man faces and the manner in which those problems are solved : old men, not caring to exert themselves unduly, require youthful hunters to bring their kill to camp before partaking of it; as tribal welfare is not compatible with neglect of initatory training, all well-bred boys are not only marked by physical means, but are also given verbal formulae by means' of which they can expose impostors; sexual morality not being otherwise insured is enjoined by formulae, group censorship, and religion; women, being quite as robust as men, require the restraining influences of mystery and the bull-roarer. For such reasons and many others, boys must study community civics. During the period of initiation the boys often receive training at the hands of one or more of the elders; at this time it is that the youth of Torres Straits are taught the elements of conduct. During the period of seclusion the old man, as sponsor or tutor, trained, the novice in tribal lore and customs, including instrcution in morality. The following is a literal transcript of the code of morals as given by the tribesman, Maino :

> You no steal. You no take thing belong another man without leave; if you see a fish-spear and take, s'pose you break it and you no got spear, how you pay man ? S'pose you see a dugong harpoon in a canoe and take it and man he no savvy, then you lose it or break it, how you pay him ? You not got dugong harpoon.
>
> Look here ! S'pose man tell you do something, you do it quick. S'pose man ask for 'kaikai' (food) or water or anything else, you give him half what you got. If you do, good boy, if you no do, no one like you.
>
> You work hard to get plenty fish and dugong and turtle. You make garden then you full-up of food. S'pose you get plenty fish you give mother and father before you given to brother, you have wife her a little and plenty to parents for they have had hard work along you. Look after mother and father; never mind if you and your wife have to go without. Give of all your fish to your parents, don't be mean. Dou't speak bad word to mother.

Father and mother all along same as food in belly; when they die you feel hungry and empty. Mind your uncles too and cousins.

You no go and talk a lie; you speak straight.

S'pose man talk to your brother you help him, too, you talk, too. If your brother is going out to fight, you help him; don't let him go first but go together.

You no play with small play-canoe, or with toy-spear; that all finish now. You no play with boy and girl now; you a man now and no boy.

You no like girl first; if you do, girl laugh at you and call you a woman (that is the young man must not propose to a girl, but must wait for her to ask first). You no marry your cousin; she all same sister. You no marry sister of your mate or by and by you will be ashamed; mates all brothers (but 'mates,' i.e., two close friends, like brothers, may marry two sisters)

Finally the 'kernge, (novice) was instructed about dealings with women. The characters of various girls were made known to the youths so that they might be forewarned. The kernge were also taught by the wadwam sponsor the following magical practices in connection with women so that the latter might fall in love wtth them : Spear the ground where the woman, or women, micturate and call her, or their, name when pulling out the spear. Mix "Medicine" with tobacco and give to the girl. Mix the medicine with sand and put it on the sand where the women are going to sit round the fire. Put 'medicine' on on the palm of the hand, and plenty behind the ears and the back of the neck, a little on the nose and plenty in the armpits, on the pubes, under the knees and on the feet. I could not get any of this "girl medicine," it was a scented substance and I think it was mainly – if not entirely—'paiwa' bark.

At the expiration of the month's seclusion the drums were beaten and the 'sobera' removed from the 'kernge', who were washed in the sea, leaves of the 'sarza' and 'urakar' trees were gathered and the boys were rubbed with these together with some sand, until they were clean and light-colored.

"My word, boy very clean," said Maino on one occasion; finally they were anointed with coconut oil and plenty girl like him."

The hunting and fishing regulations of certain African tribes are favorable to the old men of the communities. As these tabus must be diligently kept, the boys are required to master them. Talbot reports the following tabus :

There are many strict laws and tabus (Ntubi) which regulate the distribution of animals killed in the chose.

After a town hunt, one fore and one hind leg of each beast killed must be given to the townsfolk. The neck becomes the property of the man who stood nearest during the kill, the tail, belongs to the mother of the hunter, one leg and the back to the father or the head of his house, while the head and remaining fore leg are left to the actual slayer.

When a man hunts alone or with one companion, the rules vary according to the animal killed.

In the case of a boar, the tail is given to the mother, the two legs and trotters to the father or head of the house, but he usually returns the latter. The cheeks and jaws must be cooked for the hunter's age class; half of the head and the stomach is given to the wife, and the other half-head to the companion; leaving the two fore legs to the mad himself.

Both water chevrotain and bay duiker must be taken whole before the head of the house, who retuns all except the two hind legs. Much the same rule applies to Ogilby's duiker, except that this is always taken to the hunter's father. Should the latter be dead, there is no obligation to offer it to the head of the house.

The rules about porcupine, blue duikerbok, and monitor flesh are similar, but not so strictly kept.

Elephant, buffalo, yellow-backed duiker, pangolin, civet cat, and genet must also be brought before the head of the house.

Should these rules be infringed, a Juju will catch the hunter and give him a sickness. from which he will not recover except by confession and sacrifice. In the case of a genet, the illness is supposed to take the form of elephantiasis....

Should a man keep to himself a male drill ape or chimpanzee, certain death is supposed to follow, and an illness from which recovery is unlikely, if the kill be female.

When a leopard or python is killed, the heart and gall cut out, buried in a deep hole, and the earth berth beaten over them. Any-one eating of these would die. Only slaves eat leopards; for free men they are tabu.

Of birds, the Monkey-killing Eagle and the Greater Plantaineater must be taken to the head of the house.

Neither man nor woman may feed on any scavenger bird, such as the vulture, nor on the owl, because it is a witch's familiar. If killed, the latter must be offered up on two posts at the entrance to the town. The Kingfisher also is forbidden food. When killed its skull is dried, powdered, mixed with leaves and given as cough medicine.

Members of the Juju Mfam are forbidden to eat called "Aru."

Many persons may not eat the fish called Ecchan or Mbonn, the heads of which are ground up and used as "medicine".

Of tabus for men alone, the principal ones are—the fish Eddokk, of which, should a hunter eat, he will be killed in the bush, and crab, "The Father of all Jujus," the eating of which would cut a man off from partaking in any ceremonies.

A woman may not eat the following: "nandinia binotata," as a child born afterwards would surely die; wild cat, lest she should become barren; anything killed by leopard or wild cat, otherwise her child would be still-born; crocodile, as her child would be born with a scaly skin and die; the Greater Plantain-eater; the first thing caught in her husband's new trap.

The greater number of these tabus probably arose from totemic causes, others from sanitary reasons, and some, obviously, from the desire of the old men to obtain a full share of what was killed by their juniors.

One day, Obassi Nsi called all the people on earth together. He said, "I make a law concerning the food which is proper for you. Of the fruits of the earth you may eat, both men and women, but of living creatures women alone may eat fish, and men only may eat the flesh of animals."

Now there was a women named Aiya Ita, who had a husband named Atu Utup (Efik word for hunter). One day each of them went out, she to the river, and he to the bush. After she had been fishing for a little while she caught a fine fish. This she took home and boilded in her pot. When it was done, she ate some of it, and some she left for the morrow.

In the evening Atu Utup came home. He had hunted all day, but had killed nothing, and was very hungry. He saw the fish which his wife had left, and he took a piece and ate it.

Now a bird came out of the bush, and settled on the branch of a tree which grew close to the house. Through a small hole in the wall he saw what the man had done. At once he flew away to Obassi Nsi, and told what he had seen.

Obassi sent for the hunter and said, "You have gone against the rule which I made, that no man should eat fish, Therefore, you must die."

After the man was dead, Obassi thought, "The rule that I had made is too hard for my people." So he sent and called them again before him, and said:

> "From to-day I remove the law. Men may eat fish. Women may eat meat. Only let no woman eat the genitals of an animal slain by a hunter. Should she do so, the hunter will never be able to kill again, unlesss he finds out from the charm who it is who has transgressed my law and makes due sacrifice, that the curse may be taken off him."

The boys of the Thonga tribe of South Africa are taught how to undergo the six main trials,--blows, cold, thirst, unsavory food, punishment, and death. Besides such training Junod reports that these boys are also taught the formulae of their tribe.

Every morning the candidates are brought together to the place of the formulae "nau-milau, law, prescription." There is a tree in the midst of this square. A special instructor, whose father has already exercised this function, climbs on the tree and begins to teach the boys. He says:

"Little boys, do you hear me. I say..."

Then come the words of the secret formulae which are a great taboo and which they must learn by heart, sentence after sentence. I have collected some of them, Thonga and Pedi. Here I will only reproduce the Thonga. They are partly incomprehensible, even to the initiated. The first one is called 'Manhengwana'. It is the name of a bird. (Junod gives the original in native language; only the translation is here reprinted.)

The little bird has sung.

It has stirred the handles of the lances which are like lions....

They pierce each other....

The bird....

Forged at the lodge.

?... in the sand. The great sand of the ploughmen....

The runing of the wild pig....Of the frog which cries....

They are walking in good order, they go to visit the mysterious hut.

They find it like the twisted rings of the adder.

As far as they have sense, Junod says that the words of this formula seem to extol the tribe and its lodge. The opening lines indicate that the bird of winter heralds the opening of school. "The running of the wild pig" is the life of the boy who was idling on the spot till the initiation makes a man of him. "The croaking of the frog" is his childish stupidity. By the rites of the initiation he will become like this frog, an invulnerable and untamable adversary. In the last lines are portrayed the circumcised boys, penetrating into "the mysterious hut," and wondering at the extraordinary wisdom which is found there. The laws, rites, and trials are like the inextricable intermingling of many snakes. Still further mysteries are next unfolded to the boys.

These formulae and others like them constitute the principal passwords by which the initiated recognize one another. There are also formulae which refer to such matters as marital relations and hunting expeditions. It is clear from these examples that the boys of this tribe thus acquire little except charm words and that the training does not rationally explain the problems of social life.

5. ***Religion.*** It was the sound of the bull-roarer that announced the opening of the secondary school which was described freely rather than literally in the opening paragraph of this chapter. The bull-roarer itself the alleged supernatural

origin of its sound, its significance to the women of the tribe, and its different significance to the men of the tribe are shown in the accounts which follow. The religious or even the magical aspects of the bull-roarer are not always clear in the accounts of its use. That this simple instrument has a fundamentally religions significance is clear from the observations of witnesses of primitive ceremonies. As Marett says, following the anthropologist, Tylor : "I have to confess to the opinion with regard to 'Daramulun, Mungan-ngana, Tundun, and Baiamai', those divinities whom the Kurnai, Murrings, Kamilaroi, and other Australian groups address severally as 'Our Father,' recognizing in them the supernatural headmen and lawgivers of their respective tribes, that their prototype is nothing more or less than that well-known material and inanimate object, the bull-roarer," The following account is drawn from Spencer's report of a ceremony which he witnessed, and which had religious significance to the natives who participated.

The following account was given to me by an old man who was well acquainted with what formerly took place, and ...I was able to watch a representation of the performance of a part of the ceremony during which the sacred bull-roarers, called Bidu Bidu by the Larakia, are shown to the initiates. As in the case of the Melville and Bathurst Islanders and the Kakadu and allied tribes on the the mainland, the Larakia ceremonies do not include any multilation of the body.

There are two grades of initiation admitting a man respectively to the status of Belier and Mullinyu.

The Belier ceremony was, apparently, held once every year at a time decided upon by the old men, who also determined what youths should be initated at any given ceremony, though all men of the rank of Belier, Mullinyu, and Lariba knew what was taking place.

As usual in such circumstances, the opening of the ceremony, which is called Makulauri, is marked by the holding of an ordinary corrobboree at which all members of the local camp, as well as visitors from other tribes, are present. At this corrobboree the selected youths are picked out by the old men and given into the charge of special guardians, who are called Birra-pirra-pirra. As soon as the corrobboree is over the youths are taken out into the bush by their guardians, the women, from under whose control they are now passing, weeping and wailing.

A camp is made out in the bush and here the boys are kept, except that every now and then they are taken to the main camp and shown to the women, but no intercourse of any kind is allowed with the latter, who are carefully watched over by certain old men, told off for the purpose. The youths, meanwhile, are allowed to eat but little and are even supposed to give to their guardians a part of the small supply of food with which they are provided. The old men tell them that, if eat much, some one will come up and kill them during the might, and that they, their guardians, will not prevent this from being done or be angry with the doer. They are continually instructed in tribal customs and are told, time after time, that they must not steal, must not interfre with other men's lubras, but must imitate the old men. They are made to sit down quietly, are continually hit with spear throwers, and kicked and cuffed so as to hurt them a great deal, but, whatever may be done to them, they must on no account show any resentment or they will be still more seriously dealt with. This is supposed to have the effect of making the youth a "good" black-fellow. During this period, also, the guardian cuts the Belier on the chest so as to make the two raised cicatrices that are the mark of a Belier.

When they have been a considerable time in the bush the youths are brought back and led to a special camp in the scrub, hidden from the sight of women and strangers. First of all they are made to sit down in a row on the ground with their faces turned away from a space that has been cleared in the scrub, in which the important ceremony of showing them the sacred bull-roarer is to be enacted.

A young man who has attained the status of Belier is now in charge of each youth, lest he should feel frightened and run away. The old men, four or five in number, who must have reached, at least, the status of Mullinyu and who are to swing the bull-roarers, go away into the bush where the youths cannot see them and paint themselves. The bull-roarers are thin flat slabs of wood from a foot to eighteen inches in length. They are two or three inches in greatest width, are rounded at one end and truncate at the other, through which a hole is bored for the attachment of three or four yards of string. They are ornamented with alternate lines of red and white.

The old men emerge from the scrub so that they cannot be seen by the youths, who have their backs turned to them. Their eyes also are covered by the hands of the Beliers in charge of them. Out in the open ground the men begin to swing the bull-roarers round and round, gradually approaching the youths as they do so. The latter are supposed to be very frightened, because they, like the women and children, have been taught to believe that the sound is the voice of a great old man who has come to take them away into the mangrove scrub.

Suddenly their guardians turn the boys round; take their hands away from their eyes and tell them to look at the old men whirling the Bidu Bidu. They stand up and for some time the whirling goes on, the youths watching in silence. Presently the old men come close up to the boys, who stand in a row. Each old man, holding one of the Bidu Bidu, comes up to a boy and stands in front of him.

First of all he rubs the stick through his own armpit and then across his stomach. If he did not do this, it is supposed that the strong magic of the Bidu Bidu might enter the boy's body and cause him to swell up. He then rubs the stick through the boy's armpit and pokes his stomach with one end of it, after which the boys are told to hold out their hands and the sticks are placed on them. Each one is told that it is Bidu Bidu, that the noise is not a voice, but is made by the stick, and that on no account whatever are the lubras to see the sticks or know anything about them.

Meanwhile the boys are told that they may take the sticks, which will help them to catch fish and secure food. They carry them about in the scrub, avoiding the women and children, for two or three months, after which they are completely destroyed by fire, no trace of them, string or wood, being left.

Further beginnings in religious instruction were witnessed by Howitt, who describes the awe inspiring scene in which the boys are introduced to the deity and the rigorous religious and moral pronouncements of the deity. This deity, the *Daramulun* referred to above in Marett's comment, is a fearful being whose name can be lawfully spoken only in sacred places. Much of the ritual is performed so that *Daramulun* will look with favor upon the boys. As a crude representation of this deity is a part of the initiatory surroundings, the boys conduct themselves circumspectly, because *Daramuluu* is cognizant of all these ceremonial proceedings. Although the teachings, mainly tabus, of this deity are to be observed throughout life, no representation of it is permitted within the tribal camp; as Gunjerung warned the boys near the close of the ceremony, "If you make anything like that when you go back to the camp, I will kill you."

Although the activities just described may not impress all students as quite religious, the indisputable fact remains that the natives themselves so regard them. The literature of primitive peoples is replete with accounts of analogous beliefs and practices. The native boy or girl who is tempted to disregard the "higher powers," spirits, or magic of his tribe has only to recall the solemn warning of Gunjerung. If the fear-inspiring practices of these peoples are thought to be crude and incompatible with the moral and aesthetic practices and beliefs common to other religions, let it be remembered that the examples here cited are drawn from tribes which have only approached the "threshold of religion."

6. *Fine and applied arts.* The art of primitive man has been carefully studied by anthropologists because it indicates so much of the status of his culture. If this section were devoted

to primitive art in general, there would be great difficulty in choosing from a wealth of material which is most truly representative. As the purpose of this section is to portray briefly the place of art in the education of primitive youth, there is difficulty in finding any suitable accounts which indicate clearly how training in art work is offered. The art of primitive tribes is, of course, restricted by the stereotyped activities of their dwarfed lives. Typical activities of this kind are body decorations on wearing apparel, weapons, and other instruments; and drawings such as those executed on rocks.

During their initiation the boys of Central Australia participate in elaborate ceremonies in which body paintings are impressively displayed. The boys also witness the actual painting, as shown in the following account of the closing rites of the initiation.

In the Engwura camp it was a busy and also a picturesque scene. The leader had, during the day, consulted the older men who were especially associated with him, and it had been decided what brands should be painted on the various young men. Each brand was distinctive of some special totem, but the most striking point in connection with the painting was that the brand of any particular individual had no relationship of necessity to his own totem, or to that of the man who painted him. It was purely a matter of what the old men, and especially the leader of the Engwura, decided upon. The following cases will illustrate the point :—

A Panunga man of the snake totem decorated an Umbitchana man of the plum tree totem with a brand of the frog totem.

A Kumara man of the wild cat totem painted a Bulthara man of the emu totem with a brand of the kangaroo totem.

An Appungerta man of the witchetty grub totem painted an Umbitchana man of the wild cat totem with a brand of the Hakea totem.

A Kumara man of the little bat totem painted an Appungerta man of the bandicoot totem with a brand of the frog totem.

A Bulthara man of the wild cat totem painted a Purula man of the native pheasant totem with a brand of the same totem, this being the only instance in which a man was painted with a brand of his own totem, and the old men said that there was no special reason for its being done in this special case.

A Purula man of the emu totem painted an Uknaria man of the lizard totem with a brand of the frog totem.

For this strange want of relationship between the totems of the men who did the decorating and those who were decorated, and still more for the totatal absence of any between the man who was decorated and the totem with a brand of which he was decorated, we could find out no reason whatever. Certainly the natives have no idea why it is so.

The materials used in the painting were charcoal, red and yellow ochre, white pipeclay and wad. In some few cases bands of wad edged wito white down were drawn on the chest, but in almost all cases the totemic brand was confined to the back, so that, as the *Illpongwurra* might neither speak to, nor in the presence of, their *ab-moara* men who were doing the painting—a rule strictly observed during the decorating—none of the men, unless they could detect it by the feel, were aware of what design they were personally branded with, though each one could of course see the brands on the other men.

An even cruder form of art is the body decoration which is sometimes referred to as tattooing. As no ink is used in this decoration, certain anthropologists object to the term "tattoo" in this connection and use instead the term "cicatrice." Weeks describes briefly this practice of decorative scarification.

Tattooing was begun in earliest childhood by the parents, but not more than sufficient to show that the child belonged to the tribe. Later on the boys and girls were urged to cut their own tattoos, and were taught to bear the pain unwhimperingly.

I have seen boys and girls sitting by the river's edge summon-ingly. I have seen boys and girls sitting by the river's edge summoning up the necessary courage to make the incisions, and when they failed to do so they were ridiculed by the others until at last they would run the knife, by the aid of a bit of looking-glass or the reflection in the river, along the old lines in the forehead. At the age of 18 or 20 the person—man or woman—who wished to be thought fashionable would work away every week or so, cutting the flesh deeper and putting wads in the cuts to cause the flesh to stand up, until they had a veritable *likwala*, or cock's comb, which would be the envy of those who had not attained to such a fine decoration.

These peoples who stand at the threshold of art possess many highly decorated specimens of wearing apparel, charms, weapons, musical instruments, wallets, and bags. As certain tribes and certain persons specialize in the making and decorat-ing of one or more of these articles, it can reasonably be assumed that some form of transmission of skill is early entered upon by the young members of the tribes. As the work of these peoples is generally conducted in open view of all, the opportunity for observation and imitation of adults is far greater than among more complex social groups like our own.

The applied arts, which are regularly taught by means of transmission from father to son, or to other near relatives, consist of making string wearing apparel and ornaments, weapons, utensils and implements, musical instruments, baskets, mats and so on. Many of the arts are carefully guarded against interference or too wide usage. For example, the Congo cannibals of the last generation held the smith in very high estimation, and thought that he required not only skill and wisdom for his work, but that he also practiced witchcraft. Consequently, no one was allowed in any way to interfere with the smith's work by stepping over his furnace, by blowing it, or by spitting into it, because, by thus polluting the fire, any of these actions would cause bad workmanship. This workman taught his son or his nephew, but would accept no apprentices.

7. ***Physical education.*** For the good of the tribe, physical education has long been a matter of grave concern. None but the fit were encouraged to continue their existence, and for these severe ordeals and training were provided. A portion of this training consisted of cultivating a stoical indifference to pain; other features of the training seem to have been conducted for the purpose of physically "hardening" the youth; still others seem to have had for their purpose the selection of the fit by means of eliminating the unfit; finally, the dances seem at times to have had some connection with physical exhilaration for the coming trial of prowess.

Examples of some of these forms of training have already been cited : the self-scarification or cicatrizing provides formal training in withstanding pain; the exposure to blows, to cold, to extreme thirst, to a diet of only unsavory food, to punishments, and to other rigors approaching death, probably serve at once to harden the fit and to eliminate the unit.

The place of the dance is most forcefully illustrated by its use as a preparation for battle. The true war dance consists of the representation of deeds of valor by warriors who have killed an enemy in battle.

The massed chorus of the guba is most imposing, but still more deeply does the *gila* impress one by its wildness. Look at this elderly man who suddenly detaches himself from the circle, stamping with all his might on the ground. His feet beat the earth in cadence, one blow being long, the three following ones short: ....He goes on, making the ground shake, brandishing his weapons with all his strength, perspiring from his efforts and pronouncing Zulu words which the throng interrupts by wild shouting, as if to encourage him ....Then he returns to his place and the whole army concludes the performance by a kind of whistling : *zu.........iiiii* .... prolonged on a high and piercing note, which suddenly descends to a deep and guttural tone : *i*... . ...*aaaa* ....He has hardly resumed his place in the ranks when a young man springs into the circle, jumping like an antelope, holding his assagai and gesticulating all the while, as if transfixing an invisible enemy. His eyes are glaring as if he were a wild beast, and immediatly the army intones a song, his song, the one which has been composed to glorify his deed. Possibly his return to the ranks will be greeted by another shout: "*I.........a......* *Nda-ul – Lion*" comparing him to a lion returning to his forest and which nobody will dare to attack. The encouragement given by the warriors to the *bagili* and their final cry are called *khuza* or *khunzela*.

"At that very movement," says Mankhelu, "the hearts of the young men tremble in their breasts ! Their hair stands on end.......An extraordinary war spirit comes over them all." ....And every one having witnessed those performances in the Thonga or Zulu mukhumbi will confess that they are wonderfully impressive. It is a mixture of dramatic, epic, and lyric poetry, three literary *genres* which are still confounded, the whole being enhanced by a deep, wild music and subject to the laws of the certain artistic style.

The fighting instincts are excited to the highest pitch by these patriotic choruses and dramatic representations. Thus should the troops be slow in making a start, the young men go dancing to the chief and beg him to "grant them permission" to go forth and slay, or rather to "give them men" to slaughter (ku nyika). The native idea appears to be that the chief holds the lives of the enemies in his hands: without his permission they cannot go forward, but, this once given, they rush enthusiastically to the fray. They even go so far as to taunt him with being an old woman, a coward, because he will not let them go at once.

When this stage of excitement is reached, the war-medicine is applied and the son-of-battle goes forth to war.

More joyous forms of physical education are found in the games. Among the Congo boys three favorite games are "The Pig East Mealie Cobs," *Hom ne* and *tlhuba holwane.*

Somewhat similar games are found everywhere. In the first of those games :

> one child plays the part of the pig; crawling along, covered with a mortar and piece of cloth, he goes from one hut to another followed by the throng of his friends who clap their hands and sing the foregoing words. People give food to the pig. It is received by its friends. When they have visited all the yards, they assemble on the central place of the village and eat the food together. Sometimes the pig suddenly turns back and attacks his followers who flee in terror.. ... ..

The games of *homane* is very similar to the English hockey. The fruit of a palm tree, which is round and very hard is used as a ball and hit with a stick into the opposite camp. If the *homane* falls between the two camps, the players rush upon it and, with their sticks, try to send it into their opponents' quarters ....

In another boys' game, the *tlhba halwane*, which is played mostly by moonlight, they also take two sides. A stick is planted by the one side in the earth and a piece of charcoal placed upon it. One of the opponents comes, hopping like a frog, takes out the stick and still hopping goes and plants it in his own ground. If he reaches the goal without falling, he has won. An opponent will take his turn, pull out (tlhuba) the stick and bring it back to his partners. Evidently the Ronga children find this comical !

Primitive Practices as the Thremshold of Modern Curricular

In concluding the discussion of primitive education, it seems desirable to warn the reader against accepting the specific practices and subject matter described in the foregoing pages as necessarily typical. The initiation is a typical customs -it varies, however, from tribe to tribe; tests of endurance are typical, but the specific tests vary among different tribes. Like the educational development of the American colonies, wherein each colony had certain general practices, but differed in many respects from most other colonies, so the education of each tribe exhibits certain general characteristics, but differs in many particulars from most others tribes.

We have dignified primitive lore by the term "course of studies" and have proceeded to divide this course into eight branches. This procedure was adopted merely for the purposes of achieving clearness and brevity. Perhaps another writer would classify primitive subjeet matter differently. Certainly, the primitive man did not so classify his material. We are, however, definitely looking for the origins of our own curriculum. Some of the origins have been definitely located by means of our procedure. It is to be hoped that the notion of the threshold of the curriculum will be retained in the reader's interpretation of the preceding pages. Were content, such as that described, now seriously proposed for modern youth, objection might well be made; yet a beginning had to be made—the germs of culture are here shown.

It is clear not only that much of the teachining of primitive boys the conducted by the old and influential men of the tribe, but also that it is of such a character as to impress upon youth the importance of meeting the physical needs of these men. While it may, therefore, be said that the training of boys is for the good of the tribe, it can more certainly be said that the training is for the good of the elders. In any case, important consequences follow this kind of training : the solidarity of the tribe is insured, conservation rules, crabbed age thrives though youth may suffer.

Whatever one's philosophy of personal or of group life, one cannot but be impressed by the through immediate utility of tribal teaching. The tribal philosopher may favor change, but he is at once halted even in his thoughts by the grim vision of gods and men in a deathly attack upon him and his people. He knows that continued existence under a settled regime is likely if not certain. Why, then, turn his back upon the passably good when nothing save evil lies in the direction of change ? But the urge for variation is not, we are assured, very strong among boys whose initiative has been well-nigh quenched in youth– or, at anyrate, originality in social and political matters is lacking in primitive men who have been thus nurtured. Perhaps the stronger minds find a safer adventure than political originality by turning their attention to the arts and crafts and story-telling. Certain it is that primitive man, like some of his descendants, has little time for the untried, the dreamer's vision, the unsafe. So it happens that the primitive teaching is immediately practical because it preserves the tribal solidarity and the tribal lore, arts, and customs which under-lie solidarity. Before severely criticizing these practices, one should consider some of the certain results of individual or group variation in an age that is quite without the knowledge possessed by Europe for over twenty-five centuries.

Alongside the training for the arts of life, was training which included the products of the imagination of these men who lived in an age of wonder. Indeed, their science was like ours as far as beginnging with what was only dimly felt is concerned; unlike our men of science, however, these pioneers did not test thoroughly, but instead decreed the truth of a guess. The consequence of this acceptance of a guess was a story or legend or myth to support the explanation of the work of nature or of man. Instead of true elementary science, many stories or folklore are the reward or the penalty for guessing without testing. When one looks for the imaginative literature of primitive tribes, one finds, therefore, a strange mixture of science, art, literature, philosophy, civics, and history. This lore together with works of art aids one in judging both the cultural level of the tribes and the cultural value of the tribal curriculum.

That much or little of the folklore was acquired incidentally affects not at all the final result. The fact is that it was acquired and transmitted. As compared with the modern high school, primitive institutions offered little. That a beginning was made is clear. That premature standardization appeared as an obstacle to progress is equally clear. The remainder of Part I will supply some of the connecting links between this primitive beginning and the curriculum of the modern American secondary school.

3

Concepts of the Curriculum

The Place of the Athenian Age in the History of Curricula

Many years before the age of glory which we now approach, man hurled questions at his tribal gods and, while waiting for an answer, found himself, an individual. And nevermore could priest or pagan god claim all that all men had. A Greek had come to show a sodden or, at best, a narrow, practical world what is meant by living man. Prehistoric man had kindled the fire of human living—dimly had the somthered embers shone ; the Greek below these smouldering embers into flame. From human blindness to clear vision leads the course from primitive man to Greek ; from brutalizing tests of animal endurance to ennobling tests of mental insight ; from unvarying, restricted group life to personally responsible civic conduct ; from guidance by blind gods to leadership by men who far transcended tribal gods—such is the transition from the life and thought of primitive man to the life and thought of the Age of Pericles.

In making the transition from an age of prehistoric rudeness to an age of Athenian grace, the studies that made men of boys changed no less than did the general forms of life and methods of instruction. By passing from present-day primitive practices, which are not unlike those of prehistoric peoples, to those of Athens, one accents the sharp contrasts among curriculum practices as well as the contrast between cultural levels. By tracing outstanding changes during the Athenian Age, one finds additional contrasts and characteristics of a progressive era. These contrasts and characteristics constitute the foundation of this chapter. Their special importance lies in the fact that this period was one of continuous curriculum reconstruction as well as an era in which many practices of early man were dropped. For all succeeding eras of progress this age is, consequently, a significant period.

Free use was made in the opening paragraphs of Chapter 2 of the term primitive, so that the term connoted life which is culturally rather than chronologically antecedent to the life of pre-Christian Greece. The period of Greek life selected for this sketch is likewise relatively extended so that it includes Thales of the sixth century and also Archimedes of the third. As far as the forming of the curriculum is concerned, this four-century period covers the true Athenian Age, even including the first publication of Homer's poems. Athenian education is selected for this sketches because, educationally, it is the most important of all Greek systems.

Greek education of this period was a course of training which began at the cradle and continued, for boys, well into manhood. Not all boys were endowed with sufficient wit or funds for such extended training. Only boys who caught the challenge of liberated and liberating intelligence were urged into meditations with the sages or into oratory with the masters of that art. For that sixth of Athenians known as citizens—Athenians who voted, argued in the market-place, accepted embassies, and talked or taught philosophy—for such as these the years of childhood were all too short a term in which to learn to live : and thus they spent their entire lives in intellectual pursuits. The divisions of Athenian schooling which are fairly well exemplified in the actual practices of authentic accounts were as follows : elementary education for pupils of 7 to 13 or 14 ; secondary education for pupils of 14 to 18 ; higher education for older students.

It should be understood that the Athenian period under discussion covers four centuries and that, as stated above, the Greeks progressed during these years. Their schools did not remain stationary. The content of the subjects of instruction as well as the names of the subjects themselves underwent changes. As there was no formal system of state education for elementary and secondary school pupils, there were great variations of practice. For this reason an extended account of their practices is significant for the student of curriculum reconstruction in America. As present-day knowledge of Greek education is limited to accounts written over two thousand years ago, our knowledge of certain aspects of it is far less detailed than our knowledge of the education of primitive peoples who are still living- no modern anthropologist can witness the life of ancient Greece. No great are the difficulties

CHART I

Chronological Chart Showing the Centuries in which Certain Greeks Flourished

	Sixth Century, B.C.	
Anacreon	Thales	Pythagoras
	Fifth Century, B.C.	
Pindar	Heraclitus	Thucydides
Aeschylus	Empedocles	Gorgias
Sophocles	Socrates	Pericles
Euripides	Democritus	Hippias
Aristophanes	Herodotus	Hippocrates
	Fourth Century, B.C.	
Antisthenes	Aristotle	Isocrates
Terpander	Zeno	Isaeus
Menander	Epicurus	Demosthenes
Plato	Xenophon	Euclid
	Third Century. B.C.	
Archimedes	Eratosthenes	

which result from these facts, that one finds wide diversity in modern published accounts of Greek education. In interpreting the outline of organization just given, one should, therefore, bear in mind the fact that the outline indicates general practice, and also that the subjects pursued were taught simultaneously in some schools though not necessarily in all schools. In reading the subsequent descriptions of the subjects, the student should notice the dates of sources in the cases where sources are given. As a chronological guide, Chart I may be valuable to some readers. Since an account of curriculum developments must trace changes in subject matter as well as in academic practices, the following accounts deal not only with what all pupils studied, but also with what knowledge was extant in certain departments of thought.

What Grecian boys Studied

In describing the subjects pursued by the Greeks, the same plan will be continued as was followed in the case of primitive education : that is, since this is an account or origins, subjects which are now found in secondary schools will be discussed even though the Greeks may have pursued these subjects in their elementary or higher schools. With these considerations in mind, one may include nine branches as comprising Athenian subjects which are analogous to those now offered in secondary schools. These branches are : literature, composition and rhetoric, mathematics, science, social studies, religion, fine arts and applied arts, physical education, and music.

1. *Literature*. Throughout this period, the Homeric poems were recited, studied, and discussed in schools of all grades and at public gatherings. By an ordinance of Solon in 594 B.C., the rhapsodes, or "readers," at festivals were required to recite passages consecutively so that each rhapsode took his cue from the preceding reader. In additlon to hearing these interpretative readings of Homer, boys read in school the works of the great poets. Later, other literary works, including lyric poetry, were read and interpreted. The following passages

show something of the quality of Greek literature, the study of which has never ceased.

The place of prose in Greek reading was distinctly subordinate to that of poetry. This subordination Sandys ascribes, in part at least, to the belief that the poets were not only teachers, but also inspired beings. As the lore of Greece was early turned into verse, the need for prose in teaching national or tribal traditions was slight. As a consequence, little prose save Aesop's fables seems to have been taught.

Quotations from the literature which has been the study of the nations' youth for centuries is justified by the present tendency to overlook entirely the people who have been called the source of all things good. The first passage is a famous parting scene which depicts Hector's leave-taking of his wife, Andromache. This passage can never be without appeal to youth as long as men respond to duty's call—whether to the call of drums or to the challenge of a peaceful task ; whether the sacrifice is made by him who goes or by those who stay behind.

HECTOR'S FAREWELL TO ANDROMACHE

"Alas ! my parents, brothers, kindred, all
Once more will perish if my Hector fall.
Thy wife, thy infant, in thy danger share :
Oh, prove a husband's and a father's care !
That quarter most the skilful Greeks annoy,
Where you wild fig-trees join the wall of Troy :
Thou from this tow'r defend th' important post ;
There Agamemnon points his dreadful host,
That pass Tydides, Ajax, strive to gain,
And there the vengeful Spartan fires his train.
Thrice our bold foes the fierce attack have giv'n,
Or led by hopes, or dictated from heav'n.
Let others in the field their arms employ,
But stay my Hector here, and guard his Troy,"

The chief replied : "That post shall be my care,
Not that alone, but all the works of war.
How would the sons of Troy, in arms renown'd,
And Troy's proud dames, whose garments sweep the ground,
Attaint the lustre of my former name,
Should Hector basely quite the field of fame ?
My early youth was bred to martial pains,
My soul impels me to th' embattled plains ;
Let me be foremost to defend the throne,
And guard my father's glories and my own.
Yet come it will, the day decreed by fates,
(How my heart trembles while my tongue relates !)
The day when thou, imperial Troy ! must bend,
And see thy warriors fall, thy glories end.
And yet no dire presage so wounds my mind,
My mother's death, the ruin of my kind,
Not Priam's hoary hairs defil'd with gore,
Not all my brothers gasping on the shore,
As thine, Andromache ! Thy griefs I dread :
I see thee trembling, weeping, captive led,
In Argive looms our battles to design,
And woes of which so large a part was thine !
To bear the victor's hard commands, or bring
The weight of waters from Hyperia's spring !
There, while you groan beneath the load of life,
They cry, 'Behold the mighty Hector's wife !
Some haughty Greek, who lives thy tears to see,
Embitters all thy woes by naming me.
The thoughts of glory past and present shame,
A thousand griefs, shall waken at the name !
May I lie cold before that dreadful day,
Press'd with a load of monumental clay !
Thy Hector, wrapp'd in everlasting sleep,
Shall neither hear thee sigh, nor see thee weep."

Thus having spoke, th' illustrious chief of Troy
Stretch'd his fond arms to clasp the lovely boy.
The babe clung crying to his nurse's breast,

Scar'd at the dazzling helm and nodding crest.
With secret pleasure each fond parent smil'd,
And Hector hasted to relieve his child ;
The glitt'ring terrors from his brows unbound,
And plac'd the beaming helmet on the ground.
Then kiss'd the child. and, lifting high in air,
Thus to the gods proferr'd a father's pray'r :

"O thou ! whose glory fills th' ethereal throne.
And all yet deathless pow'rs ! protect my son !
Grant him, like me, to purchase just renown,
To guard the Trojans, to defend the crown,
Against his country's foes the war to wage,
And rise the Hector of the future age !
So when, triumphant from successful toils,
Of heroes slain he bears the reeking spoils,
Whole hosts may hail him with deserv'd acclaim,
And say, 'This chief transcends his father's fame':
While pleas'd, amidst the gen'ral shouts of Troy,
His mother's conscious heart o'erflows with joy."

He spoke, and fondly gazing on her charms,
Restor'd the pleasing burthen to her arms ;
Soft on her fragrant breast the babe she laid.
Hush'd to repose, and with a smile survey'd.
The troubled pleasure soon chastis'd by fear,
She mingled with the smile a tender tear.
The soften'd chief with kind compassion view'd,
And dried the falling drops, and thus pursued ;

"Andromache ! my soul's far better part,
Why with untimely sorrows heaves thy heart ?
No hostile hand can antedate my doom,
Till fate condemns me to the silent tomb.
Fix'd is the term to all the race of earth.
And such the hard condition of our birth :
No force can then resist, no flight can save;
All sink alike, the fearful and the brave.
No more—but hasten to thy tasks at home,
There guide the spindle, and direct the loom;

My glory summons to the martial scene,
The field of combat is the sphere for men.
Where heroes war, the foremost place I claim,
The first in danger as the first in fame."

The importance of the drama in Greek education can be estimated in the light of what might be accomplished in America by powerful motion-picture dramas if motion pictures were shown only at festival seasons and witnessed as now by the multitudes. The character of the dramatic productions cannot here be fully illustrated—a single gem selected from the *Oedipus* must suffice to indicate the beauty of thought thus rendered to the people; the tragic force of this powerful drama is only suggested by this excerpt in which Creon tries to justify his actions in the presence of his brother, Oedipus, the king of Thebes.

...Is life like mine a thing
To cast aside and plot to be a King ?
Doth a sane man turn villain in an hour ?

For me, I never lusted thus for power
Nor bore with any man who turned such lust
To doing.—But enough. I claim but just
Question. Go first to Pytho; find if well
And true I did report God's oracle.
Next, seek in Thebes for any plots entwined,
Between this seer and me; which If he find
Then seize and strike me dead. Myself that day
Will sit with thee as judge and bid thee Slay !
But damn me not on one man's guess.—'Tis all
Unjust : to call a traitor true, to call
A true man traitor with no cause nor end !
And this I tell thee. He who plucks a friend
Out from his heart hath lost a treasured thing
Dear at his own life.

But Time shall bring
Truth back, 'Tis Time alone can make men know
What hearts are true; the false, one day can show,

2. ***Composition, rhetoric, grammar, and public speaking.*** The science of language lingered far behind fine usage. This science as well as the antecedent practice seems to have grown directly from the civic life of ancient Greece. In early Greece, for example, Achilles was so trained that he

> .. mightst speak, when speech was fit, and do when deeds were done;
>
> Not sit as dumb for want of words; idle for skill to move.

In later Greece, skill in speech was needed by all who sought their rights in court; of the origin of rhetoric as an art, Jebb says,

> The law-suits which followed the establishment of the democracy are said to have given him (Korax, about 455 B.C.) the idea of drawing up, and committing to writing, a system of rules for forensic speaking.
>
> This work contained rules (1) for the arrangement of a speech into five parts—proem, narrative, arguments, subsidiary remarks, and peroration, and (2) the topic of *general probability*—the question as to the probability that a case or event was thus and so.
>
> The somewhat lowly origin of this art seems to have determined too largely the judgments rendered by later Greeks upon the sophists who taught and practiced rhetoric. As Isocrates asserts.
>
> They undertook to teach the mode of conducting law-suits thus confining their subject to its most odious branch.

In a later discourse, ***On the Antidosis***, Isocrates shows clearly the distinctions to be made between himself, a teacher of superior quality, and certain sophists of his time; his literary skill has, he says, been used for no bad or lowly purposes. His curriculum was not a preparation for making law-speeches, but was instead designed for the youths who were to become the nation's pilots. For the training of such youths, this great teacher organized a general curriculum rather than one in which specific skills were perfected. He required three things to make a great speaker—

> Capacity, training, and practice. Capacity—which includes intellect, voice, and nerve - is the chief requisite. Practice, however, can by itself make a good speaker. Training is by far the least important of the three. It may be complete, and yet may be rendered useless by the absence of a single quality – nerve ?

What Isocrates meant by training is clear from many implications in his discourses : this training included all that makes good men just—"breadth of view; nobleness of moral tone; practical thoroughness of method; encouragement of solid work"—work that is well done and that will have a permanent value. He appears to have belonged to that large group of teachers who are annoyed by, if not suspicious of, attempts to become definite in teaching. For the somewhat unspecialized life, of the Athenians whom he instructed and before adequate analysis of life activities and needs had been introduced, this attitude toward the curriculum may have been more fully justified than it would be at present.

Meanwhile, the science of grammar developed so that by Plato's time the schoolboy's life included both grammar and composition, in the modern meanings of the two terms.

> ...when the boy has learned his letters and is beginning to understand what is written, as before he understood only what was spoken, they put into his hands the works of great poets, which he reads at school; in these are contained many admonitions, and many tales, and praises, and encomia of ancient famous men, which he is required to learn by heart, in order that he may imitate or emulate them and desire to become like them. Then, again, the teachers of the lyre take similar care

that their young disciple is temperate and gets into no mischief; and when they have taught him the use of the lyre, they introduce him to the poems of other excellent poets, who are the lyric poets; and these they set to music, and make their harmonies and rhythms quite familiar to the children's souls, in order that they may learn to be more gentle, and harmonious, and rhythmical, and so more fitted for speech and action; for the life of man in every part has need of harmony and rhythm.

As Plato recognized the parts of speech, number, tenses of verbs, and voice of verbs, and as Protagoras had already distinguished between the moods of verbs and the genders of nouns, one may conclude that, by the fourth century, though not long before that time, grammar as now understood was taught to Athenian youth.

Aristole in his *Rhetoric* carried grammatical analysis still further by distinguishing among deponent and neuter verbs, conjunctions, connecting particles, and connecting clauses. He describes also the art of paragraphing. In rhetoric, in the modern sense, Aristotle's work is foundational. It includes an elaborate terminology with definitions and examples, an extended discussion of propriety of style and of meter and rhythm in prose, and a treatment of the formal divisions of a discourse.

3. *Mathematics*. In a systematic account of the history of mathematics as a formal subject, few chapters can precede that in which the work of the sages of Greece is recorded. Early in the Athenian period, Thales, one of the "seven wise men," betook himself to Egypt on a commercial enterprise. While there he allowed himself to wander among the haunts of Egyptian priests. Ere long he passed his masters and won the admiration of others by his skill as a geometer.

The second great geometer, Pythagoras, was, so tradition says, taught and inspired by Thales. From his master he went also to Egypt and, like Thales, excelled his masters and amazed all casual workers in geometry. Although much of the work of Pythagoras was associated with philosophical speculation and mysticism, he was able to add greatly to mathematics and, according to the historian Proclus, gave to his science the name of mathematics.

As a result of the work of these two men and their pupils, geometry had, by 480 B.C., arrived at the following state. The subject matter included the bulk of the first two books of Euclid, portions of the fourth and sixth books, and a sketch of the doctrine of proportion. Little was known of the properties of the circle; for example, the theorem which states that the angles in the same segment of a circle are equal to each other was unknown to mathematicians of this time. Approximations were then employed in solving such problems as that involving the relation between the circumference of a given circle and the perimeter of a square of equal area. The form of geometry underwent an important development prior to this time. Instead of being a purely practical, rule-of-thumb procedure, it had become a science with definitions and proofs which had universal application. The use of the equation in connection with proportion was introduced to Greece by Thales. The organization and method of geometry comprised, as early as the time of Pythagoras, the combination of arithmetic and geometry. This early combination of arithmetic and geometry by Pythagoras leads Allman to rank him alongside Descartes to whom we owe the combination of algebra and geometry. From this time forward geometry flourished, and in the fourth century Euclid callected and wrote what is still known as the *Elements* of geometry. Under Archimedes of the following century, further refinements, extensions, and applications of geomerty were made. The content of this branch of learning is now too well known to require illustrction. Among the Greeks, geometry was taught in secondary schools and arithmetic in both elementary and secondary schools.

The development of arithmetic from the period of primitive groping to the time of Archimedes can be judged by comparing the samples of primitive reckoning described in Chapter

2 with the following proposal of Archimedes. This proposal, called the *Sandreckoner*, which was made to King Gelon of Syracuse, indicates incidentally something of the status of science among the Greeks.

There are some, King Gelon, who think that the number of the sand is infinite in multitude; and I mean by the sand not only that which exists about Syracuse and the rest of Sicily but also that which is found in every region whether inhabited or uninhabited. Again, there are some who, without regarding it as infinite, yet think that no number has been named which is great enough to exceed its multitude. And it is clear that they who hold this view, if they imagined a mass made up of sand in other respects as large as the mass of the earth, including in it all the seas and the hollows of the earth filled up to a height equal to that of the highest of the mountains, would be many times further still from recognising that any number could be expressed which exceeded the multitude of the sand so taken. But I will try to show you, by means of geometrical proofs which you will be able to follow, that, of the numbers named by me and given in the work which I sent to Zeuxippus, some exceed not only the number of the mass of sand equal in size to the earth filled up in the way described, but also that of a mass equal in size to the universe.

Now you are aware that "universe" is the name given by most astronomers to the sphere the centre of which is the centre of the earth, while the radius is equal to the straight line between the centre of the sun and the centre of the earth. This is the common account, as you have heard from astronomers. But Aristarchus of Samos brought out a book consisting of some hypotheses, in which the premises lead to the conclusion that the universe is many times greater than that now so called. His hypotheses are that the fixed stars and the sun remain uumoved, that the earth revolves about the sun in the circumference of a circle, the sun lying in the centre of the orbit, and that the sphere of the fixed stars, situated about the same centre as the sun, is so great that the circle in which he supposes the earth to revolve bears such a ratio to the distance of the fixed stars as the centre of the sphere bears to its surface.

4. *Science.* The teaching of science among the Greeks was subordinated to the teaching of linguistic subjects. Science was not a subject which determined the success of an Athenian citizen. It was not yet a subject with diversified practical applications. Men of science were highly speculative; men of the applied arts were highly practical. Men of science and men of practice were further divided by the ancient notions of the wise who held that the arts, being matters of mere skill, were inferior to speculative matters. This divorce of science and practice seriously restricted the development of both : science neglected the simple testing of conclusions; applied arts were deprived or intelligent guidance. For example, Aristotle with his great wisdom overlooked the need for testing his conclusions about falling bodies and by doing so thrust upon the world a misconception which had to wait until Galileo's day for correction. Meanwhile, neither science nor any one of the applied arts was generally taught to adolescent boys. Consequently, this discussion of science deals with the progress in science rather than with the general teaching of science.

The procedure of the Greeks was prompted by their mistaken notion in regard to the "essence" of things. If any object were submitted to the speculative scrutiny of a philosopher, its essence was likely to be determined, and thereafter the object was required—so far as speculative science was concerned – to conduct itself according to the alleged essence. If, therefore, by the essence or nature of things, it were found that a heavy body fell more rapidly than a lighter body, then it was easy to see that of two bodies of different weight, the heavier must fall the more rapidly. From this point it was easy to see also that for two such bodies the rate of acceleration would be greatest for the heavier body.

Had Aristotle been less encyclopedic in his pursuit of science – had the essence of more objects been left undetermined —fewer obsessions might have cramped the centuries succeeding him. It would be quite misleading, however, to leave the impression that no scientific applications or first-hand observations were made by the Greeks.

Despite a lack of keenness in science comparable with their keenness in speculation, the Greeks possessed scientific knowledge which was far in advance of that possessed by primitive man. Despite the fact that as a subject of study by schoolboys science lagged behind linguistics, far more than a beginning was made in many of the branches of science. Despite the fact that the Greeks in certain cases merely transferred science from primitive superstition to dogmatic speculation, the advances made by this people are worthy of a brief outline here.

By their own genius and with the assistance of other peoples, particularly the Egyptians, the Greeks developed a large body of scientific knowledge. At this outline is based upon the work of a very few men of outstanding achievement, the subject, as treated by most teachers, even in higher schools, was probably inferior to that which is here sketched. A first-rate man of science who tested and applied his science—who even derived much of his science by experimentation—was Archimedes. But this third-century scientist, like his contemporary Eratosthenes, was too late to influence Athens during her period of intellectual supremacy. An earlier scholar, Aristotle, made extensive first-hand studies in biology, as will be seen later. As stated above, this outline is given as a sketch of samples of the available knowledge of science among the Greeks, and not as an outline of an actual school course in science.

a. In *physics*, the Greeks knew certain properties of light as evidenced by their use of lenses and mirrors; for example, Aristophanes refers in *The Clouds*, Act II, to the burning-glass by which fires can be kindled and wax melted. In electricity and magnestism, it was known by Thales that amber, when rubbed, will attract light bodies, and the story of the discovery of magnetite by Magnis the shepherd was current'. In mechanics, Archimedes knew many of the laws of levers and pulleys—"Give me a fulcrum on which to rest," he is alleged to have said, "and I will move the earth." His study of floating bodies and his knowledge of the water displacement of metals are matters of common knowledge. In sound, Pythagoras is credited with an investigation of the relation between the weights of hammers and the pitch of sounds produced by them as they struck an anvil. In physical, Democritus set forth an atomic theory of matter.

b. In *biology*, the study of medicine and surgery seems to have prompted investigation which was carried to a high degree by Aristotle, in whose works are found classifications of plants and animals and accounts of their development and structures. Aristotle's work in biology was based largely upon direct observations of some five hundred living forms, fifty of which he dissected. These animal forms he classified upon such bases as dentition, the presence of vertebrae, and "family" likenesses.

The following excerpt indicates something of the nature of Aristotle's encyclopedic and foundational work :

> The urchins are devoid of flesh, and this is a character peculiar to them; and while they are in all cases empty and devoid of any flesh within, they are in all cases furnished with black formations. There are several species of the urchin, and one of these is that which is made use of for food; this is the kind in which are found the so-called eggs, large and edible, in the larger and smaller specimens alike; for even when as yet very small they are provided with them. There are two other species, the *spantangus*, and the so-called *bryssus*; the animals are pelagic and scarce. Further, there are the *echinometrae*, or "mother-urchins," the largest in size of all the species. In addition to these there is another species, small in size, but furnished with large hard spines; it lives in the sea at a depth of several fathoms; and is used by some people as a specific for strangury. In the neighborhood there are sea-urchins of a white color, shells, spines, eggs, and all, and that are longer than the ordinary sea-urchin. The spine in this species is not large nor strong, but rather

> limp and the black formations in connexion with the mouth are more than usually numerous, and communicate with the external duct, but not with one another; in point of fact, the animal is in a manner divided up by them. The edible urchin moves with greatest freedom and most often; and this is indicated by the fact that these urchins have always something or other on their spines.

c. In *earth sciences*, Eratosthenes computed the circumference of the earth and placed the zones mathematically. Strabo, in the first century, prepared an extensive account of the geography of Asia Minor. These two citations indicate the expansion of the "known" world, and, taken with the common knowledge which must have been disseminated by travelers, show the Greeks to have possessed a sufficient volume of geography for educational purposes.

5. *Social studies*. During the era of sophist teaching, training for citizenship was the prime motive of education. Much of the rhetoric already referred to was undertaken specifically for this purpose. Besides this training there was that offered as Grecian traditions through the national poetry. In addition to the reading about and discussion of historical and contemporary problems, the boys were expected to receive incidental civic training from art, music, and gymnastics. Plato in his discussion of an ideal state only slightly exaggerated the best Athenian education of his day when he described the ideal system of training as at least looking toward a time when philosophers should be kings.

Finally, the ephebic oath which was taken when the youth was eighteen years of age summarized formally the civic training of the times. At the time of taking this oath the youth was presented with spear and shield and, with due ceremony, received into citizenship. This impressive oath ran as follows :

> I will never disgrace these sacred arms, nor desert my companion in the ranks. I will fight for temples and public property, both alone and with many. I will transmit my fatherland, not only not less, but greater and

better, than it was transmitted to me. I will obey the magistrates who may at any time be in power. I will observe both the existing laws and those which people may unanimously hereafter make; and, if any person seek to annul the laws or set them at naught, I will do my best to prevent him, and will defend them both alone and with many. I will honor the religion of my fathers. And I call to witness Aglaurus, Enyalius, Ares, Zeus, Thallo. Auxo, and Hegemone.

6, *Religion*. In quite the manner in which modern cynics view the man who spends his half-Sunday in church, so Plato in one of the dialogues gently plays with the old-fashioned notions of his friend whom he finds "at prayer." This means neither that the Greek of enlightened Athens had outgrown all gods nor that Plato himself was unable to find comfort or stimulation in religion. It does indicate, however, that the old forms of ceremonies were falling into disuse.

With the decline of interest in the older ceremonies, there was a decline in the literal interpretation of the Grecian "scriptures." There was a natural refusal longer to follow the early beliefs in unethical, irrational gods. Religion came gradually to be an ethical system which though exalted and exalting lacked in appeal to all classes of society. The following quotation from Freeman indicates the character of the problem of religious education by Plato's time, the method and place of instruction, and an advanced proposal much of which was actually carried out among the more scholarly classes of the Greeks.

Plato is not prepared to rewrite the Hellenic Bible, but, as Freeman continues, he proposed canons which should be followed in the choice of the material of instruction. "The first canon is that God, being good, cannot be the cause or originator of any harm or evil to mankind. .. The second canon is that God is not a wizard, appearing now in one form, now in another." The application of these canons would have excluded most of Homer and Hesiod as well as many of the lines of poems of the Athenian Age. There was, of course, much religious instruction included in the actual teaching of civics and morals by all the great teachers of Greece.

7. *Fine and applied arts.* The appreciation of art was one of the most important national pastimes of the later Greeks. Their art, addressed as it was to every one who wished to look upon it, was necessarily a popular art. The importance of art in education is reflected by the belief that, even though one did not regard art as a profession, one must practice it for at least two purposes : the disciplinary purpose, to cultivate a fine nature; and the practical purpose, to avoid being duped by fakirs in art.

During the early Greek period and until the time of Socrates, art was concerned chiefly with the gods, victors in the national gymnastic contests, and heroes. During the lifetime of Socrates, art broadened so as to represent more fully the life of the great Athenian age. Contemplation rather than mere satisfaction became the artist's objective. Attached to this conception of art was the moral quality which was believed to to exist in fine art : every work of fine art was "such that its moral purpose was manifest to the average man." This notion is illustrated still further in the later paragraphs on applied arts. It was during this period that systematic instruction in drawing and printing became general in Greek schools. In the *Protagoras*, there are references to boys going to artists to receive instruction, but this was for those only who expected to become artists. From this work and from the elements of drawing taught in many earlier schools, there seem to have developed the more extensive school courses of the fourth and third centuries. By 300 B.C., Freeman asserts that art had no doubt become a regular part of the curriculum. This scholar supports his statement by references to pictures and the common use of art terms in Plato's discussions of art.

Although the educated Greeks performed distinguished service in developing the fine arts, they regarded the applied arts of the modern curriculum with mild favor and sometimes with disdain. Socrates, for example, could think of no more complete method of confounding the great orator Gorgias than by associating with rhetoric another form of art called cookery (Polus and Socrates are speeking) :

Soc. Since, then, you prize giving pleasure, are you willing to give me a little pleasure ?

Pol. I am

Soc. Ask me, then, what kind of art cookery appears to me to be.

Pol. I do ask you; what kind of an art is cookery ?

Soc. None at all, Polus.

Pol. What is it ? say.

Soc. I say, then, it is a certain skill.

Pol. Of what ? say.

Soc, I say, of procuring gratification and pleasure, Polus.

Pol. Are cookery and rhetoric the same thing ?

Soc. By no means, but a part of the same study.

Plato, in *The Republic*, was, however, solicitous about the development of ideals of craftsmanship : "Ought we not keep an eye," he says,

> on the craftsmen also, and prevent them from representing moral evil or disorderliness or bad taste or lack of harmony either in their imitation of animals or in their buildings or in any other object of their craft ? ... Must we not rather search for such craftsmen as are able by their native genius to discover what is beautiful and graceful ? For in this way our children, dwelling in a region of health, will be influenced for good by every sound and every sight of these works of beauty, inhaling as it were a healthy breeze that blows to them from a healthy land.

Taken together these passages indicate that applied arts were held to be not without merit, and that these arts were to be cultivated. In their original contex these passages indicate that training and practice in the arts belonged, however, to persons who were not destined for philosophy or other scholarly pursuits.

8. *Physical education.* Physical education received great emphasis throughout ancient Greece. By the time of the Athenian period the older customs of training boys for physical endurance had given way to physical training for the cultivation of bodily grace and symmetry. Attention to atheletics persisted, however, even throughout this period. One of the leading poets, Pindar of Thebes, is now represented very largely by the odes which were written in honor of the victors in the national atheletic contests. Not without criticism, however, was this great attention given to physical training. Socrates, for example, remarks that "It is strange that the founders of the great Festivals should have kept all their rewards for a physical prowess which serves only the athlete himself, and should have assigned no honour to the mental toil from which flow benefits to all."

Physical education was given during the elementary school years in the palaestra and during later years in the gymnasia. The types of training included practice in correct posture, setting-up exercises, running and jumping, discus and javelin throwing, ball games, rope climbing, boxing, and wrestling.

9. *Music.* Music and art fared somewhat alike when the decadent period began. Even in Plato's time certain forms of both these subjects had fallen into disrepute, the causes being that artists and musicians of fourth-century Greece catered to the crass demands for a type of realism which was analogous to that required of modern artists and musicians. Lyre playing was, however, a regular subject of study for boys. The ability to play the lyre war so common that a proverbial reference to an ignorant person was, "He cannot even play the lyre." Associated with lyre playing was the study of lyric poetry. As soon as the boys mastered the lyre sufficiently, they were taught to play and sing. Plutarch says the Athenian laws were very likely learned in metrical form in this way. The flute was at one

time a popular instrument, but the Greeks ejected it, as an intelligen modern world might eject the yelping saxophone—and for the same reason.

The respectful attitudes towards music of the three great philosophers of Greece are shown in their writings. First, Socrates, late in life, attended the music school of Konnos.

Second, in the *Protagoras*, Plato says,

> The music-master makes rbythm and harmony familiar to the souls of the boys, and they become gentler and more refined, and having more rhythm and harmony in them, they become more efficient in speech and action. The whole life of Man stands in need of good harmony and good rhythm.

Third, Aristotle pays his respects to this subject when he says,

> Music is neither a necessary nor a useful accomplishment in the sense in which Letters are useful, but it provides a noble and a worthy means of occupying leisure time,

Curricuim contributions of ancient Athens spirit and content

Primitive man found a world of chaos. To that unordered world he applied his slender skill in thought. Thought soon led to system. The pity is that the early system satisfied the thinker and became too soon the boundary line of thought. This finality led as we have seen to penalties for nonconformity, and early man remained too long a prisoner in his self-created cell. Primitive attitude, primitive subject matter, primitive life itself then turned ever inward to its ever-narrowing world—a world whose soul was destitute of the nature of the soul, self-directed thought.

To this enfettered soul, the land of Greece gave hope. How what land came to rescue man and how far short the promise was that even Athens gave will be a topic for Part II. But there it was that conformity—tribal ideals, fear, superstition, and, in many matters, downright blindness gave way to individuality and later to education planned to cultivate individuality. A striking and objective contrast between the primitive and the enlightened man is shown in the physical education practiced by the two : in one is brutality, mutilation, and at best sheer endurance ; in the other is sportsmanship, grace, and glorification of studied skill.

The men of Athens pared over problems which have persisted to modern times. What should children learn ? asked Plato and, before him, Isocreates. This question they settled by analyzing man's capacities, the effects of training and practice. and what each youth proposed to do. To the results of this analysis they brought the content then available and added more as life demanded it, or as men of literature, science, art, or philosophy discovered new items and forms of subject matter. No less than men of modern America did the men of Athens try to face the problem of education for the workaday world. But the world which they studied, unlike the scope of the student of American secondary education, was limited to a small fraction of Athenians.

For the youth of genius they decided as have men ever since : this youth's practical needs include, as Isoerates maintaind, all that makes the good man just ; and this view needs only to be fitted to each youth, as Issocrates fitted it, to lead to the modern specialized currieulum for the brilliant youth of our day. The modern problem of religious education with its host of students finds likewise its counterpart in ancient Athens. While modern scholars of all faiths forbid the use of certain Hebrew lore for ethical training, just so one finds the tales of early Greece proscribed by Athens. The place of art in the curriculum grew directly out of the Greek tendency to conventionalize the practical and give to common things a touch of grace ; their conclusions committed the schools definitely to what was then thought best in art and music. The problem of the classification of pupils led teachers to select and organize curricula and plans for pupils' lives on the bases of abilities, interests, social position, and financial rating. That the problems of individual differences were not solved is not because the problems were unseen, but because the technique of modern psychology and the attitude of the modern sociology had to be developed before these problems could be solved. The technique of viewing "with alarm," with intelligence, or with pleasure any modifications or improvement in the curriculum can be exemplified in a score of ancient works still extant.

The Greeks showed their youtn an ordered world. In physics, biology, earth sciences, and astronomy; in mathematics; in language—expresssion, forms, and interpretation; and in life itself, the ancient sages reduced to system all they saw or pondered. This rational contemplation of things within reach (science) and of things beyond reach (metaphysics) attained a quasi-culmination in encyclopedic Aristotle. And not only were science and metaphysics employed to integrate the life and thought of Greece ; art also drew together and depicted what the genius saw in nature or felt in contemplation. Art as practiced by the Greeks gave expression through literature, oral expression, music, physical education, noble living, craftsmanship, and that which connotes in a restricted sense. The art of living nobly was in this age the culmination of all art ; this branch of art included the ability to live well fully, happily, and nobody within established conventions. The best example of a man was no longer the strongest brute, but was instead he who possessed the clearest and best-ordered brain. Out of this orderly Greek world arose a dangerous tendency to allow the principles rather than a combination of principles and concrete experiences to form the curriculum.

Despite the many glories that were hers, Athens thus had her limitations, some of which find parallels in present-day practices or attitudes. Among her limitations as they affected the curriculum was a social system which excluded from education all save a sixth of her population. Limitations in educational method grew out of the tendency to pursue mathematics as a branch of mysticism with charms, the tendency to separate too completely science and practice, the failure to take time for experimentation, the lack of time and opportunity for extensive travel, and the common failure to see the ideal of the superior craftsman. The problem of religion was badly handled because of the failure of the intellectuals to the masses in the reconstruction of religion. Perhaps the most fundamental limitation was, however, the dogmatic form of scientific speculation. Although Aristotle made many direct observations and for his day left a notable record of progress, his habitual speculative procedure posited an essence or innate characteristic for every object. The innate characteristic then became the major premise in his thought about the object and, when accepted as it was in later centuries, it blocked the progress of science and became the sheerest verbalism.

Modern experts have launched a program for economy. This program deals with two forms of economy, one of which emphasizes speed, while the other emphasizes efficiency. Not all crities have, in their discussions, recognized these two forms, but have instead devoted themselves two speed. In undemocratic Greece there was no greet need for haste in completing, academic training but there, was need for the other and more basic type of economy ; namely, the economy which accompanies those mental procedures in which concepts and universal principles supplant inaccurate, rule-of-thumb guesses. It is seldom possible, however, to develop principles which have universal applications save by allowing such principles to grow out of familiar, concrete experience; and later these principles, to have significance, must be applied by the learner. Such a process entails a heavy expenditure of time and many, as a consequence, be judged wasteful. In opposition to this view that the pursuit of abstract systems of thought is wasteful, the Grecks held that puplis who are able to master concepts which have universal application save themselves from waste of effect. That is, for all departments of knowledge which have been rationally systematized, pupils may profitably combine the study of principles and practice.

Modern men have mechanized much of life and increased the quantity of knowledge, but in certain forms of insight they have made little improvement in quality and mental economy. By their power in literature and art. for example, the Greeks reduced the number of directions of further improvement; in these fields, extensions, but not improvements, have been made. In characterizing primitive and Athenian contributions to curriculum growth, it may be said that primitive education represents the radical; Greek education then represents the strong brace roots. Each branch of this growth represents a step toward mental economy rather than toward waste and encumbrance in the training of youth. For example, mathematics was changed by the Greeks from a relatively concrete and cumbersome subject to an abstract, universal science ; the economy which followed this change is obvious. The training of youth in oral and written expression was also made efficient by the development of systematic principles which had general application in both speech and writing. As this conceptualizing or universalizing of knowledge is an outstanding characteristic of Greek curriculum developments, a search for the content of a modern program of studies constantly drives the modern educator back to Greece as a source of concepts which have led to mental economy. There it was that great economy began when a gifted race grappled with the changing conditions of life as issues in curriculum making and then drew up rational plans for formulating the objectives of education, for treating the individual differences among pupils, and for choosing the agents of instruction. Greek contributions cannot be finally appraised until their constructive criticisms and their objectives have been discussed in Parts II and III. If modern problems are found to be quite different from those of ancient times, then and then only can a program for economy be justified in discarding the content and practices of ancient Athens and returning to the cruder practices of peoples who lived before elaborate conceptual schemes of thought had been invented.

4

Principles: Basic to Curriculum Development

Characteristic Contributions from Rome

At about the age of twelve, the Roman schoolboy was promoted from the elementary to the secondary school. In the elementary school the boy had acquired the mechanics of reading and writing the rudiments of arithmetic, and had studied literature. During the early period, prior to 80 B.C., the boy memorized the laws of the Twelve, These laws, together with certain precepts and maxims, constituted the social studies of the elementary school. The study of literature consisted of two branches : the study of style and the interpretation of meaning. The secondary school to which the boy next proceeded was the first definitely organized secondary school and was known as the grammar school. As such, it was a school for adolescents and was the prototype of the modern grammar school, academy, and reorganized high school. The boys went regularly to school, paid their fees on every Ides, and received both class and individual instruction. This grammar school, whose course was three or four years in length, was followed by the school of rhetoric, whose length was usually at least two years. This Rome gave order to the secondary school.

The Curriculum of the Roman Secondary

Quintilian (35 A.D,—95) described in detail the curriculum of the later Roman secondary school. This curriculum is best understood when viewed in connection with the curricula of the pre-school and elementary school periods. The following account of these curricula is based upon Quintilian's comprehensive treatise.

Dusing the preschool period, before the child was seven years of age, the chief elements of training were the rudiments of Latin and Greek and such general information as results from carefully planned play. Many families employed Greek nurses of high intelligence and much refinement: great care was taken to see that the children learned from infancy the correct pronunciation of the languages.

During the elementary school period, ages seven to twelve, the slave companion or 'pedagogus' had general charge of the child. In this school a basis was laid, as at the present time for the work of a higher school. The subjects of study were reading, writing, and arithmetic. The reading then embraced the mechanics of reading during the earliest years and the study of literature during the later years. Greek literature, said Quintilian, was to be studied before Latin, because Greek was the origin of Latin and because Latin was certain to be learned anyway. Neither language was, however, to be so exclusively pursued as to impede progress in the other.

The secondary school was divided into two divisions, the junior division or grammar school of about four years and the senior division or school of rhetoric of about two years. In both divisions the literary studies of the elementary school were continued. Such literary study was here, as in Greece, known chiefly as grammar. The 'grammaticus or teacher of grammar had both extensive and intensive duties. Grammar embraced, first, such technicalities as the sounds and values of latters and linguistic modifications and historical changes of letters; second, the inflectional properties of the different parts of speech, with reasons therefore ; and, third, syntax and composition.

Besides attending to these technicalities, the 'grammaticus' tried to instil an adpreciation of and skill in the elements of style : excellence, lucidity, and elegance. Literary study of this sort was conducted in connection with the interpretation of the poets. The study of poets included, as it often does today, a consideration of style, philology, rhythm and meter, and historical allusions. Grammar was sometimes further extended to embrance oral expression. More frequently eloquence and rhetoric were the terms applied to the study of expression. Oral reading occupied and important place at this stage, as it did also in the elementary school ; for this work, prose and poetry were drawn from many sources. Besides literary studies, boys studied music, geometry, arithmetic, and astronomy during the junior division of the secondary school.

In the senior division of secondary education, called the school of rhetoric, the boy pursued advanced courses in oral and written expression and thus laid a solid foundation for his later activities as an orator. Here, pure Latin was studied, great care being given to choice of both words and subject. The character of this word study is indicated by Quintilian's insistence upon the specific significance, form, measure of words, and the propriety of words to both the meaning to be portrayed and the occasion of each discourse. The occasion of the discourse was the guide also to the arrangement or order of the words and the divisions of the discourse as well as to the expression of the speaker. As a basis for his academic course in composition, Quintilian provided for extensive reading of Greek and Roman poets, historians, philosophers, and orators, each of whose writings he characterized in regard to use of both content and from. Training in expession was provided by a carefully graded system of lessons in oral Latin. These lessons began with the simple, well-prepared declamation of passage of increasing difficulty and led to half-extempore speaking for which preparation had been made and finally to extempore delivery. At this final stage much attention was given to voice and gesture. Motivation for this work was afforded by the demands of the Forum, which was of compelling interest to all enlightened Romans.

The contributions of Rome are thus found to be characteristic : she organized the school itseif, she furthered the systematization of the courses, and she made her education more practical than that of philosophical Greek teachers such as Plato and Aristotle. In other words, Rome adopted and developed the aim of Isocrates. The following quotation from Quintilian presents the educational ideal of Rome's greatest schoolmaster and also of Isocrates :

> Let an orator be such a man as we may term truly wise; not only accomplished in his manners (for I think differntly from those who think that is sufficient), but in knowledge and the practice of speaking, beyond what perhaps ever any man was. But this is no reason why we should relax in aiming at perfection. It was the practice with most of the ancients to lay down maxims of wisdom, though they did not admit that any man was perfectly wise. For there is certainly such a thing as perfection in eloquence, and there is nothing in human nature that forbids our attaining it. But even though it should not be attained, yet still they who aspire to the summit, will go higher than they who, preposterously despairing of succeeding in their aim, loiter at the bottom.

The Part Played by Rome in the Development of Curricula

This account of secondary education in Rome of the first century of our era shows the genius of the Romans in organizing and furthering what had been begun by their Roman ancestors and by the Greeks. They were, in this respect, no more imitators. They developed in Rome the same rationalized forms of subject matter prior to the invasion of Greek thought as those which the Greeks had developed some centuries earlier. One reason why they appear to be imitators of the Greeks is that they had reached, by the time of the elder Cato (234—149 B.C), a stage of cultural development which was in many respects analogous to that which the Greeks had reached when the sophists began to ply their craft in fifth-century Greece. It is, therefore, to the credit of the Romans that they were able to distinguish the most excellent from all the examples of human development which were then extant and adopt and adapt certain Greek practics to attain their own ends.

To the assertion that the Romans were a narrow, practical people and lacking in originality, it should, therefore, be said that prior to the Greco-Roman period, the Romans had already traveled a very considerable distance toward the discovery and dissemination of knowledge, that they continued their journey by adaptations which they themselves made of the best of ancient lore and practice, and that they developed still further for Middle Ages nearly all the branches of Knowledge which they had inherited from the Greeks.· That the Romans added no new subjects save possibly agriculture to the curriculum is the only reason for concluding so summarily this account of the educational contributions of the Romans. As the Greeks developed and added subject matter to the means of educating youth, so the Romans continued to add subject matter, particularly literature, and also added organization and admistration.

The Seven Liberal Arts

Christian boys of the Middle Ages pursued, or, more accurately, suffered in the absorption of, the seven liberal arts. These liberal studies were among the gifts of Greece and Rome to Western Europe. The pity is that Western Europe and not Greece herself arranged the details of this gift, and that too little of the soul of Athens reappeared in the organizing and conducting of the study of these arts. Later, the curriculum of the early modern period was developed from these seven subjects.

It was Varro (116—127 B.C.), the most learned man of his century, who outlined for Rome and the West this gift from the Greeks. By canvassing Roman life he was able to search intelligently for the branches of learning which were needed to supply the proper training for Roman boys. Of Grecian learning he found nine branches with which to complement the science that was known to Rome. These nine branches of pagan learning were met by two attitudes of Christian Rome. First, there was grave concern as to the desirability of encouraing pagan thought. Second, there was full realization of the need for Greek learning as a foundation for a Christian for a Christian curriculum. Even as wise a man as Augustine (354—430 A.D.) held and expressed both views though he finally decided in favor of the second. Augustine, therefore, named six of the seven liberal arts which he thought necessary for the training of youth.

To Martianus Capella of Carthage (about 500 A.D.) was left the task of fixing the arts to the number of seven. In his somewhat veiled introduction of the seven arts, he set forth an allegorical account of the marriage of Philologia and Mercury. This supposedly beautiful setting enabled Capella to present as bride the earth-born maiden Philologia, who represented school learning. and as bridegroom the heavenborn Mercury, inventor of letters and the symbol of Greek learning. The first two books of Capella's work were devoted to the principals of the wedding, and the remaining seven presented the seven bridesmaids, who symbolized grammar. rhetoric, logic, geometry, arithmetic, astronomy, and music, respectively. In addition to Capella's list, Varro had included medicine and architecture, both of which Capella rejected as bridesmaids because they were concerned with perishable earthly things and had nothing in common with the ethereal and divine. Augustine had omitted astronomy because of its questionable astrological association, but included philosophy.

The arts thus fantastically presented by Capella were adopted both by writers on education and by schools. Although not all schools offered all these subjects, these were the basal arts, and grammar was the solid rock on which all other arts were founded. What Capella failed to mention, others were quick to see; namely, that seven was the heaven-ordained number : "Let us understand plainly that whensoever Holy Scriptures mean to set forth anything as entire and complete, as they frequently do, it is comprehended under the number, even as David says, 'Seven times in the day have I spoken praises unto thee,' and Solomon, 'Wisdom hath builded

builded her house; she hath hewn out her seven pillars." Thus it happened, Parker says,

> that the pedigree of the seven arts is an important part of history of modern literature. The doctrine that they were seven was immutably established and no one ventured to controvert it or break up the list. The family was, in fact, in the condition of the family in Wordsworth's poem.... its device was "We are seven."

The seven liberal arts were classified into two groups—the trivium, which consisted of grammar, rhetoric and logic, and the quadrivium, which consisted of geometry, arithmetic, astronomy, and music. The content of these subjects was not, however, the same as that now included under these seven names. As the early modern differentiation of subjects was based upon these seven studies, the subject matter of each will be briefly summarized.

1. *Grammar*. The basal character of grammar is attested by the common description of it by such terms as "foundation," "doorkeeper" of all the other sciences, "mistress of rhetoric," and "interpreter of theology." Parallel with the study of this Latin grammar, 'The Distichs of Cato were studied. The Distichs, also in Latin, were used as a first Latin reader from the early Middle Ages until after the opening of modern times. This collection of simple verses, as now extant, comprises four books, of forty, thirty one, twenty-four, and forty-nine morality and religious couplets. with short prefaces. After a foreword and fifty-six short proverbs, Book I opens as follows :

> If God a spirit is as poets sing,
> With mind kept pure make thou thy offering.
> Be oft awake : from too much sleep abstain,
> For vice from sloth doth ever nurture gain.

The extensive character of grammar is shown by the divisions assigned to it by the authors of the leading textbooks of the Middle Ages, Donatus of the fourth century, and Priscian of the sixth. Donatus treated the topics now included in grammar and rhetoric and to these Priscian added literary analysis and interpretation. This content was supplemented by dialogues or colloquies, fables, proverbs, and maxims. The following samples from the three most popular mediaeval books on grammar and related subject sound in part familiar and in part unfamilar to modern ears.

Two versions of *Ars Grammatici* by Donatus have come down to us. The longer form, *Ars Maior*, opens with a definition of the human voice after which letters are discussed in some detail : "A letter," says Donatus, "is the smallest part of an articulate sound. Some of the letters are called vowels ; others are called consonants.' Of the consonants, some are semi-vowels, and others are mute," etc. Later sections of Donatus are devoted to syllables, feet, accent, punctuation, parts of speech, and rhetorical matters. Priscian treats of accidence and syntax by the study of Virgil's *Aeneid*, which opens with the well-known question, "What part of speech is *arma* ?" During the twelfth century, about 1119, Alexander de Villa Dei, the "Aristotle of Grammar," wrote the *Doctrinale*, a book which, for a time, came nearly displacing Donatus and Priscian. This book, which contained 2645 lines, devotes 1073 to etymology, 476 to syntax, and 1095 to quantity, accent, and figures. The relation of the organization of this material to prevailing methods of instruction is illustrated by the fact that the popularity of this book was due largely to two features : its metrical form rendered it easier to memorize ; and the nicety of its logic accorded with the disputatious interests of mediaeval schoolmasters.

All these textbooks were in Latin, and, as the pupils rarely had copies, it was necessary for them to memorize the contents or else copy from the master's dictation. After some proficiency had been acquired, still other works were studied at the larger schools, as at St. Gall, where many of the standard Latin authors were read.

2. *Rhetoric.* The subject, so important in a Greek democracy, often declined in the Middle Ages to mere drawing

up of business forms by priests. It had. it is true, a distinct function in the preparation of the preacher, but many mediaevalists disdained an art which taught the user only to proclaim that which any inspired preacher must unaided deliver with fervor and effect. At its best, however, as exemplified by Maurus, rhetoric was the art of employing discourse effectively in daily affairs. Although Maurus defined rhetoric in secular terms, he regarded it as very important in ecclesiastical in struction. As far as the preacher expresses himself eloquently, adequately, and impressively, he owes his skill to this art.

Therefore, he who attains a mastery of rhetoric, instead of being culpable, is to be praised for acquiring power the better to proclaim the word of God. Furthermore, one may, through rhetoric, prove anything true or false. This being the case, the preacher, more than anyone else, must master rhetoric in order that he may not stand defenseless in the presence of false witnesses, and that he may not fail to present truth most effectively to his hearers. Indeed Maurus feared, that, without this art, even listening to the presentation of truth might become a wearisome exercise and faith an impossibility.

Brunetto Latini (1220–1294 ?) devoted Part III of his compend of universal knowledge to rhetoric. As conceived by Brunetto, this subject was allied with politics. This conception of the general scholar parallels the conception of rhetoric as the handmaid of religion of Maurus the churchman.

3. *Logic*. As the mediaeval scholar had many occasions upon which to defend his faith, logic—or dialectics as it was often called—was needed in the training for disputation. Important as this study was in training for the social life of the Middle Ages, is now has little attention from modern secondary-school curriculum makers. Whether it should regain in part its former place, depends upon the present need for analysis of arguments whether printed or spoken and in part upon the question as to whether this art has been taken over in sufficient

quantity by other subjects. Quite certain it is that the present day demands fine analyses of arguments. If, however, teachers of our day utilize such material as is now available, as in social studies and literature, the alleged practical values of logic of the old schools is not without a place in the modern school.

4. *Geometry*. The character of mediaeval geometry seems to receive a just treatment in the following account which is based upon Maurus. This subject is an exposition of form, beginning with observation and continuing by demonstration. The high origin of geometry is attested by philosophers who declare that Jupiter made use of it in his works. This allegation by the philosophers caused Maurus some uneasiness, and he is constrained to deny Jupiter's use of this science in favor of use by the Christian God. If this alteration in the premises is allowed, Maurus holds that the Holy Trinity also employs geometry in bestowing forms and images upon its creatures. Likewise, the demands of this rigorous science determine the course of the moving stars and the planets and assign unalterable positions to the fixed stars. Indeed, every well-ordered arrangement is determined by, and can be reduced to, the rules of geometry. The religious significance of this subject is set forth still further by Maurus, as he shows its significance in the building of the tabernacle and the temple. In those important edifices were used circles, spheres, hemispheres, quadrangles, and other figures. Hence, the pursuit of geometry, if properly correlated with religious works, will yield much for the spiritual welfare of the clergy.

5. *Arithmetic*. The arithmetic of the early Middle Ages has little more academic significance than that of the Greeks. Its special value lay in computing the problems of the Scriptures and the date of Easter, as well as from the mystical properties of certain numbers and their combinations. Capella well illustrates the addle-pated arithmetician of his age :

> What shall I call four ? In which is a certain perfection of solidarity ; for it is composed of length and depth, and

a full decade is made up from those four numbers added together in order ; that is, from one, two, three, four. Similarly a hundred is made up of the four decades, that is, ten, twenty, thirty, forty. which are a hundred ; and again four numbers from a hundred on amount to a thousand, that is, 100. 200, 300, 400. So ten thousand is made up of another series. What is to be said of the fact that there are four seasons of the years, four quarters of the heavens. and four principles of the elements ? There are also four ages of man, four vices, and four virtues.

Of a collection of "Problems for Quickening the Mind," Cajori gives the following account :

> The following is a specimen of these "Problems" : A dog chasing a rabbit, which has a start of 150 feet, jumps 9 feet every time the rabbit jumps 7. In order to determine in how many leaps the dog overtakes the rabbit, 150 is to be divided by 2. In this collection of problems, the areas of triangular and quadrangular pieces of land are found by the same formulas of approximation as those used by the Egyptians and given by Boethius in his geometry. An old problem is the "cistern-problem" (given the time in which several pipes can fill a cistern singly, to find the time in which they fill it jointly), which has been found previously in Heron, in the Greek *Anthology*, and in Hindu works. Many of the problems show that the collection was compiled chiefly from Roman sources. The problem which, on account of its uniqueness gives the most positive testimony regarding the Roman origin is that on the interpretation of a will in a case where twins are born. The problem is identical with the Roman, except that different ratios are chosen. Of the exercises for recreation we mention the one of the wolf, goat, and cabbage, to be rowed across a river in a boat holding only one besides the ferry-man. Query : How must he carry them across so that the goat shall not eat the cabbage, nor the wolf the goat ? The

solutions of the "problems for quickening the mind" require no further knowledge than the recollection of some few formulas used in surveying, the ability to solve linear equations and to perform the four fundamental operations with integers. Extraction of roots was nowhere demanded ; fractions hardly ever occur.

6. *Astronomy.* Two reasons make a discussion of astronomy desirable here : first, its connection with astrology ; and, second, its connection with theology. That is, mediaeval astronomy shows the danger to which a subject may lay itself open by treading where only guessing thrives, and, at the same time, it shows the danger of making an institutional matter of questionable suppositions. An earth-centered universe as a theoretical postulate hindered all except the rare original thinker or investigator ; the union of this false postulate with theological dogma discouraged the original thinker from disclosing any scientific variations in thinking.

Reference to the disparity between the findings of the greatest astronomers and the astronomy of the schools may also be mentioned in passing. Throughout the Middle Ages there were astronomers like Isidore of the seventh century who repeatedly mentions that heaven is a sphere rotating round an axis and having the spherical earth in its centre." The earth's sphericity seems, however, to have remained a dark secret as far as schoolboys were concerned. The alleged failure of the modern schools to offer the best that science can provide has thus a parallel in an age which we may not wish to emulate.

7. *Music.* The value of music to the church gave this art an obvious place in the mediaeval school. As Maurus indicates, music aids in training for the reading of the psalms, as well as in the strictly musical portion of the ritual. While the "choir school" offered this practical training, there was provided also a certain amount of theoretical information about intervals and the "movements" of certain tones within a scale. As heaven and earth and all that moves therein is

"nothing but music," and as the "world was created by music and can be ruled by it," no further sanction was needed for the study of this noble art!

In addition to religion which supplemented the seven liberal arts as a school subject. each of the arts themselves included certain content not now offered in these respective courses. As grammar included what is now known as language and literature, so astronomy included much science now classified under different names. Masters called upon their own resources to kindle interest and to add content to all arts. Alcuin, for example, enriched the courses considerably in the school of Charles the Great. Some portions of the enrichment must have added mirth to the life of the boys. Among his colloquies. these passages occur :

P. What is faith ?	A. The certainty of things unknown and wonderful.
P. What is wonderful ?	A. I lately saw a man stand and a dead man walk who never existed.
P. How can this be ? Please explain.	A. It was an image in the water.
P. Why did I not understand this by myself, considering that I have often seen such a man ?	A. Becausc you are a good young man, and quick of perception, I shall speak to you of other wonderful things. Try, if you can, to find them out by yourself.
P. I will try, but if I fail, please correct me.	A. Rest assured that I will do as you desire. A person unknown to me has spoken to me without tongue or voice ; he never

existed before, does not exist now, and never will exist hereafter ; I never heard nor saw him.

P. You dreamt, master, I think ; did you ?	A. Right, my son. Now hear another. I saw the dead bring forth the living, and the breath of the living devour the dead.
P. By the friction of boughs fire is produced, which devours them.	A. That is true..."

There is little reason to believe that the recorded content of these courses constituted all the content. How much of informal discussion accompanied the foregoing colloquy is not indicated. Even in that somewhat unscholarly age, reason prompts us to believe that further historical research will show that those years were far more scholarly than they have been judged to be.

Curriculum Developments during the Later Mediaeval Centuries

Mediaeval Europe has been variously characterized as a land of gloom and as a guardian of light. The early mediaeval centuries have been called the Dark Ages, while the thirteenth centuries has been styled the "greatest of centuries." Whether or not the mediaeval era appears as a plateau in human progress, a slough of despond, or a circuitous ascent depends upon one's point of view and clearness of vision—rather upon clearness of vision than upon point of view. Viewed from the vantage ground of competent historians and in the light of mediaeval writings, this period is distinguished as one of advancement in new directions and on enormous spread in territorial area—a spread which is, in certain respects, comparable with the modern attempt to extend secondary education to neglected social groups.

The Middle Ages brought forth many new problems and encountered many impediments in the solution of these problems. First, hordes of peoples of low cultural status presented themselves for assimilation—either learned men had to provide for the assimilation of these hordes or the hordes would arrange for the extermination of civilization. Second, ancient education had to adapt itself to new religious conditions —either classical learning had to show it value in promoting the new Christian religion or the new teachers would forget the past. Third, there was much to study, but facilities for study were poor - either there must have been a decay of learning or an improvement of conditions. Fourth, there were long periods of neglect of learning by kings and princes ; in an age of bellicose tumult, the rulers had little time for the cloister, and rarely could men who looked toward scholarship choose else but to live apart from politics and trade.

Confronted with problems such as these, what were the aims of medieval men ? By what means did they plan to solve their problems ? Two aims are outstanding as far as political and ecclesiastical leaders were concerned : these men sought first to build a universal empire, and, second, to establish firmly a universal church. A third aim, that of a few notable statesmen, was to establish schools worthy of their realms. A fourth aim, that of mastering eastern love, dominated a few scholars. Besides, there were the aim of the "gentle" knight to perform noble services graciously, and the aim of the traveler—pious pilgrim or rash Viking—to explore, and possibly plunder, the lands beyond their own.

But mediaevalism was not a static issue composed of problems all with their solutions patent to the wise, In addition to problems more or less clearly seen and aims which roughly paralleled the problems, there were many moving variables—human forces which at times represented the practical man's escape from the real problems. Toward the later centuries of the Middle Ages, such forces took form in the rise of towns, the development of trade, the growth of industry, and the formation of guilds; the refining of princes, the extension of travel and education and culture; the rationalization of theology and the reconciliation of religion with a rigorous logic; and the development of a "practical" curriculum.

One mediaeval institution and only one was partially fit for the age. Kings neglected learning, warrior despoiled the schools and burned the books, traders found no profit in learning which produced no successful alchemists, the unorganized masses had no means of asking for the learning away from which they most certainly would have turned. To the church, therefore, fell a double duty as defender of the new faith and preserver of ancient lore. These two, faith and ancient lore, she had to balance, and in doing so the faith was not forgotten even if pagan learning was forced to suffer. Mediaeval conformists had to scrutinize the curricula of their day to exclude and eliminate each item that was judged irrelevant to churchly learning. This care was due in part to the fact that pagan lore was believed to be spiritually harmful as well as ecclesiastically useless. When, for example, Gregory of the sixth century found a bishop teaching grammar—language and literature - he wrote, "I have been informed—I cannot repeat it without shame—that you, my brother, are teaching certain persons grammar. At this I was so grieved and felt so strong disgust that my former feelings were changed to groans and sadness; because the same mouth cannot utter the praise of Jupiter and Christ." But not all churchmen shared Gregory's objections to the classics. Anselm, archbishop of Canterbury in the eleventh century, recommended the study of Virgil and other pagan writers. Furthermore, as an aid to classical study, the laity especially as represented by leaders such as Charles the Great, Alfred the Great. and Otto the Great by mandate or example, stimulated the study of the seven liberal arts. Contrasting examples can thus be cited of men who like Hermannus Contractus wished on his deathbed to reread Cicero; and Odo of Cluny, who likened Virgil to "a beautiful vase full of ugly adders." The obvious utility of Latin finally overcame the bigoted opposition to it, so that by the twelfth century the classics were copied, quoted, studied, and discussed by scholars, and sometimes employed even in support of the Scriptures. In addition to the instrinsic lure of the classics and their utility, there was already a belief in their disciplinary power. Just as Plato wished only minds whetted by geometry, so certain scholar-teachers of the Middle Ages wished minds cleared and sharpened by the classics.

CHART II

Mediaeval Contributors to Secondary School Curricula and the Revivals of Learning

Seventh Century

Columba, founder of Irish and Scotch centers of learning
Columban, fonder of north Italian center of learning
Gallus, founder of monastery famed for its learning.
Isidore of Seville, encyclopedist and versed in Latin and Greek
Theodore of Tarsus, patron of Greek in England

Eighth Century

Bede, historian and "most general scholar of his age"
Boniface, scholar and "apostle of Germany"
Alcuin, teacher, bibliophilc, Greek and Latin scholar
Charles the great (d. 814), school administrator and patron of learning

Ninth Century

Al-Khowarizmi, mathematician and astronomer
Dicuil, popular Irish geographer
Rabanus Maursu, teacher and author of books on education
Servetus Lupus, protagonist of letters

Alfred the Great, first translator into English
John the Scot, teacher and scholar of Greek and Latin

Tenth Century

Massoudy, travel-writer; sphericist
Gerbert, scholar and patron of science, mathematics, music, and medicine

Eleventh Century

Avicenna, leader in medical literature
Constantinus Africanus, "restorer of medical literature in the West"
Omar Khayyam, mathematician and poet
Guido di Arezzo, leader in musical notation
Anselm, "the father of scholaticism"
Roscellinus, early scholastic and teacher

Twelfth Century

Abelard, dialectician, teacher, and author, and with William of Champeaux a leader in the university movement
Adelard of Bath, scholar, traveler, and pioneer translator of Arabic
John of Salisbury, scholar, publicist, and protagonist of Greek
Hugo of St. Victor, student of education and scholar
Walter Map, British writer of prose and poetry
Chretien de Troies, French poet of Holy Grail
Gerard of Cremona, translator of Ptolemy's *Almagest* and scores of other works
Averroes, Moorish popularizer of Aristotle
Moses Maimonides, physician and student of Aristotle
Daniel Morley, carrier of Arabic books to England
Robert of Chester, translator of Al-Khowarizmi's *Algebra*

Thirteenth Century

Alexander Neckam, encyclopedist
Wolfram von Eschenbach, poet-author of popular version of *Parsifal*
Thomas Aquinas, the "Angelic Doctor"
Albertus Magnus, schoolman and scientist
Robert Grosseteste, scholar of Latin and Greek, and teacher of Roger Bacon
Roger Bacon, a herald of modern experimental science
Alphonso the Wise, scholar and patron of science
John of Garland, Latin lexicographer and teacher
Marco Polo, geographer

So it was, therefore, that learning persisted and at the hands of distinguished champions shone forth in a revival. The accompanying chart indicates to the student of mediaeval history the strength of the revivals. Each of the scholars here catalogued represents a revival in his branch of study. Gallus as founder of a seat of learning, Gerbert and Al-Khowarizmi as mathematicians, Dicuil and Massoudy as geographers, Gerard all translator, and John of Salisbury of lover of the classics—all these, like the many others catalogued in the chart, represent deepening of knowledge, a spread of learning, or both. These transmitters and pioneers of scholarship were notably successful workers in science, mathematics, literature, music, art.

In science, men questioned the dogmatism of the older writers and conducted experiments for themselves. Although no scientist of these centuries shook off the magic of his age, many men disclosed certain secrets which had before been hidden in darkness and mystery. Albertus Magnus, for example, by his own experiments exposed many false notions about science; for instance, by actual experimentation he found that ostriches did not, as alleged, eat and digest iron, although he did give credence to the famous tale of the toad and the emerald :

> An emerald was recently seen among us, small in size but marvelous in beauty. When its virtue was to be tested, someone stepped forth and said that, if a circle was made about a toad with the emerald and then the stone was set before the toad's eyes, one of two things would happen. Either the stone, if of weak virtue, would be broken by the gaze of the toad; or the toad would burst, if the stone was possessed of full natural vigor. Without delay things were arranged as he bade; and after a short lapse of time, during which the toad kept its eye unswervingly upon the gem; the latter began to crack like a nut and a portion of it flew from the ring. Then the toad, which had stood immovable hitherto, withdraw as if it had been freed from the influence of the gem.

Likewise, Roger Bacon, who inspired much scientific experimentation, accepted the story of a wise man who believed with others that animals when ill or injured sought their natural remedies. This story was that a man, in seeking an herb of great virtue, dissected a serpent, leaving intact only the skin of its belly—the snake then crawled as well as it could to the herb and, upon touching it, was immediately made whole. Another scientist who looked to fact while he held to fancy was the geographer Massoudy (Al-Mas'udi). Massoudy, though a keen observer and a man versed in mathematical geography, held with Al-Khowarizmi the "dome theory"—or belief in an earth-summit in the middle of the known world. In spite of continued error in some matters, these men added to the reliable knowledge of physics, chemistry, biology, geography, and astronomy.

In mathematics there was the transmission of the unified treatment of arithmetic, algebra, and geometry which came from Pythagoras by way of Arabia and Spain to mediaeval Europe. Of the greatest importance was the transmission of the work of Al-Khowarizmi, because "Through his arithmetic, presenting the Hindu art of reckoning. he revolutionized the common processes of calculation and through his algebra he laid the foundation for modern analyses.

In the development of new literature, the vernaculars of the northern countries produced during this period such undying masterpieces as *Parsifal* and *Tristram.* These tales, as related by Wolfram von Eschenbach and Gottfried von Strassburg, indicated the wealth of literary material which lay in the folklore of the northern peoples and the possibility of using the new languages in the production of enduring literature.

In music Guido d'Arezzo and others of the eleventh, twelfth, and thirteenth centuries applied the syllables *ut*, *re mi*, *fa*, *sol*, *la*, and the successive tones of every hexachord; and, by always using mi-fa to cover the half-step, developed a plan similar to the modern "movable *do*.". Musical notation was as greatly improved during this period as was arithmetical notation. in addition to bringing about these mechanical improvements in music study, this period developed the art of melodic ornamentation and began the use of modern harmonic and contrapuntal arrangements.

In the works of mediaeval architects and craftsmen are found evidences of skill, patience, and industry which excel much of the work of the greatest men of modern times. Then it was that the work of gilds was brought to its highest point. Periods of apprenticeship varied according to the trade and locality. The cooks of Paris required only two years' service, "the carpenters four, the chandlers six, the embroiderers eight, the goldsmiths ten. A seven years apprenticeship, which had become universal amongst London crafts, was adopted as the national standard in the sixteenth century. On the continent a much shorter period of from two or six years was supplemented by the requirement of from three to five years' travel in search of fuller experience."

A significant curriculum problem in the church schools of the twelfth and thirteenth centuries grew out of the crowding of the curriculum and the demand for practical courses. It was the belief of many teachers that boys could profitably economize their time by shortening or omitting their work in grammar. The economy thus effected enabled the boys to proceed more directly to the popular "modern" courses in business. Chief of these new courses was correspondence—the "art" of letter writing came near overshadowing the training in language and composition as then included in grammar. Other modern subjects, as law and medicine, were opened to boys as soon as the rudiments of reading were mastered. To make the situation worse for sound scholarship, the teachers of the practical subjects flagrantly advertised their powers and the creditable opportunities for advancement in the practice of the law, medicine. and documentary writing. Indeed, the interest in short cuts to scholarship and the plea for practical subjects during the twelfth and thirteenth centuries are so similar to those of modern times that one may well seek counsel here in the handling of the problems of the present day. It was this decline of interest in grammar that inspired Henri d' Andeli of the thirteenth century to produce *The Battle of the Seven Liberal Arts.* In this account of an academic battle, grammar is humbled and withdraws "into Egypt, where she was born."

Of the general aims of the Middle Ages already named, those which referred to the universal church, to the acquisition, expansion, and transmission of Greek and Arabic learning, to chivalry, and to travel affected the lines of curriculum development of this period. Only a few monarchs attempted to translate the aim of a universal empire ito terms which affected the curricula of their times. By adopting Greek and Arabic learning this period distinguished itself from the early Middle Ages and at the same time prepared the way for the greater revival of letters in the fifteenth century and of science in the sixteenth. As an age of curriculum-pioneering, this age should be venerated for its systematization of knowledge as well as for its great dissemination of mathematics and science through western Europe.

An appraisal of Roman and Mediaeval curriculnm development

During the fifteen centuries which preceded the year 1300 many changes took place in secondary school curricula. Varied though the purposes of the Romans and the mediaevalists were, their characteristic skill in selecting and organizing distinguishes this long era as one of standardization of existing materials rather than as one of fertility in the discovery of new materials. They were not, however, wholly lacking in the production of new subject matter.

The early centuries of this period witnessed the addition of Roman literature to the standard program of European schools. As this literature provided a masterly treatment of subjects as diverse as agriculture and the world of departed spirits, it constitutes one of the world's outstanding gifts to civilization. The mediaeval centuries witnessed the change from pagan to Christian subject matter in things religious. The reentry of large divisions of Greek learning, the further developments of science and vernacular literature, the continued spirit of encyclopedism, and the addition of works of the Christian fathers mark the mediaeval age as one of some originality.

Ample reasons exist, however, for the prevailing notion that curricula declined in effectiveness during the Middle Ages. First, throughout the later years of this long period, the classics were so completely mechanized by teaching procedure that the original beauty of their lines was lost. But this loss of beauty was not deplored because the purpose of teachers during the mediaeval period was not to teach literature; instead, their purpose was to develop facility in the use of Latin language. Since the church objected to having her sons find comfort in pagan literature, few mediaevalists seem to have risen above this language drill in studying the classics. This condition is not a necessary indication, however, that mediaeval teaching was not good; rather, it reflects merely the policy of employing the classics for purposes of drill upon language forms and usage. For this purpose mediaevalists found Latin classics effective.

Second, this attitude toward literature is only one example of the results of the dominance of schools by a young and undisciplined institution. For the church of this period was not in control of her power; she wielded great physical and mental force, but in matters of scholarship she extended only the protection of the untrained guardian and displayed only the insight of a frontier institution. As the schools, in view of their purposes, betrayed no necessary inefficiency by employing the classics for purposas of drill, so the church betrayed no necessary insincerity or unrighteousness by her narrowly intolerant frontier attitude. In keeping with the times, as already described, life had somehow to be directed. A powerful and timely institution undertook to direct European development, and the desiccated mediaeval curriculum was the result.

Although one can easily find reasons for denouncing the effects of the church upon academic life, one can quite as readily find reasons for exonerating the church from certain defects. The general influence of the church seems to have led to a decline in interest in science. mathematics, literature, fine art, and physical education. The church seems also to have stereotyped the academic treatment of what learning she did tolerate. By neglecting great bodies of important knowledge and stereotyping what she guarded, the church has no light charge against her. She has, however, a wholly different story to relate through the lives and works of some of her greatest leaders. Among the products of the church are Gerbert, the mathematician, John of Salisbury, the scholarly publicist, Roger Bacon, the scientific philosopher, and Dante, the poet.

These leaders represent the secular mediaeval achievement at its height and indicate that individuals could and did rise above the common spirit of their times. Although the church often stood in the paths of these men, their lives show that strong, scholarly leadership rather than a change in the fundamental principles of the church was the need of this period. Had the mediaeval church been granted one hundred years of leadership by Gerbert and Roger Bacon's papal guide, the curricula of moderns times could have been produced during any century of the mediaeval era. For the church herself exhibited the spirit of her leaders and did not stand as an intrinsically impersonal institution. Owing to a lack of intelligent leadership, the gains of the Middle Ages were slowly made and were often obtained through clandestine activities. Gains there were, nevertheless, in the several branches of science, art and architecture, music and literature, and in the number of available mathematical documents. A notable reconstruction of higher education took place, and that in turn soon influenced secondary schools. Certain practical forms of education, such as commercial training, were maintained in private venture schools. The territorial extension of knowledge has already been mentioned as a contribution of mediaeval times. Unless, however, the spirit of religion has been quite misunderstood in modern times, the mediaevalists displayed their greatest lack of skill in teaching this subject which was at the center of all their academic interests.

At its worst this era appears as the silencer of leaders, Free leadership and tolerance of constructive criticism, two essentiais of progress, were lacking. At its best this era appears as an age in which undisciplined hordes were yielding to the subtle charms of learning and at times encouraging trained leaders to guide youth in the paths of learning. To these last influences are due the credit for beginning a new era in the fourteenth century.

The ancient Romans organized schools, selected subject matter, and divided the subject matter into teachable units. The later mediaevalists bequeathed to modern times a mechanized curriculum consisting of the seven liberal arts. To this bequest were added both deadening traditions and scholarly aspirations. Out of the latter, when combined with the seven liberal arts, came the interests and advancements in literature, science, and mathematics which distinguish most clearly the modern age from mediaevalism.

5

Aims of Education

The first modern scholar

Every scholar whom genius marks begets within his age a revival of learning. Thus it was tnat the mediaeval genius revived for every century of that era the learning of the past and kept aglow the zeal for deeper knowledge in his day. Either the century which produced the indefatigable translator, Gerard of Cremona, or the century which gave light to that forerunner of modern science, Roger Bacon, may properly be styled an era of revival. Indeed, the names of Isidore, Charles the Creat, and Alfred, Gerbert, and so throughout the names recorded in Chart II, all stand for men who prompted the revivals of their times. It was by these recurring stimuli to learning that modern times were generated. The man born out of the long era of gestation was Petrarch—the fourteenth-centurg scholar who served as herald of the day when human life, humah thought, and human works could be frankly used in directing adolescent schoolboys.

In Petrarch's day were Boccaccio, who served as gleaner of fascinating tales and still serves as the inspired of the novelist; Chaucer, who bedecked his native land with verse; and Vergerius, who showed the first modern teacher what to teach. As curriculum makers, these men announced a program which had been faintly seen by John of Salisbury and perhaps by other mediaevalists. Even these fourteenth-century men were not at one in estimating the worth of their own native tongues, nor were they quite agreed as individuals to desert traditions long establshed; their hesitancy illustrates the difficulty which a radical change in curricula always entails. Men of their times these men did, however, represent a balance of spirit seldom if ever found before them. This spirit leaned toward modern times and indicated the decline of mediaeval scholarship; although many mediaevalists could have developed modern schools; always in their centuries the balance lay with tradition. New learning then made its way but slowly and in the face of tradition-bound scholars. In Petrarch's day and afterward, new learning made its way rapidly, because scholars who never knew the bonds of mediaeval Europe pointed out the way to the Italian renaissance.

In characterizing Petrarch, the father of humanism, and showing the differences between mediaeval and early modern influences, Robinson says :

> John of Salisbury, for example, in the twelfth century, had known almost as many of the Roman poets and moralists and used them, in a very different fashion. He had read them, however, and used them, in a very different fashion. He had read them with no surrender to their charm, and no response to their views concerning life and uses. But with Petrarch it was other-wise. He first, among the men of the Middle Ages, was endowed with a passionate love for the beauty of ancient literature, and an entire sympathy with its rulling ideas, and at the same time, it must be observed, with a saving incapacity to foresee the disintegration of thought and faith that in the long run would inevitably result from such sympathy.

Even Petrarch was reluctant to give up the ancient language of his Roman ancestors and adopt the language of his day. Petrarch's comments upon his own vernacular and upon Latin are also especially significant, because he appreciated so fully the merits of his native tongue; for he was familiar with the work of Dante in Italian and had himself written, as a young man, in the same language. His attitude is of importance also as showing the same reluctance to adopt his vernacular as Englishmen of the sixteenth century showed in adopting the English language. As Petrarch exhibits in several other passages the same attitude as the presented in the following excerpt from a letter to Boccaccio about 1336, this may properly be regarded as characteristic.

> To be sure, the Latin, in both prose and poetry, is undoubtedly the nobler language, but for that very reason it has been so thoroughly developed by earlier writers that we nor anyone else may expect to add very much to it. The vernacular, on the other hand, has but recently been discovered, and, though it has been ravaged by many, it still remains uncultivated, in spite of a few earnrst labourers, and still shows itself capable of much improvement and enrichment. Stimulated by this thought, and by the enterprise of youth, I began an extensive work in that language. I laid the foundations of the structure, and got together my line and stones and wood. And then I began to consider a little more carefully the times in which we live, the fact that our age is the mother of pride and indolence, and that the ability of vainglorious fellows who would be my judges, and the peculiar grace of delivery is such that they can hardly be said to recite the writings of others, but rather to mangle them. Hearing their performances again and again, and turning the matter over in my mind, I concluded at length that I was building upon unstable and shifting sand, and should simply waste my labours and see the work of my hands levelled by the common herd. Like one who finds a great serpent across his track, I stopped and changed my route—for a higher and more direct one, I hope. Although the short things I once wrote in the vulgar tongue are, as I have said, so scattered that they now belong to the public rather than to me, I shall take precautions against having my more important works torn to pieces in the same way.

The bases of the revival of learning

A recital of certain conditions which existed during the twelfth, thirteenth, fourteenth, and fifteenth centuries will serve at once to indicate the continuity of modern learning with that of the Middle Ages and also to explain the directions in which the early modern curriculum expanded. First among these conditions is the emancipation, partial at least, from the narrowing influence of early interpretations of the function of learning. Although much of the force given to this narrowing influence was derived from the power of the church, it should be understood that the church was not intrinsically concerned with this matter. The leaders of the church were at times hiedered by their own prejudices or ignorance and were probably influenced by their own prejudices or ignorance and were probably influenced by their personal wishes; when such leaders expressed their views, as did the scholarly Augustine, these views became, in the hands of other men, little less than ecclesiastical dogma.

We have already seen how such views affected the attitude of certain churchmen towards the pagan classics. Among other men there was great consternation in regard to the use of the Arabic system of notation. Under cover of dogma such men used the church to shield themselves and their generations from information which, owing to prejudice or laziness, they did not desire to master. It would probably be unfair not to grant that objections to changes in academic lore sometimes arose from deeply sincere men. Be that as it may, the ascent of the learned Gerbert to the papal chair in the tenth century shows how little real significance such matters and to the church. Viewing the problem from a different angle, it may be noted that had not the church served as guardian of conservatism, some other institution would have done so, else learning would have perished. It is questionable whether any other institution could have performed this service as well as did the church. Repeated demonstrations of the fact that one could be a broadly trained scholar or protagonist of learning and also a reputable churchman seem to have been necessary to convince men of the wisdom of freeing scholarship from dogmatic restrictions.

Fortunately for the permanence of the revival of learning, these demonstrations and their accompanying revivals took place within the church. At best learning could advance but slowly; occasional misfortunes were as inevitable then as they are now – if setbacks were more frequent then than they are now, it was probably because of men's slight experience in dealing with knowledge. At any rate, by the fifteenth century the church found men of humanistic learning more valuable as enemies, and did not hesitate to raise to her highest offices men who were trained in and sympathetic with the new Greek learning.

Second, there developed during the later mediaeval centuries an interest in distinctly secular learning. Besides knowledge of law, medicine, geography, architecture, and the practical arts, which as already stated developed with occupational needs, this interest in secular learning extended to matters as heraldry and social training in connection with chivalry, and to literature, science, and mathematics as branches of "pure" learning. Interest in the last named subjects was shown by the zealous search in Italy, Greece, and the northern countries for lost manuscripts. Discoveries were hailed with delight such as scholars now experience upon the discovery of an ancient Egyptian treasure house. Additions to literary knowledge were made and disseminated by lecturers, such as Filelfo, 1429, trained in Greece. "Such a lecturer did not, as a rule, confine his labours to any one place, but accepted invitations from several cities in succession. This method of teaching began immediately after Petrarch. In the earlier days of humanism it was a necessity; there was no other way in which the first elements of the new learning could be diffused.

Such a lecturer as Manuel, Chrysoloras, or Giovanni di Conversino appealed to an enthusiasm which was still in its youth. By such men the seeds of humanism were sown far and wide." In such a lecture students were introduced, for example, to a certain portion of Cicero's text which was dictated to them. Then followed "a ccmmentary, dealing with grammar, with the usage of words, and with everything in the subject matter which needed to be explained or illustrated.

Thus, at the end of such a course, the lecturer would have dictated a fully annotated edition of the classical book, or portion of a book, which he was treating; and the diligent student would have translated it." Although of less immediate importance for tne revival of learning, the literary birth of vernacular languages was an element soon to be reckoned with in secondary schools.

Third, important patrons of secular learning encouraged, by the founding of academies, the revival of ancient lore, for, says Jebb, "it should be remembered that humanism was not cradled in the bosom of Universities." One of the most important of these academies, that at Mantua, will be described later; another was that of Lorenzo de Medici in Florence. In the academies, ancient literature and art were studied, criticized, and employed as models for new writings.

Fourth, this period witnessed a reconstruction of subject matter in terms of the needs and interests of the times. Such a reconstruction of ecclesiastical learning for universities had already taken place under the direction of such men as Abelard. At the beginning of modern times, a reconstruction of materials for secondary schools was occassioned partly by the increased volume of subject matter and partly by the shifting of educational objectives to matters of literary scholarship rather than to scholarship for ecclesiastical purposes.

Fifth, the art of printing was discovered The activity of Aldo Manuzio, the publisher, as a disseminator of the classics may be contrasted with that of Filelfo the lecturer of 1429. Aldo began his series of Greek editions in 1493 with the *Hero and Leander* of Musaeus; next came the whole of Hesiod, thirty idylls by Theocritus, poems by Theogni, five volumes of Aristotle, nine plays of Aristophanes, the works of Thucydides, Sophocles, Herodotus, Zenophon—all these productions within one decade. The prices of the volumes ranged from only about twenty-five cents to one dollar of our money. The importance of the art of printing in the territorial expansion of learning is so obvious that it needs only to be mentioned here.

Sixth, humanism. a symbol of freedom to think, feel, and express oneself through literary studies, was the dominant characteristic of the Italian revival of learning. The humanist as neo-pagan became later a pedantic and narrow-minded follower of the past, but the humanist of Petrarch's type "advocated the study of the classics as the key to a larger mental life, not contrary to the Christian, but auxiliary to it; one which should educate and exercise men's highest faculties." As Petrarch himself said in a letter to Boccaccio, "While I know that many have become famous for piety without learning, at the same time I have known of no one who has been prevented by literature from following the path of holiness."

In summary, six main bases were laid for modern times :

(1) a broadened interpretation of the function of learning;

(2) an interest in secular learning;

(3) the revival of ancient learnig;

(4) reconstruction of subject matter in terms of new needs and interests;

(5) the use of printing; and

(6) the cultivation of the humanistic attitude toward literature. Petrarch has been described as the first modern man because he embodied all these bases save the fifth. The work of Vittorino da Feltre will be discussed in the next section because he stands among the forerunners of those who as teachers disseminated the spirit of humanism. It should be noted that Vittorino was a modernist not only in his attitude toward literature, but also in his attitude toward science and mathematics.

The First Modern Schoolmaster

In 1423 Vittorino da Feltre established at Mantua the first great school of the Renaissance. Vittorino was singularly fitted for conducting the first great modern school. By nature he loved active boys, by training he loved the new learning, in matters of faith he was a devout churchman, in character and disposition he was nearly if not quite without fault. Withal he was an exacting master whose standards of scholarship, religious practices, character, and physical attainments led him to hold his pupils to strict account in all these matters.

Before going to Mantua, Vittorina had come under the influence of *De Ingenuis Moribus* by Vergerius. In this tract, written about 1404, Vergerius dealt with character and its discipline, liberal studies, physical education, recreation, and the art of studying. The following quotation from Woodward is given at this time because it shows the character of both Vergerius and Vittorino and thus orients the reader with reference to this early schoolmaster.

CHART III

Early Modern Men Whose Works Influenced Curricula

	Fourteenth Century	
Petrarch		Wycliffe
Boccaccio	Vergerius	Chaucer
	Fifteenth Century	
Vittorino da Feltre		Leonardo da Vinci
Chrysoloras		Reuchlin
Guarino		Pius II
Savonarola		Colet
	Sixteenth Century	
Erasmus		Ascham
Luther		Montaigne
Copernicus		Peter Ramus
Thomas More		Thomas Elyot

Michel Angelo
Rabelais
Melanchthon
Vives
Sturm
Mulcaster
Shakespear
Francis Bacon
Magellan
Kepler
Lily

Seventeenth Century

Galileo
Brinsley
Harvey
Ratich
Comenius
Peacham
Descartes
Milton
Dury
Hartlib
Hoole
La Salle
Boyle
Temple

Eignteenth Century

Francke
Newton
Leibnitz
Defoe
Montesquieu
Halley
Pope
Voltaire
Linnaeus
Rousseau
Diderot
Franklin
Priestley
Watts
Adam Smith
Basedow
Kant
Lamarck
Laplace
Humboldt
Pestalozzi
Richter

Vergerious, at the outside of our period, had defined a liberal education to be one which enables a men to attain to and purposue a life or moral and intellectual distinction, and which trains and develops his physical powers. Such an education will prepare men for the career of a statesman, of a solder, or of a simple citizen. But its object is not to train a mere student. This comprehensive aim is obviously suggested by the Greco-Roman ideal although it is at the same time held to be in complete

accord with spirit of the Christian life. In its practical working this education was exhibited in the most developed from in the Mantuan school. Vittorino claimed for this method, following Plutarch, the title of "encycolpaedic," in that he definitely purposed the threefold end of the moral, intellectual, and physical training of his pupils.

It was hold that the most profound truths in all, or nearly all, departments of life were to be sought for in the ancient Literatures, in which were included the works of the greater ecclesiastical Fathers, so for at least as their religious and moral contents were concerned. So whilst Letters from the dominant study upon the intellectual side, philosophy and the Fathers, the instruction in morals. gymnastic, and military exercises provide for physical culture. At the same time Mathematics, the study of Nature, and Astronomy, have their due place; and music, singing and dancing, the letter with some reserves, are admitted. Drawing is treated as a technical rather than a liberal subject. Eloquence, recitation and reading are cultivated as aids to scholarship and for their own sakes. It is by no means assumed that every student can cover the entire field of learding now thrown open to him. Illdigested knowledge is condemned, for a restless curioslty that hurries from one subject to another is hurtful to all true progress. But amidst all this veriety the essential feature of education consists in systematic discipline and practice. "Natura sin disciplina ceaca" was a doctrine universally accepted. Where this is secured, alternation of subjects, and corresponding change of masters, is desirable : indeed intellectual health demands variety. But it still remains true that to unite knowledge with style, to impart fact and truth in literary dress, was the humanist schoolmaster's ideal on the side of erudition.

The curriculum proposed for a woman was, on its moral and intellectual sides, idedtical with that of a man, with perhaps, a little less stress upon Rhetoric and more upon Religion. There was no assumption that a lower standard of attainment is inevitable as a consequence of smaller capacity. It is, however, accepted that only women of leisure or position can expect to enter upon the pursuit of learning with that undivided mind which it demands.

Vittorino, who was born in 1378, four years after the death of Petrarch, distinguished himself while yet a student by him academic ability as a pupil and as a pupil-teacher in Padua under John of Revenna. At this time there were no great teachers of Greek in Italy, if indeed there were any teachers who knew Greek. For it is recorded that Florence alone of all Italian cities had a teacher of Greek in 1400. There it was that the great Chrysoloras arrived in 1399 and continued to teach Greek until after the opening of the fifteenth century. Some time before 1411 Vittorino received his doctor's degree, although he continued to teach and study mathematics at Padua until 1415.

These years at Padua were full of revelations to all of Italy and especially to the young men who where fortunate enough to be at the center of important academic events. Such was the fortune of Vittorino, and the curriculum of early modern Europe was greatly influenced by this fact. To Padua in 1407 there came the greatest Latin scholar of the time, Gasparino Barzizza. This scholar searched for and found many lost manuscripts and shared with Paduan students the content thereof. Particularly fortunate then was Vittorino to be received into Barzizza's house together with two Greek scholars, George of Trebizond and Francesco Filelfo.

Yet another bit of good fortune accompanied Vittorino's work at Padua, for here it was that Vergerius lived and taught. As Vergerius was the author of the most significant book of his century on education, as sited above, it was important that Vittorino find this guide to curricum planning.

In 1415 Vittorino left Padua for Venice, where he taught with Guarino in the first humanist school of Venice. Here,

Vittorino studied Greek with Guarino until a year later, when the Plague drove them from the city. Later, from 1418 to 1422, Vittorino taught at Padua, whence he returned to Venice. Soon afterward came the invitation from the worldly Marquis Gonzaga of Mantua to come to that city and establish the modern school which Vittorino directed until his death in 1446.

With a view to the harmonious development of mind, body, and character, he provided his pupils with a broad curriculum. As mentioned above, the Greek notion of an encyclopedic curriculum was here exemplified. One of his pupils, Predilacqua, writes that :

> no subjects of instruction were wanting, and that special masters were provided to secure effective teaching. Arithmetic, which he valued highly for its training in accuracy and business habits of mind, was in the rudimentary stage taught by games, following the practice of the ancient Egyptians, whose method in the subject Vittorino highly commended. Geometry, in which Vittorino had gained a high reputation at Padua, and with which we may believe that he associated the elements of Algebra, he taught in conjunction with drawing, mensuration, and surveying. We hear much less than we should expect of Vittorino's teaching of mathematics, when we consider his interest in the subject and his credit as a master in earlier years. The medal by Pisanello expressly records his fame in this department of knowledge. We are told that he engaged masters to teach the elements of Natural Philosophy and Euclid. At Padua, Mathematics and Astrology had been closely associated. Vittorino discarded Astrology for Astronomy, and lessons on the heavenly bodies were included in the course. Natural history was not neglected, though we may suppose it to have been of an uncritical sort, like our own sixteenth-century "bestiaries." Music was admitted, although under careful supervision. There was much anxiety amongst educators at this time respecting the moral

influence of music and musicians. Indulgence in the art tended, it was feared, to sensuous excitement, or to mere indolence. To listen to music was an excuse for doing nothing ; to practice it might lead to loss of complete self-control. Music masters, carefully chosen, paid special attention to those likely to excel. But Vittorino held fast to the Attic distinction between base and elevating harmonies. With these precautions he admiited instrumental music, choral singing, and dancing.

As a matter of course. Latin and Greek received the major emphasis in this school. Since Greek was a very newly revived subject, its presence was one of the signs of modernity. For this course in physical education, Vittorino had the support of Vergerius as well as of classical Greece. Finally, religion was the touchstone of education, yet he was not disturbed by the disparity between the classical and the Christan ideas of life. His tolerance seems to have been due to his ability to identify the thought and morals of ancient times with the ethical teachings of the philosophers ; as he could see the consistency of these teachings with the eithers of Christanity, no difficulty arose.

Heralds of learning in the North

No mystery at all enshrouds the spread of learning from Italy to the North. Although communication by travel, books, and missives was far less common than it now is, certain scholars continued to travel and students went abroad to school just as earlier men had done since the time of Thales and Pythagoras and as modern men have done ever since. That a nation which had scholars or students to educate would soon hear of Italian scholarship was inevitable. As certain scholars had gone to Spain and others to Paris in the twelfth century, so scholars of the fifteenth and sixteen centuries want to Italy. Besides these pilgrimages to Italy, there were sojourns of Greeks and Italians in the northern countries. One other condition which facilitated the spread of learning from one nation to another was what which had existed throughout the middle Ages—the universal use of Latin as the scholar's language.

France was by nature, by language, and by training the best fitted of the northern nations to accept the new learning. So we find that by 1458 Gregory of Tifernus, an Italianated Greek, was appointed as professor of Greek at the University of Paris. Again in 1494 Charless VIII visited Italy and imbibed an enthusiasm for that country and new learning, so that for nearly a hundered years the kings of France were patrons of Italy and her learning. Other scholars who spread the humanities in the sixteenth century in France were Budaeus—author and scholarly lexicogrpher, John Lascaris—the Italian grammarian during the reign of Louis XII, Jerome Alexander—scholar. teacher, editor, and bibliophile, Robert Estienne—scholar and printer, and Turnebus—an editor and teacher who, says Montaigne, "knew more, and knew it better, than any man of his century, or for ages past."

In being transported to Germany, humanism developed two characteristics, the second of which was a major trait throughout the period. These characteristics were an interest in the classics themselves and an interest in science which was the direct outgrowth of the study of men who like Roger Bacon had seen the absolute necessity of learning about achievements of the past before lunching out upon unexplored seas. Among this group of devotees to new learning was Peurbach, a student or Arabian trigonometry, the author of *New Theorics of the Planets* and a student of Ptolemaic astronomy. Peurbach's pupil, Regiomontanus, went to Cardinal Bessarion in Italy, under whom he mastered Greek for the purpose of translating scientific treatises. Like the Polish Copernicus who, during the next generation, studied nine years in Italy, these men depended for their scientific information upon the revival of learning in which fine literature found the largest place.

The interest of Germans in a certain form of religious dogmastic prevented their showing a prompt enthusiasm for the new learning. German students in Italy there were in the fiftenth century, as Agricola and Reuchlin. But it was not until the pope decided a famous case in favor of Hebrew and Graek scholarship that Reuchlin could convince his compariots of the righteousness of his arguments for "modern" learning. Soon thereafter the alliance between humanism and the Reformation because intimate, and an important task of the learned men was the elucidation of the Bible.

Under such circumstances it was consistent for Melanchthon and Strum in the sixteenth century to launch their extensive plans for secondary education in knowledge, eloquence, and piety. The program of studies of the reorganiztd Latin grammar school of *Gymnasium* of that century has been preserved in Melanchthon's *Book of Visitation* which was published in 1528, This program of studies is simply an account of the various ways in which a variety of Latin works were studied, for Latin was the sole subject of study. The six-year curriculum of Wurtemburg in 1559 which was copied by all Germany continued six years of Latin, three of Greek, and five of music ; religion, grammar, rhetoric, logic, and conversational Lation were taught concurrently with literary readings.

The spirit of Vittorino breathed not in these German educational sanctuaries. Perhaps the school plants and teachers of Germany were not equal to the task of offering a thoroughly modern program such as Vittorino offered. At least one German prince, Duke Ernest of Saxe-Coburg-Gotha, did, in the seventeenth century however, establish a system of schools which, in its science offering, rivaled the great school of Mantua. The digested of his *Schulemetode* in Chart IV shows the breadth of the offerings of this remarkable system of schools.

CHART IV

The Curriculum of Duke Ernest's Schools, 1642-1685

Lowest Class

Bible verses	Prayers
Lord Prayer	Spelling
Articles of Faith	Reading

Intermediate Class

Luther' catechism	Penmanship
Psalms and hymns	Arithmetic
Prayers	Singing

Upper Class

Religion	Spelling (based on the Bible)
Reading	Science
Writing	Church Doctrine as it relates
Arithmetic	to ritualistic ceremonials
Civics	Warning against hard drink-
Music	ing

Composition

The science course, which follows closely. *The Great Didactic* of Comenius, included the following activities: the teacher explained the hourglass, sundial, points of compass, signs of zodiac, the rising and the setting of the sun and moon, shooting stars, thunder and lighting. Observation lessons were conducted upon weather conditions and flora and fauna, including the anatomy of a pig when butchered. Mathematical sciences included surveying. weights and measures, carpenter's rule, the plummet, angles and circles, the balance, levers and pulleys. The course in civics included community problems and personal conduct : problems of cities, ditches, steams, courts, laws, trades, merchants, and schools ; and individual conduct problems of domestic relationships, morally, prayers, manners, courtesies, cleanliness, bad language, stealing, lies, charity, relationships to rulers and to God, and obedience to parents.

These descriptions of German schools show how strong the religious emphasis was in their programs, and they show also modern tendencis in science. These discriptions suggest besides that for certain classes of German boys a different form of training must have been required. One can hardly suppose that the spiritual descendants of chivalric heroes would find such programs sntisfactory. Indeed, there were organized for the members of the gentry the *Ritterakademien* whlch were of great service in the modernization of studies and counteracting the tendency of the classical schools to sterotype all education. As similar schools for the gentry were established in many parts of Europe, this type of institution will be left for separate treatment until later.

Humanism as heralded in England by Erasmus was also far different from the humanism of Italy. Erasmus, at forty years of age and already a scholar in Latin and Greek, had spent five years (1495–1500) in England. When in 1510 he reached England as a Cambridge professor of Greek and divinity, he was a ripened scholar and, though a thorough humanist and a Christian who held self-culture valuable though subservient to religious development, he was withal practical enough to see the sterile pedantry into which many Italian humanists had fallen. It was to be expected, therefore, that he would direct curriculum development toward a thorough understanding of, rather than an imitation of, the classical works which were studied.

In order to understand the position of Erasmus in this matter, it is necessary to canvass briefly the decadence of humanism during the half-century after Vittorino's death. This period was marked by an overemphasis upon the form rather than the content of literary works. Cicero came to be regarded as the master of Latin style, and decadent humanists, or Ciceronians, attempted to cultivate a style exactly like his. This imitation of Cicero called forth from Erasmus his satire entitled *Ciceronianus, or a Dialogue on the best Style of Speaking*. This critical work will be discussed in Chapter 7. His work for secondary education included the writing of school books such as his own *Colloquies* or exercises in conversational Latin. These sketches were laden with proverbs and maxims which gave a moral tone to the dialogues. He edited Latin, Greek, and Hebrew works, and wrote besides many treatises which dealt with educational and religious topics.

Contemporary with Erasmus was Vives, whose views on education were, in regard to the importance of mathematics and experimental science, in advance of the views of Erasmus.

Another humanist of that period was John Colet, who, early in the sixteenth century, organized in London a Latin grammar school known as St. Paul's. This humanistic school was open to boys who were already far enough advanced in Latin and English to be able to read and write their own lessons. The following quotations from his Statutes sets forth the course of study of St. Paul's school.

THE COURSE OF STUDY OF ST. PAUL'S SCHOOL

As touching in this scole what shalby taught of the masters and lernyd of the scolers, it passith my wit to devyse and determyn in particular but in generall to speke and sum what to saye my mynde, I wolde they were taught all way in good literature both laten and greke, and goode auctours suych as haue the veray Romayne eliqueı ce joyned withe wisdome specially Cristyn auctours that wrote theyre wysdame with clene and chast laten other in verse or in prose, for my entent is by thys scole specially to incresse knowledge and worshipping of god and oure lorde Crist Jesu and good Cristen lyffe and maners in the Children.

And for that extent I will the Chyldren lerne ffirst above all the Cathechyzon in English and after the accidence that I made or sum other if eny be better to the purpose to induce chyldren more spedely to laten spech And thanne Institutum Christiani homines which that leryned Erasmus made at my request and the boke called Copia of the same Erasmus And thenne other auctours Christian as lactancius prudentius and proba and sedulius and Juuencus and Baptista Mantuanus and suche other as shalby tought convenyent and most to purpose into the true laten spech all barbary all corrupcion all laten adulterate which ignorant blynde folis brought into this worlde and with the same hath distayned and poysenyed the olde laten spech and the varay Romayne tong which in the tyme of Tully and Salust and Virgill and Terence was vsid, whiche also seint Jerome and seint ambrose and seint Austin and

> many hooly doctors lernyed in theyr tymes. I say that ffylthynesse and all such abusyon which the later blynde worlde broght in which more ratheyr may be callid blotterature thenne litterature. I vtterly abbanysh and Exclude oute of this scole and charge the Maisters that they teche all way that is the best and instruct the chyldren in greke and Redyng vnto them suych auctours that hathe with wisdome joyned the pure chaste eloquence.

The importance of this document is due largely to the fact that the program of this school became a model for many other institutions. The purpose of education in the American colonies over one hundred years later was also in harmony with Colet's course of study. The slight changes in the programs of classical schools for the two centuries following Colet and the contemporary liberal training will be sketched in the remainder of the present chapter.

Early modern secondary schools in England

Following upon the establishment of a modern course of study in St. Paul's, other schools reorganized their courses in accordance with the advanced notions of the day. Among the most famous of these schools was the Latin grammar school of Canterbury, which in 1541 was reorganized under the direction of Henry VIII. The text of the incorporations, statutes, and injunctions of this school has been preserved and, with Leach's translation of the document, appears in his *Educational Cearters and Documents.* This modern curriculum of Canterbury consisted of the study and reading of Latin fables, maxims, adages, comedies, poems, orations, essays, and epistles, Latin grammar and composition, conversational Latin, religion, rudiments of English, and incidental physical education and other recreation. The closing injunction suggests that Greek was a possible optional subject, although no courses in that language were mentioned in the curriculum itself. The Eton time-table of 1530 mentions no subjects of study save those in Latin and religion—if the study of the "properest hymns" indicates the study of religion,

Modern tendencies are more in evidence in the Westminster time-tabie of 1560. This time-table shows a marked advance over those of Eton and Canterbury during the reign of Henry VIII or the preceding generation. The document, whieh was originally in Latin, shows the complete offering of one of the most notable English schools of the sixteenth century and shows that the following subjects in one form or another were taught : Latin, Greek, Hebrew, English, religion, music, dramatics, public speaking, morality, and hygiene. As in all three of these early English secondary schools, Latin here included a considerable variety of content.

As compared with the best of mediaeval schools, the Westminster school is found wanting in provision for a portion of the seven liberal arts ; also as compared with Vittorino's school, many omissions are to be noted. The teaching seems, however, to be a gain over that of the Middle Ages, as Latin literature is here pursued as a subject desirable in itself and not expressly subservient to the needs of the church. If one can assume that boys of Westminster actually studied the literature of the Romans and the Greeks and not merely the Greek and Latin languages, the changed attitude toward the classics represents an enormous gain.

It should not be understood, however, that this type of school of early Elizabethan England provided for all the educational needs of youth in the sense that the 'encyclopedic" seven liberal arts of the Middle Ages attempted to do so. With the development of the universities in the twelfth century, there had come a differentiation of function of secondary schools and higher institutions, so that the attention of secondary school was devoted mainly to the trivium. Indeed, secondary schools were often called trivial schools because they offered nothing more than grammar, rhetoric, and logic.

Early American Latin Grammar School

Up to this point of the discussion of modern schools in England, reference has been made only to the Latin grammar schools, which were, in the first half of the seventeenth century, carried to America. After showing briefly the close relation between English and American Latin grammar schools, a return to England will be made in order to discuss certain more liberal forms of education which flourished there prior to 1750.

American students needs only to have the general characteristics of the early colonists suggeted to them in order to understand that but one course of study was offered. Those colonists of New England from whom we have most direct educational ancestry had been trained in the schools and the customs of England. They had been nurtured by an eductional system which offered thorough training in such content as that described above. They had also been nurtured by England at a time when men were not averse to living, fighting, or even suffering a torturing martyrdom for the sake of theological beliefs and ecclesiastical practices. Nothing could be more certain than that such scholarly churchmen would establish schools which were like those of England and that religion would be a dominant motive in both the establishment and conduct of the schools. A few quotations from contemporary writings will serve to verify this foregone conclusion.

First among the important source materials is the Massachusetts Law of 1647, which in modernized spelling reads as follows :

> It being one chief project of that old deluder, Satan, to keep men from the knowledge of the scriptures, as in former times by keeping them in an unknown tongue, so in these latter times by persuading from the use of tongues, that so at least the true sense and meaning of the original might be clouded by false glosses of saint-seeming deceivers, that learning may not be buried in the grave of our fathers in church and commonwealth, the Lord assisting our endeavors; it is therefore ordered that every township in this jurisdiction, after the Lord hath increased them to the number of fifty householdrs, shall then forthwith appoint one without their town to teach all such

> children as shall resort to him to write and read, whose wages shall be paid either by the parents or masters of such children, or by the inhabitants in general, by way of supply, as the major part of those that order the prudentials of the town shall appoint; provided, those that send their children be not oppressed by paying much more then they can have them taught for in other towns; and it is further ordered, that where any town shall increase to the number of 100 families or householders they shall set up a grammar school, the master thereof being able to instruct youth so far as they may be fitted for the university, provided that if any town neglect the perfomance hereof above one year, that every such town shall pay five pounds to the next school till they shall perform this order.

This document shows the purposes of the colonial Latin grammar-schools and in turn indicates an inevitable course of study : an interest in religion provides the motive for the legislation, and the schools are the schools are intended to prepare boys for college. In order to verify one's almost certain guess as to these requirements, one may next examine the college entrance requirements of the leading colonial colleges.

The first laws drawn up for an American college were those for Harvard College in 1642. The subjects then prescribed for college students as well as those prescribed for entrance show the absence of modern secondary school subjects in the colonial curriculum. For entrance, the requirements consisted of the ability to read Cicero or the equivalent extempore, the ability to compose and speak Latin in verse and prose, and the ability to repeat correctly the paradigms of nouns and verbs in Greek. Additional rules pertain to the student's religions education and general conduct. The college curriculum of that time is shown by the following tentative timetable :

The Times and Order of their Studies, Unless Experience Shall Show Cause to Alter

The second and third day of the weeke, read Lectures, as followeth.

To the first year at 8th. of the clock in the morning *Logick*, the first three quarters, *physicks* the last quarter.

To the second yeare at the 9th. houre, *Ethicks* and *Politicks*, at convenient distances of time.

To the third yeare at the 10th. *Arithmetic* and *Geometry*, the three first quarters, *Astronomy* the last.

Afternoone

The first yeare disputes at the second houre.
The 2d. years at the 3d. houre.
The 3d. yeare at the 4th. every one in his Art.

The 4th. day reads Greeke

To the first yeare the *Etymologie* and *Syntax* at the eighth houre.

To the 2d. at the 9th. houre, *Prosodia* and *Dialects*.

Afternoone

The first yeare at 2d. houre practice the precepts of *Grammar* in such Authors as have variety of words.

The 2d. yeare at 3d. houre practice in *Poesy*, *Nonnus*, *Duport*, or the like.

The 3d. yeare perfect their *Theory* before noone, and exercise *Style*, *Composition*. *Imitation*, *Epitome*, both in Prose and Verse, afternoone.

The fift day reads Hebrew, and the Easterne Tongues

Grammar to the first yeare houre the 8th.
To the 2d. *Chaldee* at the 9th. houre.
To the 3d. *Syriack* at the 10th. houre,

Afternoone

The first yeare practice in the Bible at the 2d. houre.
The 2d, in *Ezra* and *Danel* at the 3d. houre.
The 3d. at the 4th. houre in *Trestius* New Testamente.

The 6th. day reads Rhetorick to all at the 8th houre.

Declamations at the 9th. So ordered that every Scholler may declaime once a moneth. The rest of the day *vacat Rhetricts studiis.*

The 7th. day reads Divinity Cathecheticall at the 8th. houre Common places at the 9th. houre

Afternoone

The first houre reads history in the Winter
The nature of plants in the Summer.

The summe of every Lecture shall be examined before the new Lecture be read.

Requirements for Degree

Every Schollar that on proofe is found able to read the Originalls of the *Old* and *New Testament* into the Latine tongue, and to resolve them *Logically* ; withall being of godly life and conversation ; And at any publick Act hath the Approbation of the Overseers and Master of the Colledge, is fit to be dignified with his first Degree.

Every Schollar that giveth up in writing a *System* or *Synopsis* or summe of *Logick*, Naturall and Morall *Phylosophy*, *Arithmetick*, *Geometry* and *Astronomy* : and is ready to defend his *Theses* or positions withall skilled in the Originalls as above said : and of godly life & conversation : and so approved by the Overseers and Master of the Colledge at any publique 'Act,' is fit to be dignified with his 2d. Degree.

Almost one hundred years later, in 1734, the new laws drawn up for Harvard still showed no change from the English models. The entrance requirements then consisted of the following:

> Whoever upon examination by the President, and two at least of the Tutors, shall be found able 'extempore to read, construe, and parse Tuilly, Virgil, or such like common classical Latin author, and to write true Latin in prose, and to be skilled in making Latin verse, or at least in the rules of Prosodice, and to read, construe and parse ordinary Greek, as in the New Testament, Isocrates, or such like, and decline the paradigms of Greek nouns and verbs, having withal good testimony of his past blameless behavior, shall be looked upon as qualified for admission into Harvard College.

In addition to the requirements as stated for Harvard, Yale required by 1745 "Common Arithmetic." Other colleges of this period made similar requirements.

The Education of a Gentleman in Early Modern Times

The early modern gentleman had educational needs which were believed to be very different from those of the clergy. It was for the edification of this person that much thought was expended and many books were written by educationists and other publicists during the sixteenth and seventeenth centuries as shown by the works catalogued in Chart V. The "compleat gentelman" and his training thus provide an important topic for discussion in connection with secondary school curricula.

CHART V

Important Early Treatises on Education

Sixteenth Century

Erasmus, *Upon the Right Method of Instruction*, 1511
Castiglione, *The Courtier*, *c.* 1528
Lupset, *Erhortation to Young Men*, 1529
Elyot, *The Governour*, 1531
Vives, *The Transmisson of Knowledge*, 1531
Rabelais, *Essays*, 1533 and 1535

Humfrey, *The Nobles*, 1561
Ascham. *The Scholemaster*, 1571

Sir Humphrey Gilbert, *Queen Elizabeth,s Academy* a) proposal), *c.* 1572

Montaigne *Essays*, 1580
Mulcaster, *Positions*, 1581

Seventeenth Century

Cleland, *The Institution of a Young Nobleman*, 1607
Brinsley, *Ludus Laterius*, 1612
Comenius, *The Great Didactic*, 1632
Peacham, *Compleat Gentleman*, 1634
Milton, *Tractate on Eaucation*, 1644
Lord Herbert of Cherbury' *Autobiography*
Dury, *The Reformed School*, 1650
Hoole, *A New Discovery of the Old Art of Teaching School*, 1660

Gailhard, *The Compleat Gentleman*, 1678
Locke, *Some Thoughts on Education*, 1693

A special form of education for the gentry was not a new adventure. Besides being incorporated into the educational ideals of the Greeks and the Romans, specialized training for a boy of noble birth had existed for centuries before modern times as chivalric education. As early as the tenth century, certain refinements in the conduct of knights received attention in the upbringing of boys who were destined for knighthood. The refinements or social customs of the times are known as chivalry. The ideals of chivalric education—religion, honor, and gallantry - necessitated a form of training which could not be obtained in a monastery. To meet this need there was developed the so-called educational system of chivalry which is described or at least reflected in the works of the early troubadours and minnesingers.

This system consisted of three divisions : that of the page for boys under fourteen ; that of the squire for youths of fourteen to twenty-one; and that of the knight. The training of the page was administered in the court of the king or of a knight. A great variety of services, many of them menial in character, were exacted of the page for the purpose of training him in service, obedience, politeness, and courtesy. The boy's religious education was also begun during this period. The training of the young squire was in part a continuane of his duties as the valet of a noble, together with practice in such knightly activities as riding, hunting, and fighting, and also such refining pursuits as composing songs, singing, dancing, playing the harp, and participating in religious observances.

The training of the knight consisted principally of his passing through an elaborate initation ceremony. In preparation for the final dubbing as a knight, the young man purified himself by fasting, prayer, and suitable meditation. Finally, he vowed to devote his life to an attack upon evil and a defense for all things pure and righteous—including women. So little of the seven liberal arts was included in chivalric education and so different were the ideals of the schoolmen and the kinghts that a dual form of education was necessary throughout the later Middle Ages.

A direct outgrowth of chivalric education is to be found in the tendencies of the early modern period. Like the gentry of the Middle Ages, the high-born lads of early modern times seldom found suitable training in the formal schools of their day. Exceptions to this condition are found, however, in Vittorino's cosmopolitan school, but, as shown above, such an elaborate program of studies was not to be fonnd in the northerd humanistic schools of France, Germany, or England. Even in Italy Vittorino's cosmopolitan program declined under the direction of the Ciceronians to the mere husks of learning. While certain members of society seen for the last ten centuries to have been satisfied by such formal literary training, many other persons representing the gentry have demanded and usually found a form of training which, if not in itself always active and practical, led directly to a wordly life far removed from the pedantic tasks imposed by the proverbial school-teacher. In feudal days a nonscholastic demand led to chivaric education. In early modern times a somewhat similar demand led to types of training which are almost entirely overlooked by the historian who examines only the Latin grammar schools and the universities.

The fresh breath of realism which added charm and vigor to the thorny course marked out by later humanists came like humanism itself from Italy. There in 1528 Castiglione in his book, 'The Courtier,' gave voice to the desires of the able nonscholastic boy. This book, by describing the education of a man of the world—statesman, soldier, artist, noble, or sailor—had much to say not only of language and literature but also of skill in arms, sports—hunting, swimming, tennis, and so on—dancing, music, drawing, painting, and sculpture.

All these pursuits were advocated along with grace, politeness, and modest superiority in all things. While Castiglion was broadening the scope of education to meet the needs of pupils to whom the English grammar school must have been most odious. Erasmus and Vives were trying to popularize sound scholarship in England by showing the reality of the humanities when correctly studied. A correct view of progressive educators of the England of 1530 includes, therefore, first the works of scholars who plead for a broad general and liberalizing training in the traditional arts and the classics and, second. the works of practical writers on education who plead for all the training that letters could bestow and, in addition, training in all that gives urbanity to the courtly citizen. As the Latin grammar schools gave at best only literary and religious training, some other institution was required to train boys for courtly life.

England saw this need and set herself the task of meeting it successfully. From the date of Thomas Elyot's *The Boke Named the Governour*, 1531, publicists and teachers wrote upon and practiced the art of liberal education. Elyot recounts the virtues of humanistic training and then adds geography for its own sake and for its value to historical study, history for its own interest and for its value in counseling the future statesman, games and sports for pleasure and to adapt the "body to hardiness, strength. and agility." Thus. through his curriculum which runs from dancing to philosophy, Elyot shows how to produce "men of so excellent wisdom that throughout all the world should be found in no common weal more noble counsellors." Sir Humphrey Gilbert in *Queen Elizabeth's Academy* proposed early in the reign of that queen a curriculum of language and literature, science and mathematics (pure and applied), modern languages, English writings. music, law, heraldry, dancing. fencing, and such additional knowledge of law and grace of manner as could be acquired only in the Inns of Court.

Almost simultaneously with Sir Humphrey's proposal appeared Roger Ascham's *The Scholemaster* (1570). This book was designed to set forth a "plain and perfect way of teaching children, to understand, write, and speak, the Latin tongue, but specially purposed for the private bringing up of youth in gentlemen's and noblemen's houses." In 1581, Richard Mulcaster. the practical headmaster of Merchant Taylor's School, published his *Positions*. In this treatise the author discussed both course of study and the method by which boys and girls might be trained "either for skill in their booke, or health in their bodie," This enterprising master analyzed his broad program in a very modern manner. Particularly significant are his extended discussions of physical education and of a fairly modern course of study for girls. With the general point of view of these pleaders for a realistic education alongside the humanities, two important contemporary essayists, Rabelais and Montaigne, were also in accordance.

In the succeeding centuries other writers plead for an education not to be found in such grammar schools as Eton or Westminster. Among these writers were Lord Herbert of Cherbury, Peacham, Milton, and Locke of the seventeenth century. Lord Herbert in his autobiography tells how he obtained an education at Oxford in spite of the university, and then outlines for parents somewhat such a course as he pursued independently. He opens his course with a considerable disquisition upon the fact that religious and moral qualities are personal matters to be worked out between God and man. He then names certain subjects which the young gentleman should pursue, together with reasons for pursuing them. "It would be fit," says he, in his autobiography, "that some time be spent in learning rhetoric or oratory. to the intent that upon all occasions you may express yourself with eloquence and grace." Of physical education, he continues, the

> exercises I chiefly used, and most recommend to posterity, were riding the great horse and fencing . . . . As for dancing, I could never find leisure enough to learn it, as employing my mind always in acquiring of some art or science more useful ; howbeit. I shall wish these three exercises learned in this order. That dancing may be learnt first, as that which doth fashion the body, gives one a good presence in and address to all companies, since it disposeth the limits to a kind of *souplesse* (as the Frenchmen call it) and agility, in so much as they seem to have the use of their legs, arms. and bodies more than any others, who, standing stiff and stark in their postures, seem as if they were taken in their joints or had not the perfect use of their members. I speak not this as if I would have a youth never stand still in company, but only, that when he hath occasion to stir, his motions may be comely and graceful, that he may learn to know how to come in and go out of a room where company is, how to make courtesies handsomely, according to the several degrees of persons he shall encounter, how to put off and hold his hat ; all which, and many other things which become men, are taught by the more accurate dancing-masters in France.

Next are mentioned fencing and riding which he himself had time to learn, and later swimming which, owing to a water complex, he hid not learn. He then catalogues questionable amusements such as "running horses," hawking, and bowling, and open vices such as "dicing and carding, especially if you play for any great sum of money, or spend and time in them." To the list of desirable subjects Cherbury adds a description which indicates community civics : "It would also deserve a particular lecture or *recherche*, how one ought to behave himself with children, servants, and neighbors ; and I am confident, that precepts in this point will be found more useful to young gentlemen, than all the subtleties of schools." Incidental comments such as these on education from a scholar who before he was twelve years old was able to compose verses in Greek and Latin. and who continued his education according to established forms supplemented by his own devices, indicate how far short of the needs of the times the grammar school came.

In 1634 Peacham's *Compleat Gentleman* included an important point in the education of the young man of blood. This topic, travel, had, however, been discussed by other educationists. Although there were believed to be few persons worse than the proverbial Italianated Englishman, Peacham agreed with Locke that well-planned travel was essential for the gentlemam, for, he says, "In my opinion nothing rectifieth and confirmeth more the judgment of a Gentleman in foreign affairs, teacheth him knowledge of himself, and setleth his affection more sure to his own Country than travel doth." Peacham devotes a separate chapter of his book to each of the following subjects : literary style and history, cosmography, geography, geometry, poetry, music, drawing and painting, heraldry. physical education, travel, and fishing.

The comments of John Milton in his *Tractate* (1644) on education should be studied as coming not from a great poet but from one of the most scholarly men of his day. He was one of the scholars who accepted promising lads for teaching and was, therefore, fortified in his beliefs. A complete and generous education was according to Milton one which included training in arithmetic, geometry, Latin, Greek, astronomy, trigonometry, engineering, fortification, navigation, physics, natural history, anatomy, and the elements of medicine. To make this realistic course the more encyclopedic, Milton included in his recommendations in Latin and Greek many writers who were unknown to the schools – "These," proclaimed this schoolmaster, "be the studies in which our noble and our gentle youth aught to bestow their time in a disciplinary way from twelve to one and twenty unless they rely more on their ancestors dead than on themselves living." Little less exacting was Locke, who, in *Some Thoughts Concerning Education* (1693), wrote that "Latin and French as the world now goes, is by every one acknowledged to be necessary" ; but he had besides these subjects a generous list : arithmetic, genmetry, geology, biology, geography, astronomy, anatomy, chronology, ethics, civil and common lay, physical education, and practical arts. This curriculum, when supplemented by travel, Locke believed to constitute a well-ordered program of studies.

Finally in the discussion of the education of nobles, Defoe's *The Compleat Gentleman* (1728—1729) must be noticed. Defoe, more daring than the rest, not only advocated a modern course, but even questioned whether Latin and Greek should be studied at all :

> We find the Moderns begin to gain upon the Antients extremely, and some parts of knowledge shine brighter in English than they ever did in Latin. Our phylosophers have exploded the Ancients in many things such as in the mocion of the heavenly bodyes. the use of the magnet, and improvements of navigacion, which, are all modern, and several other things ; likewise the circulacion of the blood in physical experiments . . . . likewise the improvements in the mathematicks, fortificacion, incampments, intrenchings, millitary discipline, beseiging and defending towns . . . . Now all these studyes are made in the English tongue, and are necessarily to be received there, and in no other. Greek and Latin have nothing to do with it.

While the education of a gentleman was progressing in England, the progressive educators of other countries were not idle. In France, both the short-lived Port-Royalists of the middle of the seventeenth cen ury and the Oratorians, who appeared earlier and persisted long after the Port-Royalists, us.d French as the basic language in their teaching. They also offered their pupils a broad curriculum which included mathematics (algebra, geometry, trigonometry, analytic geometry, and the calculus), science, history (sacred and secular), and geography.

By 1650, France had as many as twelve important academies in which courses were offered especially for youth of noble birth. The curricula of the academies included natural science, mathematics, geology, French history, heraldry, modern language, riding, and other gentlemanly arts.

This knightly training of France was pursued by German boys ; some of them went to France for their training, while others attended the *Ritterakademien* which reflected much of the character of French academies. The purposes and properties of these schools are aptly sketched in Russell's account of them :

> Dissatisfaction with education at home and admiration for everything foreign soon worked a complete change in the ideals of the German nobility. The highest ambition of the young noble was to become a "perfect cavalier." To know the latest Parisian fad , fashions, and customs ; to know how to dance, fence, and ride like a born Frenchman ; to be accomplished in speech and manner—all this was of more importance than a knowledge of Latin or the art of disputation. French political ideas readily found a place in many German states, and the "perfect cavalier" gradually came to need special preparation for civil and military service. The dew ideal carried with it the desire for an acquaintance with mathematics and physics and their practical applications. The new political sciences, political history. jurisprudence, geography, and statistics, heraldry and genealogy, were all a part of the educational life of the *galant homme*. To be sure, the formal disciplines (religion, ethics, rhetoric

and dialectics) were not altogether abandoned ; nor was Latin wholly supplanted by French and the other modern languages. But the fact is these old-fashioned studies were relegated to places in the rear rank ; all that pertained to fine manners, practical conduct, and civil military functions, came to the front.

Although the Thirty Years' War (1618–1648) played havoc with these schools, they were revived in the latter half of the seventeenth century under the leadership of the pietist, Francke. Meanwhile, the Gymnasien existed, but hardly flourished. Germany was thus furnished with two systems of secondary education, neither of which could attract the diligent scholar or guide the strongest minds.

Early Differentiation of the Modern Subjects

A part of the task of early modern times consisted of the differentiation of the modern subjects. That these subjects were taught at least occasionally during these centuries has been shown by the programs of Vittorino, Mulcaster, and others. As stated above, the early grammar schools devoted their energies chiefly to the subjects of the trivium. In doing so they maintained a very conservative course of study. Other schools, however, devoted much of theis energies to the subjects of the quadrivium. These schools, especially private schools for the nobles, became by contrast schools of progress with courses in the vernaculars, science, and mathematics.

No subject seems to have caused greater travail in its birth and later development than English. Prejudices and fears such as those expressed by Petrarch in regard to his own vernacular had to be overcome, traditions of the classroom had to be broken, the ideal of a universal scholars' language had to be shattered, textbooks in English had to be prepared. Many stages separate the birth of English as a vernacular and as a literary language from its acceptance as a subject to be studied in higher schools. Most remote is the stage at which the Latin grammar schools first arrived and lingered. During that period, if the rules were enforced, English was seldom tolerated even in the play of older boys.

A second stage may be located during the early sixteenth century when Vives. in 1531, in agreement with Comenius, says of language in the school : "Let them (the pupils) at first speak in their own tongue, which was born in them in their home, and if they make mistakes in it, let the master correct them. From this start gradually proceed to speaking in Latin. They will mix up in the vernacular what they have heard from their master or read themselves in Latin, so that at first the language in the school will be a mixture of the mother tongue and of Latin. Let them speak their own language out of doors, so that they may not accustom themselves in any way to make a hotch-potch of two languages. The instructor must take all possible care that the expressions used are pure, and good Latin." With such upbringing, it is little wonder if the schoolmasters themselves could not, as the contemporary Palsgrave alleged, express their thoughts in their own vernacular. For the next fifty years during which English remained in this state of subordination, books intended for scholars were written first in Latin for permanence and then, if desirable, translated.

An interesting instance of a change in this matter is provided by Roger Ascham. When in 1545 he produced in English his book on archery, he excused himself for this vulgarity by saying that he believed many men who would wish to read such a book were not Latinists. Twenty-five years later Ascham's *Scholemaster* appeared in English with no apology for the vernacular. During this time, in 1553, there appeared the first important textbook on English composition. Many men of this time seem to have been on the borderline in the acceptance of English; if they could use a sufficient number of Latin phrases in their English, they seem to have thought themselves still within the pale of respectability. Sir Humphrey Gilbert in his proposal entitled *Queen Elizabeth's Academy* (*c.* 1572), had advocated rhetorical exercises in English because of the necessity of using English "as in preaching, in council, in parliament, in commission, and other offices of Commonweal."

By 1580 a third stage was reached in the acceptance of English. Between that date and 1600 Mulcaster went to the extreme of showing in his *Elementaire* how to teach English, and Carew, in a scholarly epistle, argued the case for English literature by cataloguing the broad range of excellent writings in English. This period was yet one of apology. Mulcaster in the *Positions* defended the use of English much as Ascham had defended it thirty years earlier; it is important to note, however, that Ascham addressed the gentry, while Mulcaster addressed schoolmen.

Within the next half century, Englishmen because so fully reconciled to their vernacular that Peacham could boldly assert his belief in training in English as essential in the education of a gentleman. This attitude may be cited as representative of a fifth stage. How difficult the convincing of schoolmen was can be determined by reflecting that this point of view was not adopted until after Shakespeare and Spenser and then only by the most advanced writers of the times. A boy might yet have attained academic honors and have been quite innocent of English literature.

Between 1640 and 1740 a sixth stage in this development was reached by enthusiasts who regarded English as a suitable foundation for all important learning. By this time the principle of Vives and Comenius that the mother tongue should be the language of the first school years had been accepted in practice, and such a writer as Defoe was ready to defend as an educated gentleman a man who based his claims to scholarship on works in English alone. Several additional stages in the development of English as a school subject have taken place since 1740, but these six stages bring the reader to the age of Franklin and his proposals that English be an important department in an academy to be established in Philadelphia.

During these successive stages, there was a transformation of the ancient subject of logic, so that, with the development of English as a secondary school subject, logic became a part of the new subject of oral and written English. That is, by the time of Elizabeth, 1558—1603, logic had been dislodged but not quite routed. Watson interprets the declamations held on Saturdays in the Westminster school, however, as a survival of mediaeval logic and disputation. This dislodging of logic was due chiefly to two causes : first, to the expansion of grammar and rhetoric which followed the extensive use of the classics; and, second, to the development of an educational psychology which held that logic was ill-adapted to "unmathematical Novices."

It is significant that logic was one of the first subjects pursued at Oxford in 1593 by the twelve-year-old Lord Herbert of Cherbury, and that he had already "attained to the knowledge of the Greek tongue and logic." This persistence of logic as well as its dislodgment was due also in part to adherence to a principle of educational psychology. The principle which led to the persistence of logic was one of the most venerable of all principles, namely, the theory of formal discipline. For example, Lawrence Humfrey, in 1561, in his treatise on the education of a gentleman says : "Rhetoric and Logic are necessary to file the talk, whet the wit and imprint order, wherewith Aristotle, the prince of pleading and reasoning, instructed his Alexander."

This view of logic, which was repeatedly set forth by prominent sixteenth-century writers on education, indicates that logic held a place similar to that which has more recently been occupied by mathematics. Still another psychological principle which was enunciated during the sixteenth-and seventeenth-century discussions of logic was that which advocates the postponement of highly abstract subjects until after a reasonably wide experience with concrete things has been attained. For example, Comenius wrote upon this matter in *The Great Didactic* (1632) : "It has already been shown that the study of facts must precede that of their combinations; that matter logically precedes its form, that this is the only method by which sure and rapid progress can be made, and that we must therefore learn our facts by observation before we can pass a sound judgment on them, or enunciate them in well-turned phrases." Survivals of logic in schools after this time, which indicate the success of the efforts of Ramus and others to make of logic a practical or applied subjects, are to be found in contemporary writings. Nevertheless, logic continued in some form as a secondary-school subject until the nineteenth century.

Science moved slowly toward the schools of early modern times. At times, as with Vittorino, science was welcome. How small a place science had in humanistic English schools has been shown by their time-tables. Science had its advocates, however, in such writers as Vives and Comenius, who proposed object nature lessons as a simple and psychological approach to abstract subjects. Hoole in 1660 suggests, as one of the reasons why London was preeminent as a place for "the full improvement of children," the fact that once a year pupils can go to a well-stocked museum of rarities. Private schools, or schoolmasters like John Milton, advocated and offered science by means of the classical works on that subject. The sources of the subject matter of science even when it was taught indicate that one might have examined a progressive school of the times without suspecting that Bacon, Harvey, Pascal, Galileo, or Boyle had ever existed.

The Promise of Scholarship in the Early Modern Period

The sad state of scholars at the close of the early modern period doubtless led numerous men to live in ignorance of the best thought of their time. There were Latin grammar schools for pedants and academies for the gentry, but there were few if any schools for the lad who would follow Bacon in the advancement of learning. Indeed, many of the intellectual leaders of that day lived a life apart from formal institutions of learning and had received much of their training outside the walls of academic respectability. As Russetl asserts, it is significant that the schools and universities of Europe "between 1625 and 1725 were not the work-shops of the leaders of thought."

Many of these leaders had nevertheless been trained in the schools and universities of their day. William Harvey (1578--1657), for example, attended the grammar school of Canterbury. where he studied Greek and Latin until he was about fifteen years of age. He then went to Cambridgee, where he spent three or four years in the study of Greek, Latin, dialects, and physics. Thereafter, he betook himself to Padua for a five-year medical course. Upon his return to England, Harvey attached himself to the College of Physicians, where he studied and lectured for twenty-five years. While thus engaged as a lecturer and also in the practice of his profession, he made his discovery of the circulation of the blood.

Other notable leaders may be cited. Leibnitz (1646—1716), though a bitter opponent of the schools of his fatherland, was an ardent educationist. He attached himself to the courts rather than to schools. He outlined curricula and wrote treatises on education, always looking toward the liberal courses of the French academies and the *Ritterakademien*. Francis Bacon (1561—1626), the courtier and publicist, who was one of the most influential educationists of his times, seems to have severed his direct connection with schools at the age of fifteen when left Cambridge. Numerous other biographical sketches of leaders, as Descartes, Hobbes, Boyle, Locke, and Newton, could be given to indicate that the schools gave these men the formal training of that day, but that the advancement of learning came not by following the methods or subject matter of grammar schools or universities.

Instead, the promise of scholarship seems throughout the latter decades of the early modern period to have been given by influences outside the decadent humanistic schools. The promise of scholarship came from such leaders as have been named—men who were for the most part outside the academic ranks when they produced their significant contributions if not during their periods of training, and from such modernized schools as those of the Oratorians, the Port-Royalists, and the Pietists.

In brief, the faith of the scholarly fathers of the humanistic period was forgotten by their pedantic progeny. Further advance lay in a renewal of the faith which fortifies all leaders in education. Decadent faith lay smouldering in the grammar schools and universities; the faith of the fathers rose as a beacon in the new schools and in the work of leaders who were unshackled by the inertia of deadening academic formalities. The classics called for rescuers, mathematics needed the continued leadership of influential scholars who were all too rare, modern literature pleaded for a place beside ancient works, science sought freedom from verbal thralldom, while history had yet to be written. Promise there was in these years, but new or reconstructed schools, subject matter, and methhds were requisite for the fulfillment of the promise. The provision of these requisites, although begun in these early years, opens a new era in secondary education. The story of that new era is recorded in Chapter 5.

6

Scope of the Curriculum

The great awakening in secondary education. Heralds proclaimed for generations before the eighteenth century a new program of studies in Europe and America. Vives, for example, in 1531 advocated a broad program of studies which included mathematics and science. Likewise, Comenius in *The Great Didactic* (1632) and Milton in his *Tractate* (1644) far transcended the restrictions of contemporary Latin grammar schools. To these notable heralds can be added such forerunners as Sir Humphrey Gilbert, John Dury. Lord Herbert of Cherbury, and John Locke. Besides these men, there were still other scholars who devoted much of their lives to the increasing of scienti^c knowledge. Among such scientists, preeminent contributors were Kepler, Harvey, Descartes, Boyle, Newton, and others whose names were cited in the closing paragraphs of Chapter 4.

So well established were the traditions of English education that even these great masters of prose and of science could only slowly free the educators of their country from extreme conservatism. Contemporary religious conditions, however, hastened the day when schools should broaden their programs of studies and organize them in conformity with existing bodies of useful subject matter and the changing needs of modern society. These religious conditions led in England to the Act of Uniformity which, as enacted in 1662, drove nearly two thousand nonconformist ministers from their parishes. Many of these ousted parsons were prepared for and interested in becoming schoolmasters, and, consequently, even in spite of unfavorable enactments, set up independent schools. As some of these parson-schoolmasters had caught the educational spirit of Vives, Milton. and Lord Cherbury, their schools offered as broad a range of subjects as had the Mantuan school of Vittorino. One of these schools, for example, the academy at Sheriffhales, from 1663 to 1697, provided training in Latin, Greek, Hebrew, and English; mathematics, pure and applied; science, including natural science and practice in anatomy; and logic and ethics.

Another seventeenth-century school was established by Charles Morton at Newington Green. This school, which was attended by the versatile Defoe and distinction of giving its boys an excellent mastery of the English language. This academy was particularly important because of its apparent influence upon Defoe. Although Defoe states that pupils left this school "not Destitute in the Languages," it was here probably that Defoe was imbued with the notion of a possible modern education without benefit of the classics. The influence of this school seems also to be shown in Defoe's *Essay on Projects*. As this essay appears in turn to have influenced Benjamin Franklin, the founder of America's first academy, its importance and the effect of the Newington school upon curriculum development in America will presently be obvious.

The program of studies of another influential English academy is important because from its influence came a famous pupil, Joseph Priestley, who was later a friend of Franklin. At this school, which was founded in 1729 by Philip Doddridge, a Miltonic program of studies was provided. Early in the course, the boys were taught short-hand so that they could more readily take lecture notes.

The French language was also taught to those who desired to learn it, Systems of logic, rhetoric, geography, and metaphysics were read during the first year, references being made to other authors whom the studentt were expected to consult. Lectures on geometry and algebra were read, and instruction give in trigonometry, conic sections, and celestial mechanics. A system of natural philosophy was read, illustrated by experiments, for which the academy was furnished with simple apparatus. ... History, natural and civil, a full system of Jewish antiquities, and the anatomy of the human frame were also among the branches which they pursued.

Also the study of "polite literature was encouraged," and lectures were delivered on civil law, mythology, and English history. The effectiveness of such realistic programs in attracting pupils who did not plan to enter the ministry is shown in Table 1.

TABLE 1

Vocational Choices of 93 Boys Who Attended the West of England Academy, Exeter, England, About 1760. (Based on Records Quoted by Parker, *op. cit.*, p. 122.)

Vocations	*Number*	*Percentages*
Merchants	24	25.8
Esquires	13	14.0
Physicians	7	7.5
Navy or navy office men	7	7.5
Attorneys	6	6.5
Ministers	4	4.3
Army men	3	3.2
Apothecaries	2	2.1
Unknown	27	19.1
Total	93	100.0

The present section of this chapter is entitled "The Great Awakening in Secondary Education" because the curriculum innovations just described were indicative of conditions which soon afterward became general, and because these changes marked the beginning of an emancipation of schools from linguistic formalists. Although many academic experiences of this period attest that these nonconformist schools were in advance of their times, somewhat as Vittorino's was in the fifteenth century, still the movement toward an enriched program of studies had greater force and extent than ever before. In the fifteenth century the broad curriculum of the Mantua school shrank on its journey to Germany, France, and England to a narrow and formal classico-religious program. In the eighteenth century, however, the enriched curricula of English academies lost little if any of their content on their journey to Scotland or America. As stated at the beginning of this chapter, the strength of the curricula of eighteenth-century academies was no sudden development; Comenius (1592-1671) and his successors on the continent had laid the basis of curricula in learning that was broad and deep. Alongside Comenius, the educator, were Kepler (1571-1630), the scientific discoverer, and Jungius (1587-1657), the founder of the first natural science association of northern Europe. From this combination of humanism as represented by Comenius and science as represented by Kepler and Jungius came an influence which was promptly recognized by the gentry who had been trained in the Franco-German *Ritterakademien*.

These progressive nobles became supporters of a liberal rationalism which was far removed from narrow classicism. Strangely enough, there was joined with the liberal spirit of the nationalists an influential group of German dissenters, known as Pietists. The Pietists, under the leadership of Francke (1663-1727), teacher and philanthropist, perceived the value of science, mathematics, and modern languages in a Latin school. And, as a sesult of Francke's efforts and his advocacy of schools which should fit the youth of the middle classes for practical life, "there has since grown up in Germany a class of *Real*-schools. Herein

Francke acted in conformity with the rationalistic spirit of his times.

Whatever may have been his opinion of the *Ritterakademie* as an institution for the practical training of the nobility, he certainly believed in the wisdom of a practical training for the learned professions, for the business occupations of the citizen class, and for the needs of the people generally. The *Real*-school, therefore, is the direct response to the educational ideal that lays special emphasis on the mastery of environment. It is the outgrowth of one phase of the rationalistic mode of thought." Accordingly, within the next generation (1747), Hecker, another pietist, established in Berlin a *Realschule*, which offered instruction "in religion and ethics, the German, French, and Latin languages, writing, arithmetic, drawing, history, geography, and the elements of geometry, mechanics, and architecture. An important feature of the founder's pian was a series of optional courses designed to give pupils an insight into the practical workings of the various trades and occupations of burgher life." Within a few years many similar schools were established, and from that time to the present day *Realschulen* have represented much of the spirit of the early English academies and of the Scottish and American academies which are yet to be described.

When in 1760 the town council of Perth Scotland, decided that it would be of "great utility to the youth to have an academy for literature and science established at Perth," there was begun a series of foundations of liberal Scotch schools. As the contemporary burgh records of Perth continue, "Not long ago, all learning consisted in the grammatical knowledge of dead languages and in skill in metaphysical subtleties; now things begin to be estimated according to their value. The time necessary for completing a course of education at the universities and the expense of such attendance prove an insurmountable bar in the way of the greater part who have inclination for these studies."

It was expected that the academy would offer a vuluable nonclassical curriculum. This curriculum "consisted of the higher branches of arithmetic, mathematical, physical, and political geography, logic, and the principles of composition; algebra, including the theory of equations and the differential calculus; geometry, consisting of the first six books of Euclid; plane and spherical trigonometry; mensuration of surfaces and solids; navigation, fortification, analytical geometry, and conic sections; natural philosophy, consisting of statics, dynamics, optics, and astronomy; and subsequently chemistry was added." Several other similar six-or eight-year programs are cited by Grant. Some of the programs, like that of Perth, omitted Latin and Greek, while others included Latin, Greek, and French.

During the period of popularization of academies in Europe, a similar popularization took place in America. The first American academy was proposed by Franklin in 1743 and opened eight years later in Philadelphia. Although Franklin would gladly have made the curriculum of this school like that of Perth, he was persuaded to add both ancient and modern languages. When in 1749 Franklin redoubled his efforts he proposed a program of studies which in breadth and modernity stands in striking contrast with contemporary Latin grammar school and college curricula. The importance of the Franklin Academy in the curriculum development of American secondary education warrants the including of the founder's long account of his curriculum views :

That a House be provided for the ACADEMY, if not in the Town, not many miles from it; the Situation high and dry, and if it may be, not far from a River having a Garden, Orchard, Meadow, and a Field or two.

That the House be furnished with a Library (if in the Country, if in the Town, the Town Libraries may serve) with Maps of all Countries, Globes, some mathematical Instruments, an Apparatus for Experiments in Natural Philosophy, and for Mechanics; Prints, of all Kinds, Prospects, Buildings, Machines, & c.

That the RECTOR be a Man of good Understanding, good Morals, diligent and patient, learn's in the Languages and Sciences, and a correct pure Speaker and writer of the *English* Tongue; to have such Tutors under him as shall be necessary.

That the boarding Scholars diet together, plainly, temperately, and frugally.

That to keep them in Health, and to strengthen and render active their Bodies, they be frequently exercis'd in Running, Leaping, Wrestling, and Swimming, &c.

That they have peculier Habits to distinguish them from other Youth, if the Academy be in or near the Town: for this, among other Reasons, that their Behavior may be better observed.

As to their Studies, it would be well if they could be taught *every Thing* that is useful, and *every Thing* that is ornamental : But Art is long and their Time is short. It is therefore proposed that they learn those Things that are likely to be *most useful* and *most ornamental*, Regard being had to the several Professions for which they are intended.

All should be taught to write a *fair Hand*, and swift, as that is useful to All. And with it may be learned something of *Drawing* by Imitation of Prints, and some of the first Principles of Perspective.

Arithmetick, *Accounts*, and some of the first Principles of *Geometry* and *Astronomy*.

The *English* Language might be taught by Grammar, in which some of our best Writers, as *Tillotson, Addison, Pope, Algernon Sidney, Cato's* Letters, &c should be classicks : The *Stiles* principally to be cultivated, being the *clear* and the *concise*. Reading should also be taught, and pronouncing, properly, distinctly, emphatically; not with an even Tone, which *under-does*, nor a theatrical, which *over-does* Nature.

To form their Stile, they should be put on Writing Letters to each other, making Abstracts of what they read; or writing the same Things in their own Words; telling or writing Stories lately read, in their own Expressions. All to be revised and corrected by the Tutor. who should give his Reasons, explain the Tone and Import of Words, &c.

To form their Pronunciation, they may be put on making Declamations, repeating Speeches, delivering Orations, &c. The Tutors assisting at the Rehearsals, teaching, advising, correcting their Accent, &c.

But if HISTORY be made a constant Part of their Reading, such as the Translations of the *Greek* and *Roman* Historians- and the modern Histories of antient *Grecce* and Rome, &c,, may not almost all Kinds of useful Knowledge be that way introduced to Advantage, and with Pleasure to the Student ? As

GEOGRAPHY, by reading with Maps, and being required to point out the Places *where* the greatest Actions Were done, to give their old add new Names, with the Bounds, Situation, Extent of the Countries concern d, &c.

CHRONOLOGY, by the Help of Helvius or some other Writer of the kind, who will enable them to tell *when* those Events happened; what Princes were Comtemporaries, what States or famous Men flourished about that Time, &c. The several principal Epochs to be first well fix'd in their Memories.

ANTIENT CUSTOMS, religious and civil. being frequently mentioned in History, will give occasions for explaining them; in which the Prints of Medals, Basso Relievo's, and antient Monuments wiil greatly assist.

MORALITY. by descanting and making continual Observations on the Causes of the Rise or Fall of any Man's Character. Fortune, Power, &c,, mentioned in History; the Advantages of Temperance, Order, Frugality, Industry, Perseverance, &c. &c. Indeed the general natural Tendency of Reading good History, must be, to fix in the Minds of Youth deep Impressions of the Beauty and Usefulness of Virtue of all Kinds, Publick Spirit, Fortitude, &c.

History will show the wonderful effects of ORATORY in governing, training and leading great Bodies of Mankind, Armies, Cities, Nations. When the Minds of Youth are struck with Admiration at this, then is the Time to give them the Principles of that Art, which they will study with Taste and Application. Then they may be made acquainted with the best Models among the Antients, their Beauties being particularly pointed out to them. Modern Political Oratory being chiefly performed by the Pen and Press, its Advantages over the Antients in some Respects are to be shown; as that its Effects are more extensive, more lasting, &c.

History will also afford frequent Opportunities of showing the Necessity of a Publick Religion, from its Usefulness to the Publick; the Advantages of a Religious Character among private Persons; the Mischiefs of Superstition, &c., and the Excellency of the CHRISTIAN RELIGION above all others antient or modern.

History will also give Occasion to expatiate on the Advantage of Civil Orders and Constitutions, how Men and their Properties are protected by joining in Societies and established Government; their Industry encouraged and rewarded, Arts invented, and Life made more comfortable : The Advantages of *Liberty*, Mischiefs of *Licentiousness*, Benefits arising from good Laws and a due Execution of Justice, &c. Thus may the first Principles of sound *Politicks* be fixed in the Minds of Youth.

On *Historical* Occasions, Questions of Right and Wrong, Justice and Injustice, will naturally arise, and may be put to Youth, which they debate in Conversation and in Writing. When they ardently desire Victory, for the sake of the Praise attending it, they will begin to feel the Want, and be sensible of the Use of *Logic*, or the Art of Reasoning to *discover* Truth. and of Arguing to *defend* it, and convince Adversaries. This would be the time to acquaint them with the Principles of that Art. *Grotius*, *Puffendorff*, and some other Writers of the same kind, may be used on these Occassions to decide their Disputes. Publick Disputes warm the Imagination, whet the Industry, and Strengthen the natural Abilities.

When Youth are told, that the Great Men whose Lives and Actions they read in History, spoke two of the best Languages that ever were, the most expressive, copious, beautiful; and that the finest Writings, the most correct Compositions, the most perfect Productions of human Wit and Wisdom, are in those Languages which have endured Ages, and will endure while there are Men ; that no Translation can do them justice, or give the Pleasure found in Reading the Originals ; that those Languages contain all Science ; that one of them is become almost universal, being the language of Learned Men in all Countries; that to understand them is a distinguishing ornament, and c. they may be thereby made desirous of learning those Languages, and their Industry sharpen'd in the Acquisition of them. All intended for Divinity should be taught the *Latin* and *Greek* ; for Physick; the *Latin*, *Greek* and *French* ; for Law, the *Latin* and *French* ; Merchants, the *French German* and *Spanish* ; and though all should not be compell'd to learn *Latin* and *Greek*, or the modern foreign Languages ; yet none that have an ardent Desire to learn them should be refused ; their "English", Arithmetick, and other Studies absolutely necessary, being at the same Time not negelected.

If the new "Universal History" were also read, it would give a connected Idea of human Affairs, so far as it goes, which should be followed by the best modern Histories, particularly of our Mother Country ; then of these Colonies ; which should be accompained with Observations on their Rise, Encrease, use to *Great Britain*, Encouragements, Discouragements, and c., the Means to make them flourish, secure their Liberties, and c.

With the History of Men, Time, and Nations, should be read at proper Hours or Days, some of the best *Histories of Nature*, which would not only be delightful to Youth, and furnish them with Matter for their Letters, and c., as well as other History ; but afterwards of great use to them, whether they are Merchants, Handicrafts, or Divines ; enabling the first the better to understand many Commodities, Drugs, and c., the second to improve his Trade or Handicraft by new Mixtures, Materials, and c., and the last to adorn his Discourses by beautiful Comparisons, and strengthen them by new Proofs of Divine Providence. The Conversation of all will be improved by it, as Occasions frequently offer of making Natural Observations, which are instructive, agreeable and entertaining in almost all Companies. *Natural History* will also afford opportunities of introducing many observations, relating to the Preservation of Health, which may be afterwards of great use. 'Arbuthnot' on Air and 'Aliment, Sanctorius' on Perspiration, 'Lemery' on Foods, and some others, may now be read, and a very little Explanation will make them sufficiently intelligible to Youth.

While they are reading Natural History, might not a little 'Gardening, Planting, Grafting, Inculating, and c., be taught and practised, and now and then Excursions made to the neighboring Plantations of the best Farmers, their Methods observ'd and reason'd upon for the Information of Youth ? The Improvement of Agriculture being useful to all, and Skill in it no Disparagement to any.

The History of *Commerce*, of the Invention of Arts, Rise of Manufactures, Progress of Trade, Change of its Seats, with the Reasons, Causes, &c., may also be made interesting to Youth, and will be useful to all. And this with the Accounts in other History of the prodigious Force and Effect of Engines and Machines used in War, will naturally introduce a Desire to be instructed in *Mechanicics*, and to be informed of the Principles of that Art by which weak Men perform such Wonders, Labour is savd', Manufactures expedited, &c., &c. This will be the Time to show them Prints of ancient and modern Machines, to explain them, to let them be copied, and to give Lectures in mechanical Philosophy.

With the whole should be constantly inculcated and cultivated, that 'Benignity of Mind,' which shows itself in 'searching for' and 'seizing' every opportunity 'to serve' and 'to oblige' ; and is the Foundation of what is called 'GOOD BREEDING' ; highly useful to the Possessor, and most agreeable to all.

The Idea of what is 'true Merit,' should also be often presented to Youth, explain'd and impress'd on their Minds, as consisting in an 'Inclination' join'd with a 'Ability' to serve Mankind, one's Country, Friends and Family ; which 'Ability' is (with the Blessing of God) to be acquir'd or greatly increas'd by 'true Learning,' and should indeed be the great 'Aim' and 'End' of all Learning.

In accordance with the general tenor of the proposals of 1749, the academy was organized in three schools, the English, the Latin, and the mathematical, each with a separate master. In 1754, a fourth school, the philosophical, was organized to offer logic, rhetoric, and natural and moral philosophy to advanced students. Although the conduct of this school fell short of Franklin's modern notions, it set up standards which were influential in ushering in a new era in American curriculum practice. Other academies which were established during the remainder of the eighteenth century also showed much independence of tradition in thei curricula and set up such objectives as preparation for the real business of living and acquaintance with an expanding body of knowledge. The academy at Exeter, for example was provided in 1778 by its constitution with the following objectives and curriculum : "the 'first' and 'principal' object of this Institution is the promotion of true 'PIETY' and 'VIRTUE'; the 'secon ',' instruction in the English, Latin. and Greek Languages together with Writing, Arithmetic, Music, and Art of Speaking : the 'third,' practical Geometry, Logic, and Geography ; and the 'fourth,' such other of the Liberal Arts and Sciences or Languages, as opportunity and ability may hereafter admit, and as the 'TRUSTEES' shall direct."

The curriculum of the conventional, early modern school represents the need for an army of Swifts, Defoes, and Franklins. While scientific discovery was progressing at a rate seldom if ever equaled, schoolboys were still forced to rely upon the inexact although at the time picturesque accounts of the Middle Ages. The makers of the textbooks of this period show greater reliance upon the "properties of things" as revealed by imagination, anecdotes told by travelers to a gullible world, and early guesses than upon the more exact reports of experimentalists who had read or acted upon Bacon's suggestions for the advancement of learning. While science was remaking the world outside the school, the schools were being more completely cast in the molds of ancient customs and lo.e. Fifty schoolmasters such as Vittorino of the fifteenth century, if organized as the present National Education Association is organiz d, could have revolutionized and modernized the schools of any country or century from that century to the nineteenth. But complacency rather than criticism ran in the veins of teachers. Despite activity which led the preparation of new books for use in the schools, these books were patterned closely after their predecessors and based entirely upon content centuries old. Le Grand (1694), for example, in his 'Entire Body of Philosophy,' announced that Egypt has a dry climate because the earth is so compact that no vapors can be transmitted by it. Gordon (1730, 12th edition), n his 'Geography,' found a place for such infallibly true paradoxes as this : "there is a certain place of the earth, at which if two men should chance to meet, one would stand upright upon the soles of the other's feet, and neither of them should feel the other's weight, and yet they should both retain their natural posture." Guthrie (1792), in his 'Geographical Grammar,' informs his readers about the strange inhabitants of Connecticut, a place in which deformities rarely develop because the women have learned from the Indians how to keep their infants straight "by means of a board," and that the citizens of this commonwealth are disallowed to "converse about whist, quadrilles or operas." These samples of content should, however, be judged in the light of the entire courses of which they were but a small part. Other portions of the books tereated many topics in a fashion that was as accurate as the existing knowledge would permit ; mathematical, physical, and political geography were included in these early compendiums.

The whole of the science came from tiny rootlets far down in the mold of ignorance and superstition. A struggle it was with generally accepted religion and with srongly intrenched conservatism for this little plant to push its way up on a level with the humanistic branches. Latin had been in the saddle for centuries, practically alone, beating off every aspirant who wished to share that honor, Greek never climbed up alongside her ; logic, ethics, and philosophy even were only adjuncts. Mathematics had but little more success. Finally from the outside comes forward in the guise of science. At first he had to wear the Latin garb and to follow the beaten track of question and answer, of dogmatic statement ; of directions without reasons, of dead memorizing of the words of the printed page or from the master's lips. Slowly inventiveness came to the aid with apparatus, and eventually with laboratories, but not until for into the nineteenth century. There is no evidence whatever that any of this apparatus was used by the students. Very likely the class only viewed portions of it as the teacher performed experiment in front to illustrate some point.

Of the scientific attitude as it is cultivated to day, of cold, dispassionate study of nature without the lingering flavor of authority or of religion, our colonial ancestors knew nothing. Of the great of subjects now in profusion in one-half of our colleges the colonial youth had no conception. Substantially, he had no geology, no zoology, no chemistry, and but little botany. Physics alone was prepared for him with anything like the fullness of to-day. For a long time it was an off-shoot of mathematics from which it originally sprang. But in the dim light of the dawn the soils was beieg stirred and the seed being dropped from which we have reaped so abundantly. To that extent are we indebted to our colonial ancestors for preparing the way.

Curricula of the early National Period

During the early national period America maintained two forms of secondary education. One of these, the decadent classical education of the Latin grammar schools, was in a weakened state. Certain outstanding schools were, however, exceptions and successfully withstood the competition of academies and the indifference and rigors of the later colonial and early national periods. Such schools were the Hopkins Latin Grammar School of New Haven and the Boston Public Latin School. Of the latter school, records of the complete curriculum of 1789 have been preserved. At a meeting of the school committee in that year it was voted that the boys at entrance to this school should be at least ten years of age, that the school should be divided into four years, and that the following books should be used in the respective classes :

First year—(Latin only). Cheever, *Accidence*; Corderius, *Colloquies*; Nomenclator, *Esop's Fables*; Ward, *Latin Grammar*, or Eutropius.

Second year--(Latin only). Clarke, *Introduction*; Ward, *Latin Grammar*, Eutropius; Selections from *Old Testament History* or Castilio, *Dialogues*; Carretson, *Exercises* - in Latin Composition.

Thrid year - (Latin and Greek). Caesar, *Commentaries*; Cicero, *Epistles* or *Offices*; Ovid, *Metamorphoses*; Virgil, *AEneid*; Latin Composition based upon King, *History of the Heathen Gods*; Greek Grammar.

Fourth year—(Latin and Greek). Virgil, *AEneid*; Cicero, *Orations*; Horace; Latin Composition, continued; *Gradus ad Parnassum*; *Greek Testament*; Homer.

Between 1814 and 1828 this Boston school, under Headmaster Gould, added several courses in English, mathematics, history, and geography. His own account of the curriculum is summarized in the following five-year program of the school :

First year

Latin Grammar | Geograph
Arithmetic | Penmanship

Second Year

Latin | English | History

Third Year

Latin	Greek	English

Fourth and Fifth Years

Latin	History	Algebra
Greek	Geography	Geometry
English	Arithmetic	Trigonometry

This program of the Boston Public Latin School represents the conditions in only a few outstanding schools. Brown cites the Princeton grammar school as another in which similar curriculum enrichment took place, but concludes by saying that the classical instruction of this period was generally "flat and unprofitable in the extreme".

The other form of secondary education of this period was that provided by academies. Although the Franklin academy fell somewhat short of the hopes of its founder, it opened to America such realistic education a· had already been provided by similar schools in Europe. At the close of the eighteenth century when Latin grammar schools still limited their curriculum to the classics, the academies were offering, in addition to the classics, the following courses : English, geography, arithmetic, history, natural and moral philosophy, logic, astronomy, and natural law. By 1811 the program of studies of Exeter were divided into two curricula :

Classical Curriculum	*English Curriculum*
(Four years)	(Three years)
Latin	English Grammar, Rhetoric, and
Greek	Composition
English Grammar and Composition	Declamation and Forensics Arithmetic
Declamation	Algebra
Arithmetic	Geometry
Algebra	Plane Trigonometry
Geometry	Mensuration

Ancient History	Surveying
Geography	Navigation
	Ancient, Modern, and United States History
	Geography
	Natural Philosophy
	Chemistry
	Moral Philosophy
	Political Philosophy
	Logic

Although contemporary classical schools attempted primarily to meet college entrance requirements, the academies generally went far in advance of those requirements. In addition to the case of Exeter as just cited, many other institutions offered curricula which were either more realistic than the courses then offered by colleges or else were paralleled by such curricula. As far as American education is concerned, this period was dominated by a 'laissez-faire' policy : some schools were vigorous and liberal ; others were weak and formal. Decadent humanism was still cramping the development of the schools of the old order, and the new schools, being subject to no external standardizing agency, were dependent almost soley upon the leadership of their own successions of masters.

Foreign schools of this period fared better only in Germany. In England the nonconformist, eighteenth-century academics had waned, and "the public schools were in a parlous state." This narrow classical curriculum could not attract the boys of families outside the direct influence of the public schools :

> The work of the sixth and fifth forms, which were taken together by the head master, gives the best indication of the standard which a classical school of those days aimed at. There were ten construing lessons in a full week : Homer's 'Iliad', 35 lines, two ; Lucian, 40 lines, two; Vergil's 'AEneid', 30 lines, two; 'Scriptores Romani,' 40

lines, two; 'Poetoe Groeci,' 35 lines, one; Horace (hexameters), 60 lines, one; and seven repetion lessons, viz., in the pieces translated from Homer, Vergil, Horace. and the Greek poets, and in the Greek Testment (one) and a book of Latin selections (two). Horace's 'Odes and Greek' plays were substituted for some of the other books during a part of the year. Three compositions were written each week, an original Latin theme, a set of Latin elegiacs, and for the sixth a set of Greek iambics or for the fifth of Latin lyrics. Declamations and speeches came at the end of the term.

It was this education that the *Edinburgh Review* in 1830 criticized relentlessly as fragmentary when considered as classical training, and antiquated when considered as training for modern life. No integrating course in ancient history was provided, so that it was "doubtful if any boy" knew "what the Persian and Peloponnesian wars were." The works were not arranged in a logical order, nor were adequate explanatory suggestions given about anything save "grammatical and materical trifling." In this way attention was "distracted from the really important lessons of history and philosophy" and directed to the same husks of learning that have for nearly two thousand years attracted the attention of certain pedantic Latinists. Worse than some pedants, these did not, according to the *Review*, even keep themselves abreast of pedantry—their books and notes "contain much that is useless and much that is inaccurate." If, as Archer observes, the reviewer had condescended to discuss the teaching of the lowest classes as well as that of the upper school, he might have found a year of forms and rules before the simplest Latin was read. Some of the historical foundations for the pedantic method of trying to teach pupils to read by depriving them of an opportunity to read thus appears ! "The absence of all non-classical subjects save as despised 'extras' was too obvious a point of attack to be missed. Only one possible merit is allowed—the compositions stand out above the rest of the work. The Latin prose is very fair, and the verses may even be good."

France made an abortive attempt, in 1802 to reconstruct her secondary education. The law of that year stated that "Every school established by the communes or conducted by private individuals wherein are taught French, Latin, the first principles of geography, of history, and of mathematics, will be considered as a secondary school." This law, although superseded by regulations made in 1808 and 1810, established certain modern subjects in the curriculum. By the further regulations of 1828 and 1840, the sciences and modern languages, respectively, were placed upon standards which approached those of the classics.

The success of Germany in reviving and continuing her development of education during this period was due largely to the belief that her military defeats early in the mineteenth century were an indictment of her educational policy. Two lines of reform took place in reply to this indictment : "first, the centralization of the school system, the conversion of a vast collection of schools of all grades into a single system capable of direction, supervision and management by a central authority acting for the state ; second, the selection of materials for instruction, the formation, of courses of study and the methods of teching best calculated to subserve the needs of the different classes of society while promoting the interests of the state." The second line of this reform, the changes in subject matter, was a part of the widespread attempt to develop and include in school programs a larger and larger amount of the *Realism* or "real" subjects.

The modern formative period of secondary school curricula

The years from 1820 to 1890 can be denoted as the modern formative period of secondary school curricula. In America this period stretches from the establishment of the high school in 1821 to the agitation which led to the appointment of the Committee of Ten in 1892. In England, in extends from the notable revival of about 1830 to the somewhat general adoption by 1890 of the reform which had for a quarter of a century been advocated by crities of the old curricula and pedantic methods. In Germany, the period is more extensive and begins with the reconstruction of the modern German educational system after the defeat at Jena (1806) and extends to the revision of the higher school programs in 1882. In France, the modern formative period opens with the law of 1802 which laid the basis for modern secondary education in that country and extends to the program of 1890-1891 which attempted to end the "eternal controversy" between the advocates of classicism and realism. Owing to the fact that excellent accounts of these curriculum developments in Europe are of easy access, attention will here be given only to the forming of American curricula. Three causes of development in America will be considered :

(1) legislative enactments;

(2) collegiate influences ; and

(3) educational prophets and publicists. Finally, actual curriculum practices will be presented.

1. *Legislative enactments.* The legislative enactments insofar as they affected curriculum practices varied from state. Certain New England commonwealths are able, however, to point with pride to the continuance of pioneering in things good. When the Boston School Committee reported in 1821 that the mode of education then practicted was not sufficiently extensive or otherwise calculated "to bring the powers of mind into operation nor to qualify a youth to fill usefully and respectably many of those stations, both public and private, in which he may be place," that committee heralded the American high school. In accordance with this plan, the English Classical School was opened in May of that year, and in 1824 this school was named the English High School.

This new secondary institution so favorably impressed the legislators of Massachusetts that, in 1827, they enacted a law which required the establishment of high school in "every city, town, or district, containing five hundred families." The same law required, furthermore, that such schools should offer instruction in United States history, bookkeeping, algebra, geometry, and surveying ; and, in towns of four thousand inhabitants, the law required also that instruction be given in Latin, Greek, rhetoric, logic, and an additional course in history. Few permanant and significant legislative changes were made until 1857, when United State history and algebra were transferred to the elementary school and the following subjects were required in the high schools located in towns to five hundered families : Latin, natural philosophy, chemistry, botany, and civics; schools located in towns of four thousand inhabitants were compelled to offer also French, astronomy, geology, intellectual and moral science, and political economy. Save for placing high-school history on the elective list in 1859, no further important legislative changes were made until 1898.

Despite the notable record of Massachusetts in pioneering by placing the new public secondary school upon a statutory basis, other states, as New York, provided equally potent regulative devices. Following upon a series of mandatory enactments by which the regents of New York had developed the academies into college preparatory institutions, the legislators of that state passed an act of 1827 "whereby the higher English branches were put on a par with the classics as a means of qualifying a schaol for state aid." As a result of this law, the regents, in 1828, passed an ordinance which provided that academies should receive state aid upon the basis of the number of pupils who were pursuing relatively advanced courses in English and Latin. As this legislation did not essay to prescribe complete curricula, the schools, as will presently be shown, generally exceeded the requirements of these regulations.

Still greater freedom was given to local authorities in the developments of curricula in other states. For example, the "curriculum was not usually specified in the articles of incorporation (of the earliest high schools in Ohio), but was frequently hinted at in the right given to the trustees to determine what branches of the 'arts and sciences' should be taught, or sometimes the phrase ran 'learned languages, arts and sciences,' or branches of a 'polite and liberal education'. Another example of this freedom is found in Mississippi, where nothing in the charters granted to secondary schools (academies) indicates "the curricula of these schools. A few charters authorize the boards of trustees to 'ordan the course of study,' but this function is usually left by implication to the faculties, wiih no suggestion from the state as to what the curriculum should contain. The distinction draw in 1821 as to requirements for a license to teach in the common schools and in the academies indicates the chief difference in the minds of the legislators of the time between the academy and the common school; in addition to the common-school subjects, the teachers in academies were required to be qualifiid to teach Latin and Greek." If, as one is included to believe, the foregoing examples are representative of legislative practices in different regions of the United States, one can readily grant that legislators have wisely refrained from enacting laws which would unduly cramp either local authorities or state supervisory agencies.

2. *Collegiate influences.* Collegiate influences during the nineteenth century can conveniently be devided into two groups : those which existed before 1870 ; and those which existed after that time. The influences prior to 1870 are comparable roughly with the tendencies of Latin grammar schools; the influences after 1870 are comparable with the liberating tendencies of the academies. The reasons for the formal tendencies of the first seven decades grew out of the traditional character of college methods and studies; the reasons for the broadening dendencies of the last three decades are found largely in the post-war realistic influences and in the appointment of Charles William Eliot as president of Harvard University.

The academy which Defoe attended in the seventeenth century and scores of academies and high schools in America before 1850 far exceeded in breadth if not in depth and character the requirements for admission to leading American colleges during the greater part of the nineteenth century. For example, four great colleges—Columbia, Harvard, Princeton, and Yale required in 1800 nothing save Latin, Greek, and arithmetic, Harvard only omitting arithmetic unill 1807.

The additional requirements up to 1870 included only algebra, geometry, geography, English grammar, and, in Harvard only, ancient history. If, therefore, one can judge the influnce of college requirements upon scondary school practices, one can conclude that the influence was unfavorable to the continuance of the comprehensive courses offered in secondary schools. Both the academy and the high school had been established to meet demands which were overlooked by college preparatory courses; both of these young secondary institutions soon became so engrossed in the preparation of pupils for college that they tended to neglect their own original plans and purposes. The failure of colleges to recognize the preparatory value of certain forms of subject matter was largely responsible for this perversion of secondary schools.

Three points which favor the position of colleges in this matter are, however, worth mentioning. First, it was probably important that secondary schools provide college preparatory training; and yet, if it can be proved that preparatory training for the colleges was not the best trainlng for pupils who did not go to college, then it is unfortunate that the colleges monopolized the attention of secondary schools. Second, the colleges were probably correct in insisting that secondary schools provided sound training in the subjects which pupils pursued.

If the contention of scholars that the science teaching was poorer than the teaching of the classics is true, the colleges may have been justified in requiring secondary schools to specialize in the classics. It was obvious, however, to followers of the international realistic movement which has been described above that this procedure of colleges was extremely reprehensible. A third defense of the colleges can be mentioned, although its ramparts have long since been shaken : it was sincerely believed by college administrators of the past century that only certain subjects provided the mental discipline which was required as preparatory to college tasks. Throughout the seventy years under discussion, it was possible, as it still is, for the college man to say magnanimously that higher institutions do not object to a broad secondary school program of studies and the colleges do not seek undue favor from secondary schools. The greatest difficulty with this position is that it shows utter lack of leadership and thus opens to opponents of higher education an analogous course of reasoning. That is, if secondary schools neglect one important function in order to perform another the assumption of leadership by supporters of hitherto neglected functions may lead to a reversal of favoritism.

If, however, one continues to trace the relationship between secondary and collegiate institutions to the end of the nineteenth century, one finds that a lack of curriculum leadership did not persist long beyond the middle of the century. The last three decades of that century are marked not only by college leadership in curriculum problems, but also by a notable infiuence of secondary schools upon college entrance requirements Indeed, the strength of the leadership of colleges during those decades may be attributed in no small degree to President Eliot's ability to recognize the values of realistic subjects, to show how to improve the teaching of those subjects, and to recognize the protagonists of old and new subjects.

From 1870 to 1900 three important groups of subjects gained a recognized place in college admission requirements : English literature and composition, modern languages, and natural science. At the same time, changes took place in the original admission subjects. In the classics, mastery rather than specific readings became the requisite; quadratics was added to the requirement of 1870; in geometry, the whole of plane geometry became a general requirement, and to this some colleges added solid geometry; all branches of social studies were either increased in amount or changed in character, or both. Broome summarizes the work of these decades as follows :

During the last thirty years (1870—1900) the tendencies in the development of college admission requirements that were prominent up to 1870 have continued. The addition of new subjects has widened the range of entrance requirements. The amount required in the original subjects has increased. In mathematics, history. and science the advance has been considerable, while even the classical requirement has increased slightly. Colleges which still require both Latin and Greek for admission not only require more in these languages, but considerably more in mathematics, history, and English, as well as modern language and perhaps, some branch of science. This continued advance in entrance requirements is due, of course, in general, to the rapid development of higher education and the constant broadening of the field of knowledge; but what has influenced admission requirements most has been the gradual transformation of the American college into the American university. In order to meet the demand for advanced study and research the college has constantly pushed the work of a distinctly secondary character into the preparatory school. This movement has been accelerated also by the increased popular demand for advanced studies in what has sometimes been called the "people's college," the public high school; for that institution is at home, is easily accessible, and is free. A third tendency, which belongs more strictly to the method of the entrance examination than to the subjects is that examinations are becoming tests of power rather than mere acquisition of facts. Instances of this tendency are the emphasis placed on sight translations in the language examinations, the growing importance of English composition, of the solution of original problems in geometry, and of independent experimental work in science.

As a result of this latter tendency in college admission requirements there has been a significant revolution in preparatory school methods of teaching, a shifting of the emphasis from stultifying memoriter work to that more quickening sort which calls for independent thought and constructive ability. In the teaching of foreign languages the actual use of the language and wide readings in its literature have supplanted much of the old-time exhaustive study of formal grammar; and the study of science has moved from the library to the laboratory.

3. *Educational prophets and publicists.* The work of several American prophets and publicists commands the attention of students of nineteenth-century curricula. During the generation which closed 1840 three men, John Griscom, Josiah Quincy, and Alexander Bache fused the ideas and practices of Europe and America into plans for secondary education in New York City, Boston, and Philadelphia. Griscom's book, *A Year in Europe* (1819), which Henry Barnard named as the most influential educational book of the first half of the nineteenth century, contains an extended account of the Edinburgh (Scotland) High School. This account, together with Griscom's personal influence, seems to have led to the naming of the first high schools of Boston and New York City and to a well-defined attitude in regard to the curricula of these new schools. This attitude was that the chief purpose of the high school was to prepare pupils for such activities as they were destined to pursue after their schooldays were over. As pupils enter the school with different plans, it appears plain that "their circumstance must require corresponding classifications of scholars and of studies."

Consequently, the High-School Society grouped the studies as constants and electives. President Quincy's intimate and general agreement with Griscom indicates that his own support of a school "to enable the mercantile and mechanical classes to obtain an education adapted for those classes" and his later support of an elective system at Harvard were due in part to Griscom's influence.

Although Bache's *Report on Education in Europe* (1839) was made to guide the trustees of Girard College in formulating a program of studies for that college, this report had a wide influence upon all grades of instruction. In the portion of this document which is devoted to secondary education, Bache reported in detail upon both classical and realistic curricula as he observed them in Europe. In recognizing the value of secondary instruction as preparatory for both professional and practical occupations, he gave due attention to the views already expressed by Griscom and Quincy. In attempting to show the value of both classical and scientific studies to students in general, he supported the policy finally adopted in American secondary education. One of the most significant issues raised by Bache was that certain countries of localities often regard as experimental and radical the long-established and successful practices of other countries. Despite many differences in the details of education in different countries, the major problems are, Bache asserts, too much alike to admit of certain curriculum differences. By comparing the educational problems of different countries, Bache finds that there are :

> high general purposes to be served in the mental training of youth, on the more or less successful modes of applying which, comparison will throw the light of experience. If a satisfactory intellectual education at Berlin requires the study of Latin, Greek, the vernacular, French, geography and history, mathematics, physics, natural history, and intellectual philosophy it is not likely that the same can be accomplished elsewhere by the study of Latin, Greek, geography, a small portion of history, and less of arithmetic and geometry. If it is possible at Berlin to devote sufficient time to the branches enumerated in the Prussian program, to make them really sources of mental culture and of positive knowledge, consistently with a thorough knowledge of the classics, it must be so in the same interval of time anywhere else. Hence there need be no apprehension even on the part of those who consider the attainment of classical knowledge for itself as the great end of instruction, in regard to the effects of an increased attention to other branches of knowledge, unless it can be

shown that the German youth are inferior in these attainments, which has never, I believe, been even attempted, or unless it can be proved that they are naturally of higher intellectual powers than those of other countries.

The most important prophet and publicist of secondary education during the middle of the nineteenth century was Henry Barnard. His views on curricula were given in a letter which he wrote to Principal Capron of Hartford in 1847. The following passage from the epistle shows this scholar's point of view:

> The course of instruction which is here provided for the physical, intellectual, and moral training of the pupils .. and rising and spreading out into all of those studies which in one direction take hold of all the occupations of society, the farm, the workshop, the counting-room, the deck, the home on the other discipline and inform the mind ..—such a course seems to me eminently judicious. It meets the demand of our age for an education in science which shall make the wind and the stream, and the still more subtle agents of nature, minister to our material wants...And the same time it does not ignore those apparently less practical studies, especially the mathematics and the classics .I do not believe that any amount of applied science, and the largest amount practicable should be given in this and other institutions of higher learning, or that any attention which may be bestowed on the English language only -and whatever else is taught or omitted, the English language and literature should ever hold a prominent, the prominent place in the actual aims and results of your scheme of study— can ever train the three great faculties of reason, memory, and imagination, to their full, natural, and harmonious development. But while I hold this not hastily formed opinion, I see no reason why the instruction of our schools, from the oral or primary, up to the university, should not deal with common things, with the principles,

the phenomena and duties of everyday life:—why sewing, and a practical knowledge of domestic economy should not find a place somewhere in the training of every girl; and a "round about common sense," the power of applying the mind and the hands readily to all sorts of work in helping himself and other people, about the house, the shop, or the farm, be the result of the house and school training of every boy. This was, and still is to some extent, the glory of our best New England schools and domestic education. And to all this should now be added the modern development of science in their application to all our great national industries.

Four women of the nineteenth century, Catherine Beecher, Mary Lyon, Emma Willard, and Almira Phelps, added their arguments to those of the leaders already named in the battle for equal rights of realistic and classical school studies. Particularly vigorous was Mrs. Phelps in her criticism of the "affectation and frivolity" and superficiality of certain female seminaries of about 1840. This advocate and teacher of science worked with her sister. Emma Willard, to provide scientific as well as classical and literary curricula for girls. At the same time Mary Lyon labored in the same way at Mount Holyoke to make her school a "plant for development not of intellectual gymnasts but of enlightened useful women."

The last of the prophets to be discussed in this section is President Eliot. In setting forth his notions of a liberal education in 1884, he described the long periods of apprenticeship which had been undergone by Greek, science, and mathematics before these subjects were granted places of respectability in curricula. Greek, for example, as he asserts, was entirely neglected in Italian schools until about 1400. although Petrarch and his enthusiastic comrades labored in its behalf during the middle of the fourteenth century. And not until long after that time did Greek enjoy a high place in the schools of any country of western Europe. The sciences were not yet fully admitted to the curricula even at the time of the address under discussion. Mathematics was recognized as a valuable discipline until it was reconstructed by western Europeans: after that time the conservatives doubted its educational value.

All three of these subjects, Greek, science, and mathematics, as offered in 1884 had been compelled to submit to ridicule as frivolous, heterodox, and useless for discipline! Furthermore, the Middle Ages defined a liberal education in terms of seven formal subjects organized in ways which in 1884 were no longer held to be liberal. Instead of the mediaeval liberal arts, there came the "new learning" of the early modern times. This new learning, which is content was largely a revival of ancient classics and mathematics, came in turn to be the program of conservatives, and looked disdainfully upon prospective newcomers to the curricula. This situation led Eliot to assert that, "History teaches boldness in urging the claims of modern literatures and sciences to full recognition as liberal arts.

Intelligent boldness in a modern world justified one, in Eliot's opinion, in admitting to high respectability English language and literature, French and German, natural science, and history. The wise men of the fifteenth century took the best intellectual and moral materials of their day and made a curriculum; if, in 1884, one followed the same procedure, this prophet believed that liberal amounts of the subjects just named would fall into secondary school curricula.

American curricular practices for the last one hundred years are recorded in catalogues and other brochures of different schools. For the sake of brevity, the practices of this period will be set forth chiefly in tabular form. The formative period of curricula-making as here limited opened with a new institution which later became the high school. The first program of studies for this three-year school was as follows:

First year—English, arithmetic, and geography. (English included reading, literature, composition, and declamation.)

Second year - English, mathematics, history, and logic. (English included the same branches as in the first year; mathematics included algebra, geometry, trigonometry, and applied mathematics, as navigation and surveying; history included ancient and modern history and chronology.)

Third year -- English, mathematics, history, natural science, and philosophy. (English, mathematics, and history included the same as for the preceding year; philosophy included logic and moral and political philosophy.)

Except for the following additions, the program remained unchanged until 1852 : the school report of 1829 states that masters may at their option add philosophy of history, chemistry, intellectual philosophy logic, and drawing; to these, trigonometry, French, and study of the constitution of the United States were added in 1836. In 1852 the school added one year to its course and then adopted the following program of studies :

First year—Review of common elemetary branches, ancient geography, general history, algebra, French, and drawing.

Second year—Algebra (completed), French, drawing, geometry, trigonometry, bookkeeping, rhetoric, constitution of the United States, and Paley's *Evidences of Christianity.*

Third year—Trigonometry, Paley, drawing, astronomy, natural philosophy, moral philosophy, political economy, natural theology, English literature, and French or Spanish.

Fourth year—Astronomy, intellectual philosophy, logic, Spanish, geology, mechanics, engineering, and higher mathematics.

Five years after the opening of the first high school, the Girls' High School of Boston was opened (1826) with the following program of studies :

First year—(Required) Reading, Spelling, Writing words and sentences from dictation, English grammar, with exercises in the same, Composition, Modern and ancient geography, Intellectual and written arithmetic, Rhetoric, History of the United States.

(Allowed) Logic, or botany.

Second year—(Required) Reading, Spelling, Composition, Modern and ancient geography, Intellectual and written arithmetic, and Rhetoric continued. Elements of geometry, Natural philosophy, General history, History of England, Paley's *Natural Theology*.

(Allowed) Logic, Botany, demonstrative geometry, algebra, Latin or French.

Third year—(Required) Reading, Composition, Natural Philosophy, and Paley's *Natural Theology* continued, Astronomy, Treatise on the globes, Chemistry, History of Greece, History of Rome, Paley's *Moral Philosophy*, Paley's *Evidences of Christianity*.

(Allowed) Logic, algebra, principles of perspective, projection of maps, botany, Latin, or French.

This program, together with that of the boys' school, seems to represent the best practices of the early high schools.

During the generation which followed the opening of the first high schools, these new schools assumed their dual function of college preparatory and finishing schools. Following this came, in turn, the division of the programs of study into classical and English curricula. Table II shows such curricula as they were offered in three superior schools of New England about 1850. Each of these curricula was but slightly modified for many years after the dates given in this table. Excellent reasons can be found in this table for the distinction between preparatory for college and preparatory for life. In the case of college preparatory students, the subjects of the high-school English curriculum were usually pursued in a more advanced fashion during the last two years of college.

Table II

The Curricula of three Representative New England High Schools+

Subjects	*Worcester (1845)*		*Cambridge (1852)*		*Hartford (1858)*	
	Classical	*English*	*Classical*	*English*	*Classical*	*English++*
Latin	4	—	4	—	4	$4\frac{2}{3}$
Greek	2	—	2	—	3	$4\frac{2}{3}$
French	—	$\frac{3}{4}$	—	4	—	4
German	—	—	—	—	—	4
English	$\frac{3}{4}$	$1\frac{1}{4}$	4	4	—	$2\frac{1}{3}$
Mathematics						
Arithmetic	$\frac{3}{4}$	$\frac{1}{4}$	$\frac{1}{2}$	$\frac{2}{3}$	—	$\frac{1}{3}$
Algebra	1	$\frac{1}{2}$	2	2	—	1
Geometry	$\frac{3}{4}$	$\frac{3}{4}$	$1\frac{2}{3}$	1	—	$1\frac{1}{3}$
Trigonometry	—	$\frac{3}{4}$	—	$\frac{2}{3}$	—	1
Science						
Astronomy	—	$\frac{1}{2}$	—	$\frac{2}{3}$	—	$\frac{2}{3}$
Botany	—	$\frac{1}{4}$	—	—	—	$\frac{1}{3}$
Chemistry	—	$\frac{1}{2}$	$\frac{2}{3}$	$\frac{2}{3}$	—	$\frac{1}{3}$
Geology	—	—	—	—	—	$\frac{1}{3}$
Natural Philosophy	—	$\frac{3}{4}$	$\frac{2}{3}$	$\frac{2}{3}$	—	$\frac{1}{3}$
Physical Geography	—	—	—	—	—	$\frac{1}{3}$
Physiology	—	$\frac{1}{4}$	—	—	—	$\frac{1}{3}$
Zoology	—	—	—	—	—	$\frac{1}{3}$
Social Studies						
History	—	$\frac{3}{4}$	1	1	2	$1\frac{1}{3}$
Civics	—	$\frac{1}{4}$	—	—	—	$\frac{1}{3}$

Political Economy	—	¼	—	—	—	⅓
Moral Philosophy	—	½	—	⅔	—	—
Mental Philosophy	—	¼	—	⅔	—	⅓
Logic	—	—	—	—	—	⅔
Geography	½	—	1	1	1	—
Bookkeeping	—	¼	—	⅓	—	⅓
Drawing	—	—	—	1	—	—

+Based upon catalogues of these schools. Here adapted from E.D. Grizzell, *Origin and Development of the High School in New England before 1865*. The Macmillan Company, 1923. Chapter XIV.

++ Five-year course. Many optional subjects.

Table III

Percentage of Schools Offering Certain Subjects in 1866-1867 Based upon Programs of Thirty Representative Cities for that Year+

Subjects	*Percentages of Schools Offering*	*Subjects*	*Percentages of Schools Offering*
Algebra	100	Logic	23
Arithmetic	77	Mechaics	13
Astronomy	83	Mensuration	20
Bookkeeping	60	Mental Philosophy	87
Botany	80	Mineralogy	13
Calculus	17	Moral Science	67
Caesar	50	Music	43
Chemistry	87	Natural Philosophy	100

Cicero	40	Natural History	30
Composition	80	Natural Theology	7
United States Constitution	53	Navigation	23
		Ovid	13
Declamation	63	Pedagogics	7
Drawing	33	Penmanship	33
Engineering	7	Political Economy	43
English Grammar	80	Physical Exercises	13
English Literature	70	Physical Geography	83
English Synonyms	17	Physiology	93
Etymology	27	Reading	47
Evidences of Christianity	13	Rhetoric	93
French	70	Sallust	27
Geometry	100	Science of Government	23
Geology	70	Spanish	7
German	50	Spelling	20
Greek	60	Surveying	47
History, Ancient	50	Tacitus	7
History, Modern	87	Trigonometry	73
Homer	53	Virgil	47
Horace	17	Xenophon	60
Latin	90	Zoology	13

+Baltimore, Boston, Cambridge, Chicago, Cincinnati, Cleveland, Dubuque, Fond du Lac, Hartford, Indianapolis, Lewiston, Maine; Louisville, Madison, Wisconsin; Manchester, New York, New Haven, Newark, Niles, Philadelphia, Portland, Providence, Rochester, Sandusky, San Francisco, Springfield, Illinois; St. Louis, Terre Haute, Troy, Washington, Worcester.

Adapted from Barnard's *American Journal of Education*, XIX, 463. 1869.

During the year 1869 Henry Barnard issued a special report upon the curricula of "the principal cities of the United States." In the published digest of the rules and regulations of these cities, extracts are quoted from reports of the thirty cities named in the footnote of Table III. At that time, as this table shows, certain subjects were well established in high schools: mathematics, English, Latin, history, mental philosophy, and many branches of science. Other courses, as evidences of Christianity and natural theology, represent survivals of the dominant interests of an earlier period, while courses such as science of government and physical exercises stand as fore-runners of courses which have now become all but universal. Still other courses are subsumed under different titles and in some cases united to form new courses, for example, no less than six of the courses in this table are now introduced to pupils under a single title "general mathematics."

The development of curriculum offerings in the North Central states is summarized in Table IV, which is based upon reports from thirty to forty schools for each period. As the schools whose reports were available are widely scattered and of varying sizes, the practices here reported were judged by Stout, from whose monograph the data were adapted, to be representative. Only the more striking contrasts between the curricula of 1860 and those of 1910 are shown by the modal offerings and ranges of offerings of schools of those two periods. If this table were enlarged to include miscellaneous subjects, there would, of course, be many subjects in only the 1860 column. An analysis of Stout's data shows that great changes have taken place in all the subjects which are catalogued in Table IV. Mathematics, for example, changed from a subject in which many schools devoted from one term to one year to each of five branches to a subject in which many schools offered from one semester to one and a half years in four of the original branches. The changes in this subject were due chiefly to greater concentration upon algebra and geometry. English was reorganized into a four-year course with increased emphasis upon extending pupils' literary acquaintance. The amounts of both English and science offered were doubled. In science the organization of year courses in physics and chemistry is somewhat analogous to the reorganization of the course in English and was in fact a precursor of still further organization

Table IV

Contrast between Curriculum Offerings of 1860—1865 and those of 1906—1911+

(Percentages show the proportions of schools offering each subject, modes and ranges show the number of years in courses.)

Subjects	*1860—1865*	*1906 – 1911*
Mathematics		
Percentage	100	100
Mode	3	4
Range++	1—4	2—5
English		
Percentage	100	100
Mode	2	4
Range	$\frac{1}{3}$—$3\frac{1}{3}$	3—4
Science		
Percentage	100	100
Mode	$2\frac{1}{2}$	4+
Range	2—5	2—7
Social studies		
Percentage	90	100
Mode	1	3
Range	$\frac{1}{3}$—2	$1\frac{1}{2}$—5
Latin		
Percentage	80	98
Mode	3	4
Range	2—4	4
Other languages		
Percentage	90	100
Mode	2+	6
Range	2—13	4—19

Commercial subjects		
Percentage	45	88
Mode	⅓	6
Range	⅓—1	½—10½
Manual arts		
Percentage	0	58
Mode	—	(2) (4)+++
Range	—	1—4
Home economics		
Percentage	10	45
Mode	?	2
Range	⅓—⅔	1—4

+Based upon tables in Stout, *op. cit.*
++ Range for schools offering.
+++Bi-modal.

of science into a few long courses, In social studies this period opened with many nondescript courses and closed with several well-systematized year-courses.

The amounts of work offered both in classical and modern and foreign languages increased. Save for very slight offerings at the beginning of this period, commercial and practical arts courses sprang into being during these years. By examining still more closely the data contained in Table IV, it can be seen that many of the changes just referred to took place after 1890 and that many courses underwent few significant changes between 1860 and 1890. Many of the great changes which took place after 1890 were due to a great inventory of secondary education, a brief exposition of which will be given in the next section.

Beginnings of the great Cooperative Inventory of Secondary Education

The periodical invoicing of any human institution is essential for its continuous progress. In invoicing educational institutions, an inventory can be conducted by or with reference to a single school or many schools. If the inventory is conducted by or with reference to many schools, the application of principles and plans derived from the inquiry is likely to meet fewer theoretical and practical difficulties, and to have wider usefulness than if the inventory is by and for a single school. The great secondary school inventory of the past thirty-six years has been a cooperative attempt to measure the effectiveness of widely varying schools, to place the results before the academic world, and to base workable recommendation upon observed results. The characteristics and outcomes of this continuous, cooperative inventory will be convassed in this section.

The preceding section of this chapter provides a sketch of the development of programs of study during the past century. During that century, many cities systematized their curricula into well-integrated sequences ; the program of studies of Worcester in 1845, as shown in Table II, is a sample of such systematization.

Not all schools were able, however, to organize their courses as well as Worcester did hers. Besides, great variations occurred among the types of organization of courses effected in well-systematized schools. For example, the programs of Worcester, Cambridge, and Hartford show striking differences in the offering in certain subjects. Far greater differences in curriculum practices are shown in Table III, which gives a tabular summary of Barnard's report upon thirty schools in 1867 ; among these differences are those shown by the percentages of important schools which offered English literature, a standard course in Latin, and history. Diversities in practice are still further emphasized in Stout's original data, as the percentages for the offerings in English vary as much in the eighties as in the sixties.

Although variations in practice are probably desirable and will continue to exist in different schools, there seem to be valid reasons, theoretical and practical, for agreement and standardization among schools upon certain matters. Such standardization has been desired especially by higher institutions to which admission is sought by candidates from many secondary schools.

Out of this urgent need for standardization grew the great inventory. Although many appraisals of secondary education had already been made, the appointment of the Committee of Ten in 1892 marks the beginning of an appraisal which has continued to the present time. This committee was delegated to report "on the general subject of uniformity in school programmes and in requirements for admission to college." This committee, which consisted of six members of collegiate institutions and four members of secondary schools, organized nine subcommittees of ten members each on the following subjects: Latin; Greek; English; modern foreign languages; mathematics; physics, astronomy, and chemistry; natural history (biology, including botany, zoology, and physiology); history, civil government, and political economy; and geography (physical geography, geology, and metereology). The following list of questions was adopted as a guide for the discussions of all the subcommittees:

1. In the schools course of study extending approximately from six years to eighteen years—a course including the periods of both elementary and secondary instruction—at what age should the subject of the Conference be first introduced?

2. After it is introduced, how many hours a week for how many years should be devoted to it?

3. How many hours a week for how many years should be devoted to it during the last four years of the complete course; that is, during the ordinary high-school period?

4. What topics, or parts, of the subject may be reasonably covered during the whole course?

5. What t pics, or parts, may best reserved for the last four years?

6. In what form and to what extent should the subject enter into college requirements for admission ? Such questions as the sufficiency of translation at sight as the test of knowledge of a language, or the superiority of a laboratory examination in a scientific subject to a written examination on a text-book, are intended to be suggested under this head by the phrase "in what form ?"

7. Should the subject be treated differently for pupils who are going to college, for those who are going to a scientific school, and for those who, presumably, are going to neither ?

8. At what stage should this differentiation begin, if any recommended ?

9. Can any description be given of the best method of teaching this subject throughout the school course ?

10. Can any description be given of the best mode of testing attainments in this subject at college admission examinations ?

11. For those cases in which colleges and universities permit a division of the admission examination into a preliminary and final examination, separated by at least a year, can the best limit between the preliminary and final examinations be approximately defined ?

In submitting their several reports upon these elementary questions, the subcommittee presented these recommendations for the time allotments of their own subjects. Naturally, the sum of the time allotments exceeded some-what the possibilities of a four-year course. These recommendations were, therefore, reduced by the general committee and organized into the four curricula as shown in Table V.

Many possible criticisms of this report were anticipated by the committee. In the first place, it was recognized that certain subjects, as history and English, suffered serious contraction in the classical curriculum. It was believed also that in the English curriculum the foreign languages were seriously

TABLE V

Curricula Recommended by the Committee of Ten

Year	*Classical* *Three Foreign Language* *(One Modern)*		*Latin-Scientific* *Two Foreign Languages* *(One Modern)*		*Modern Languages* *Two Foreign Languages* *(Both Modern)*		*English* *One Foreign Languages* *(Ancient or Modern)*		Year
	Latin	5 p.	Latin	5 p.	French (or German) begun	5 p.	Latin, or German, or French	5 p.	
	English	4 p.	English	4 p.	Engfish	4 p.	English	4 p.	
I	Algebra	4. p.	Algebra	4 p.	Algebra	4 p.	Algebra	4 p.	I
	History	4 p.	Hlstory	4 p.	History	4 p.	History	4 p.	
	Physical Geography	3 p.	Physical Geography	3 p.	Physical Geography	3 p.	Physical Geography	3 p.	
	Total	20 p.	Total	20 p.	Total	20 p.	Total	20 p.	

	Latin	5 p.	Latin	5 p.	French (or German)	4 p.	Latin, French, or German	5 or 4 p.	
	English	2 p.	English	2 p.	English	2 p.	English	3 or 4 p.	
	*German (or French) begun	4 p.	German (or French) begun	4 p.	German (or French) begun	5 p.	Geometry	3 p.	
II	Geometry	3 p.	Geometry	3 p.	Geometry	3 p.	Physics	3 p.	II
	Physics	3 p.	Physics	3 p.	Physics	3 p.	History	3 p.	
	Historp	3 p.	Botany or Zoology	3 p.	Botany or Zoology	3 p.	Botany or Zoology	3 p.	
	Total	20 p.	Total	20 p.	Total	20 p.	Total	20 p.	

(*Contd.*)

Latin	4 p.	Latin	4 p.	French (or German)	4 p.	Latin, French, or German	4 p.
+Greek	5 p.	English	3 p.	English	3 p.	English	5 p.
English	3 p.	German (or French)	4 p.			as in other 3; additional 2	
German (or French)	4 p.	Mathematics	4 p.			Mathematics	4 p.
		Algebra 2; Geometry 2		German (or French)	4 p.	Algebra, 2 : Geometry 2	
		Astronomy 1/2 yr. and				Astronomy I/2 yr. and	
III Mathematics	4 p.	Meteorology	3 p.	Mathematics	4 p.	Meteorology 1/2 yr.	3 p. III
				Algebra 2; Geometry 2			
Algebra 2 Geometry 2		History	2 p.	History	2 p.	History	4 p.
				Astronomy 1/2 yr. and		as in the Latin-Scientific	2
				Meteorology	3 p.	additional	
	——		— —		— —		— —
Total	20 p.	Total	20 p.	Total	20 p.	Total	20 p.

	Latin	4 p.	Latin	4 p.	French (or German)	3 p.	Latin, French, or German	4 p.	
	Greek	5 p.	English as in Classical additional 2	4 p.	English as in Classical additional 2	4 p.	English as in Classical additional 2	4 p.	
	English	2 p.	German (or French)	3 p.	German (or French)	4 p.	Chemistry	3 p.	
	German (or French)	3 p.	Chemistry	3 p.	Chemistry	3 p.	Trigonomy and Higher Algebra	3 p.	
	Chemistry	3 p.	Trigonometry and Higher Algebra	3 p.	Trigonometry and Higher Algebra	3 p.	History	3 p.	IV
IV	Trigonometry and Higher Algebra or History	3 p.	or History, Geology or Physiography 1/2 yr. and Anatomy, Physiology, and Hygiene 1/2 yr.	3 p.	or History, Geology or Physiography 1/2 yr. and Anatomy Physiology, and Hygiene 1/2 yr.	3 p.	Geology or Physiography 1/2 yr. and Anatomy, Physiography and Hygiene 1/2 yr.	3 p.	
	Total	20 p.	Total	20 p.	Total	20 p.	Total	20 p.	

+In any school in which Greek can be better taught than a modern language, or in which local public opinion or the history of the school make it desirable teach Greek in an ample way, Greek may be substituted for German or French in the second year of the Classical program.

contracted. The defense for this condition was chiefly that four years is a very short period for secondary education; it was argued, however, that the curricula omit all short information courses; that they provide four long sequences in language, science, history, and mathematics; and that they meet almost all college admission requirements. Second, the years for beginning different subjects were defended upon the principle that the final choice of curricula should not be made until after the pupil had been given an opportunity to exhibit his quality and discover his tastes by exploring all the principal fields of knowledge. In conformity with this principle, the subjects of the first two years were made representative and as similar as possible.

The order of subjects was defended also by calling attention to heavy elimination of pupils during the first two years, it was held that a representative course of study would be of greatest possible benefit to such pupils. Third, a preference of the committee for the Classical and Latin-scientific curricula, though somewhat dogmatically defended, was clearly stated. Fourth, the omission of music, drawing, and elocution was explained as indicating only that the committee believed that local school authorities should determine the amounts of time to be devoted to these subjects; it was pointed out also that much incidental training could be given certain subjects which are omitted : the hopeful case of drawing was emphasized. Fifth, the lack of flexibility within this program of studies was shown to be only apparent, because, it was said, the experienced teacher would make necessary or desirable transpositions of German and French, the sciences, and the historical subjects.

If one compares the orderly character of the four curricula as recommended by the Committee of Ten with curricula which are summarized in Table IV and are described in greater detail by Stout, one must grant that this report was an important achievement. It appeared at the close of a long period of expansion of subject matter and purposes of schools. It pointed out the way of standardization and added valuable recommendations concerning the improvement of teachers and teaching.

Owing to the weight of the influences which led to this document and the merit of the report itself, the work of the Committee of Ten can fairly be called the beginning of the long period of invoicing of secondary schools in America. Directly from the report came plans for the reorganization of programs of studies and, as soon as marked defects were seen in the new plans, still further modifications were prepared.

Although the curricula proposed by this committee show unmistakable evidences of college influences and of the supremacy of the defenders of the classical languages, yet the curricula cannot be called traditional or mediaeval. It is much nearer the truth to say that these curricula represent the best of nineteenth-century curriculum thinking, and that the suggestions are both scholarly and modern.

Despite the admitted values and merits of this report, it has received the following criticisms :

(1) As a result of the strong influence of higher institutions it overemphasized the standard college-preparatory subjects and neglected practical arts of "vocational" curricula (it is possible, of course, that, as far as the particular curricula provided are concerned, this college influence was justifiable and correct); but

(2) in spite of an avowed interest in pupils who remain in school for two years or less, no differentiation of work for such pupils was provided; and

(3) the differentiation made for students was in every case in terms of subject matter and not in terms of the interests, needs, or equipment of pupils.

All these criticisms should be viewed in the light of what the committee attempted and the general conditions which existed in 1892. It should be clear that the committee had the virtue of logical organization and that systematization was the objective most desired. But these facts suggest to the present-day educator she criticism that the committee was somewhat lacking in its vision of what the secondary school would become. While these criticisms deserve to be recorded, it should be remembered by critics that the American secondary school is still held by able foreign and American observers to be in an experimental stage. The rapid extension of secondary education from 1890 when only 300,000 pupils were enrolled in secondary schools to the present time when nearly 4,000,000 pupils are enrolled has contributed to the disparaging of the formality of curricula proposed by the Committee of Ten.

As a direct result of the standardizing influences of the Committee of Ten in combination with changes in the purposes, administration, and population, and population of secondary schools, the period since 1893 has been one of reorganization. The subject matter of each secondary school department has been reconstructed and new administrative units have been organized. The great cooperative inventory of secondary education during the last three decades and the changes affected by it constitute the general subject matter of the later sections of this book. This subject will be divided into the following topics : educational objectives, the school population, teaching conditions, the reconstruction of subject matter, and the administration and program of studies. Critics of education have, however, been so important in educational development and reform that Part II is devoted to a brief account of their work and the problems raised by them.

7

Pupil Purposes

Critics and progress

Unlike the well-tempered lover whom every one admires, the critic, though a saint and an inspirer of progress, neither expects nor receives admiration from the crowd whose acts he questions. Indeed, instances of unapplauded critics flood the mind : Anaxagoras, Pericles' teacher, critic of a people who mistook the solar ball of fire for a god ; Protagoras, the agnostic in a land of pagan gods ; Jonah of Nineveh, critic of a city dying from its own corruption ; Jesus the shepherd, a critic who placed life above the letter of the law ; Roger Bacon, neither poet nor profligate, but only an allegeted bearer of light in a darkened age ; Servetus, whose ominous crown of straw, leaves, and sulphur was award for attempting to separate truth from error ; Copernicus, with irreverence for a Ptolemaic universe.

Darwin, with his hesitant announcement of a great revolutionizlng scientific theory ; Rice, discloser of waste in certain formal drills ; and Wilson, critic of deadening diplomacy. It is not here maintained that these critics are without followers, but that such critics are seldom popular with the crowd whose thoughts and acts they criticize and whose good they seek. "Change of view in any direction usually causes some pain at first," or as Jebb says, "Popular sentiment is universally against new subtleties." Even though constructive critics of secondary school curricula be the mainspring of a period of progress which stamps their day as a golden age, any, temporary unpopularity of such reformers should, therefore, cause no wonder.

Despite repeated assertions, that constructive criticism leads to reform and progress, the critic gives little immediate comfort and often finds none in a world which stands in need of the freeing of thought by minds qualified to sift error from truth. Despite the social philosopher's praise of variations in thought as precursors of progress, an uncritical veneration for the solid and enslaving thought and customs of the ages protects ancient darkness against modern light. Why should our race venerate its fetters when open paths lead to light ? Why has the critic so little comfort among his own ? Why has the student of education been shackled whenever he has projected to clear cold light of criticism upon the school ? Certain scholars have much to say of the ills which arise from vested interests in property : what can be said of vested interestes of teachers in unprofitable subject matter.

But can we accept the critic as a guide ? Is the critic truly a herald of progress ? Of late, our country has heard criticms of pacifism and of war, of divorce and of domestic tranquillity, of Latin and of forge work in schools. Where lies truth when diverse proclaimers basn their criticisms upon udon "scientific data"? Who can distinguish Socrates from the mountebank ? What procedure enables us to find out and profit by the second principles of curriculum construction? Long and difficult though this procedure be, it must be followed if it can be found. For its derivation, one may search in the literature of progress. If it be found that constructive criticism has either a necessary or a frequent connection with progress, we shell find in the discovery sufficient grounds for examining carefully the criticism of curricula.

The value of criticism as shown in the literature of progress

The literature of progress has been reviewed for the

purpose of deriving a procedure of dealing with criticism of the secondary-school curriculum and for the purpose of discovering whether or not the critic carries light to darkened places. Such a review calls attention to striking differences between the types of human activities during different periods of history. At times, as during the political and eccelesiastical tumult of the Middle Ages, there has apparently been much unprofitable activity combined with exceeding slow progress toward any defensible educational goals.

At other times, as during the Renaissance, there has apparently been much profitable activity. Accompanying these two periods were equally different types and amounts of mental stimulation. A review of the works of certain partially suppressed mediaevalists shows that their years were barren times for cirtics. Those ceturies were times of extreme intolerance on the part of scholars of any nonconformity to the strict and comprehensive tents of the major institutions of that period. Outspoken criticism was rare; written criticism were often burned by or with their authors. The Italian Renaissance was characterized; on the contrary, by great freeom from institutionalized tenets as far as the occupations of scholars were concerned.

The lives of Petrarch and Vittorino stand forth as proof that their years wers one long open season for critics of mental sterility and joyless schools. Criticisms of academic practices were then freely made by certain scholars, and the reconstructed courses of instruction of the fifteenth century were among the results. In Chapters 1 to 5 is given a detailed discussion of the curricula of different historical periods. It is sufficient to say here that the scholarly constructive critics of the thirteenth and fourteenth centuries appear to have been directly and chiefly responsible for the emergence of the enlightening, humanizing curriculum of the early modern centuries; while the general lack of sympathetic attention ta critical thought during the seven preceding centuries was responsible for the attempted suffocation of practically all proposed changes in subject matter taught in secondary schools.

The historical survey presented in the foregoing chapters supports the statement that few school practices are of the greatest possible value unless they have been subjected to the unfettered criticisms of the generation in which the practices are found. Periods of intolerance toward criticism are periods of stagnation, while periods of free criticism are likely to be periods of great progress.

The literature of progress enables one to classify much of the activity of the Middle Ages as irrationai in the larger sense of the term—as instigated by fundamentally instinctive tendencies rather than by high ethical and social ideals. The activity of the Renaissance was, by contrast, indelibly marked by the social impulse of evangelizing superior minds in the interest of subject matter which possessed high ethical appeals, high literary appeals, and appeals to the so-called rational self. A convincing lesson is taught by these two periods: humanity needs guidance to enable men to avoid unprofitable and harmful activity; criticism should form a part of such guidance.

Criticism varies, however, in quality, and even when apt it is not automatic in producing good. Criticism which is violently opposed to existing conditions has often been overlooked as far as practical results within the lifetime of the critic are concerned. Such criticism fails to ally itself with current forces even for the purpose of directing them. While this somewhat extreme or Bohemian form of criticism may ultimately lead to progress, it lacks certain leadership values which charaterize the criticism of Erasmus, Spencer, or Dewey. That is, to be of greatest value, criticism must be based upon a thorough examination of the past and the present, together with a consideration of the probable tractability of the critic's own generation. Criticism, like legislation, is most effective when directed against practices which are generally recognized as undesirable. The radical critic is often classified as radical only because he has too early become dissatisfied with existing practices and has undertaken prematurely to correct certain evils.

The constructive critic, as distinguished from the radical critic, is he who marshals the strong forces of his day against the generally undesired practices. When, for example, Comenius launched his criticism against the badly organised Latin teaching of the seventeenth century, he utilized the contemporary interest in Latin in the improvement of Latin teaching, instead of attempting too early to bring about an abandonment of Latin in favor of the undeveloped vernacular languages of northern Europe. Comenius employed also another device of the successful constructive critic : he made his criticism effective by utilizing established means—the schools—in advancing his criticisms. If Comenius can be accepted as a typical constructive critic, it may be said simply that such a critic is a practical thinker who recognizes both things and people as they are and tactfully directs the people in the acceptacce of his criticism.

Before constructive critics of the curriculum can be successfully located and their recommendations accepted, it is necessary to see that they have gone somewhat beyond the requirements just stipulated as defining constructive criticism. It must be decided, if possible, whether the critics are themselves looking toward progress. In order to arm ourselves for this test, it is necessary to examine the nature of progress. The literature of progress produces no magical formula for testing progress. Instead, the concept of progress must be set up and then the directions of any activity or critical thought, whether progressive or decadent, must be measured by that concept : "Progress is evolution measured by an assumed standard of human values." Or, as another student of progress says, "Progress is better adaptation to given conditions. Change may be adaptations—at first, perhaps, very imperfect - to new conditions."

If, therefore, change be wisely directed, progress is most likely to follow. "An age of progressive thought demands a fearless search for truth unhampered by dogma or class prejudice or organized hindrance....Humanity can move forward only as it generates imagination, moral imagination, clarified by untrammeled critical thought, daring imagination, based upon fact and enlarged by scientific faith. Only when the majority of the members of a social group are provided with the means of finding out truth for themselves and actually develop the capacity for constructive thought can we hope to realize the noble vision of the idealists." This author closes his extended survey of the literature of progress by saying that progress, as nearly as it can now be described, "is the identification of personal interest with social interest to an increasing degree." A constructive critic is, therefore, one who adds to his practicality a clear vision of personal and social needs as revealed during a high-minded, moral, and scientific approach to contemporary problems. Just what will be the critic's point of view upon specific problems depends upon his personal philosophy of life. If, however, he is practical, intellectually honest, moral, and scientific, his criticisms are the best available suggestions to progress.

It is believed that the foregoing discussions of the relation between criticism and progress, together with the important fact that critics are among the best sources of curricula problems, justify an approach to curricula by way of the critics. As there are two sides to every question, conservative as well as progressive critics must be heard in any complete discussion of secondary education. For two reasons, first place will be given to critics who represent mainly progressive tendencies :

1. the progressive provide targets for the conservative; and
2. problems can most readily be found in the literature of the progressive critics. The remainder of Part II will, consequently, be devoted to the critics, their opponents (the conservatives), and the problems raised by the critics.

Criticism of Secondary Education is no New Adventure

1. *Reasons for criticism.* Why should anyone criticize an institution whose officers are continuously devoting their services

to the welfare and improvement of mankind ? How can one be as ungrateful as to look with disfavor upon the well-meant activities of the school curriculum ? Three general reasons for such criticism may be cited in advance of the criticisms themselves : first, secondary education is a vital institution in any time or place and it must, therefore, be as nearly correct as possible; second, since secondary education is vital, it must change as time change; third, men have special interests, fears, aversions, and attitudes and some observers are certain to stand aghast at that which pleases others.

2. *The beginnings of criticisms are unrecorded.* Unfavorable comments upon the training of youth must have been made during the time which intervened between the primitive ancestors of the Greeks and the Greeks themselves. At some time a man, probably a young man, took issue with the elders about the initiation cremonies for boys, or about a primitive lecturer's views on some other educational matter, or possibly the young man crossed over the mountains which separated his tribe from another and learned the folly of his tribe's taboos. At some time the complexity of the customs which prevailed in the primitive valley of ignorance was exchanged for a complexity in which reason had a larger place than that accorded it by primitive man. Whatever the earliest experiences with criticism may have been, it is certain from our knowledge of primitive man that no one without a heavy purpose undertook to leave the trodden path.

The criticisms which are reviewed in the succeeding pages are cited as outstanding examples of the reactions of intelligent men to the subject matter studied in secondary schools. As schools often fail to realize the highest purposes of contemporary society, one may look for criticism and advancement in any intelligent and progressive age. The forth coming criticisms are here presented for three definite purposes. First, these criticisms have for the most part actuated educators to better curriculum practices. Second, these criticisms have in most cases been acted upon by leaders whose regimes still stand for progress—in many cases, however, a century or more elasped between the advancement of the criticism and any action upon it. Third, these criticisms have been so intimately bound to periods of advancement, and the technique of dealing with these criticisms has so fully characterized educational reforms, as to prove that no educator can afford to neglect the technique of dealing with criticisms unless he desires to have his school rot as have the schools of countrless, forgotten pedagogues whose stupidity has demand humanity ever since the first self-satisfied old man turned teacher.

3. *Early Greek critics and the curriculum.* As far as historical records show, the Greeks were the first people who drove out complacency by frequent, repeated, and well-directed attacks upon beliefs and customs. Thales, for example, found that his people failed in important crises because of the effects of superstition-laden courses of study. As a case in point, the Greeks, having failed in an attack upon Syracuse, were preparing to save themselves by a retreat; the retreat was intercepted, however, by an eclipse which, declared the prophets, indicated the wrath of Diana who could be placated only by twenty-seven days of peace. While the Greeks, ignoring the plain teaching of science, maintained this peace, their enemies continued their activity so vigorously that all the Greeks were either massacred or sold into slavery. The generations later, in 364 B.C., a similar defeat was suffered by the Thebans, because Pelopidas was unable to convince his men that eclipses have nothing to do with the relations between men and their divinities.

This persistence of primitive lore among the populace after the advent of science to scholars illustrates two important matters : first, advances in knowledge are frequently thwarted by the ignorance of the masses; and second. the best thought of a given period may still be unknown to the smug, "practical" man hundreds of years later. Had Anaxagoras been able to direct the training of as many pupils as are now enrolled in the schools of any large American city, he might have opened to at least one hundred leaders what he showed to four of his great pupils—Euripides, Thucydides, Aspasia and Pericles. But these early critics confined their attacks to subject matter, instead of including the administration of schools among their targets —their fields of operation were restricted by ineffective machinery.

4. *Protagoras.* A critic who advanced the technique of criticism itself was Protagoras. This critic extended the scope and the rights of thinkers by asserting that man is the measure of all things. By developing this notion as a teacher, Protagoras, who was also a tutor of Pericles, was able to lay the foundations for a philosophy which was certain to undermine all edifices based on superstition and fear. It is easy to see, however, that any nation whose science is believed to have emanated from the gods must have difficulty in accepting this principle of criticism. It is quite in keeping with primitive survivals among the Greeks that Protagoras, like Anaxagoras, was banished and that Socrates, who practiced the same theory of measurement, was given a potent glass of hemlock.

As the direct line of advancement of thought and understanding proceeds through these free-thinkers, it is evident that their criticisms were milestones in the path of progress. The direct effects upon the curriculum are two. In the first place, these sophists laid bare certain superstitions of their day and substituted for ignorance their rational beginnings in science. That certain sophists committed errors and that they were at times guilty of using very large measures in measuring their own fees is shown by recorded evidences, but such mistakes as these were simply the errors that all men makes when they leave a well-marked road. These men have to their credit, in the second place, the fact that they stimulated such men as Isocrates to take a sober view of life and also to be discontented with things as they were.

5. *Isocrates.* It was Isocrates who saw beyond the horizon of earlier critics and heralded a new view of criticism. He saw that the critic himself is not beyond the pale of criticism and that the advances made by the critic are open to still further

correction and modification. By alleging that the sophists disregarded truth and that they professed knowledge of which they were ignorant, he also chastened those teachers who attempted advances for which science had not yet prepared them. As a constructive critic, Isocrates asserted that a youth should seek teachers who knew how to compose orations, who knew how to practice oratory, and who in all their teaching were no less perfect than the youth whom they essayed to teach.

6. *Socrates.* By individual analysis, Socrates, and older contemporary of Isocrates, showed his pupils—or listeners—how to strike below the veneer of opinions which blinded truth-seekers to real knowledge. Unfortunately for Socrates, although fortunately it may be for later generations, he was unprepared to reconstruct a program or body of knowledge for the persons whose veneer he pierced.

Although he held that virtue was based upon convincing and energizing knowledge, he could recommend no general body of knowledge to supersede the error and opinion which he disrupted. So far, Socrates was, according to Plato, a destructive critic. He showed how to teach and, it part at least, what should not be taugh. He was perhaps in the position of one who is well grounded in the art of teaching, but is deficient in subject matter for instruction. An immense service would have been performed by Socrates even had he gone no further. He had cleared away blinding defense mechanisms and he had helped his pupils to see problems.

But a real difficulty lay in the fact that many of his pupils were unable or unwilling to solve their problems—only an adventurer willingly travels an unmarked road. It appears, however, from the account of another of Socrates' pupils, Xenophon, that it was the hope of Socrates to preserve the good elements of conservatism as they were found in morals and religion. Xenophon makes Socrates appear as a guide who would apply a pragmatic test to ideas and practices to discover the good. Lacking the well-organized objectives which typify the logical scholar, Socrates was unable to reconstruct a system of thought which might have enabled him to attain his two ideals of social stability and a searching individual freedom.

7. *Plato.* To Plato, and then to his pupil, Aristotle, fell the task of further constructive criticlsm. Plato's criticisms of education can be understood only as a part of his general philosophy. His problem was that of finding out how men can live best. This problem drove him, in turn, to that of discovering the nature of the soul or the living principle of man. The soul is, he found, a tripartite being characterized by a desire for satisfaction—its appetitive nature, by self-assertiveness, and by receptivity.

As these three elements are not by nature in proper quantities or proportions in the soul, education is needed in order to bring them into correct coordination and to develop or weaken specific tendencies according to one's nature. Education thus became avowedly a process of soul-culture. Formal disciplining of the powers or characteristics was recommended by means of the right amounts of subject matter. Upon this basis which provides for individualized instruction, Plato outlined a course of study which would, he believed, develop justice, right, and virtue.

Whatever entered Plato's proposed curriculum had to meet the requirements of his general philosophy of life for specific virtues require specific training. Music and literature were valued because they soften and refine the emotions as gymnastics refines, steadies, and directs physical activities. Each passage selected for the literature course was to be employed because it expressed ethical sentiments and could therefore help to form the desired character in the developing child. Heroic examples of high living were to be taught to the child.

This principle of selection led Plato to reject many questionable Greek stories of agds and men and also to reject false and superficial views of life as represented by certain poets. As religion, myth, and history, were badly interwoven in Plato's time, he had the task of formulating criteria by which to organize religious and historical materials for instructional purposes. These criteria were based upon the following moral qualities: filial respect, good-will toward fellow-citizens, courage or manliness, truthfulness, and self-control.

With these standards as bases for judging literature, the old story of the treatment of Cronos by his son Zeus became a hateful and demoralizing falsehood which had to be banished, accounts of quarrels among the gods were dismissed because they could never be used in teaching good-will, and ghostly stories of Hades were cast out because they could not be used to inculcate manliness and courage. Truth could be taught only by telling "what is" and avoiding "the thing that is not." Self-control was to be taught by practice in obedience and self-restraint. As the needs of society were shown by these criteria, it became the duty of the masters of language and literature to select suitable subjects from the lives of great and heroic men and give suitable expression to them.

In addition to the disciplines already enumerated, Plato advocated as much of mathematics and science as each child's nature could be induced to undertake, although he held that, "the acquisition of knowledge ought not to be made a slavery to any free man." As often stated, Plato held that no pupil was ready for the higher training which he offered until the youth's mind had been whetted by geometry. Finally, the ablest pupils were to be selected for still further training in philosophy, mathematics, and science, beyond the age of twenty. In the pursuit of these studies intellectual progress rather than the rule-of-thumb achievements of Babylonians and Egyptians was the objective. Intellectual progress comes, Plato believed, only by a mastry of ideas, that is, the ultimate forms of things—universal modes. Consequently, the study of geometry must not be for the purpose of learning how to measure land as crude Egyptians might practice mensuration, but instead for the purpose of acquiring a universal mode of thinking. This theoretical training is not of course to be given to the soldier or builder, but to the statesman—the philosopher who is to be a king in Plato's ideal state; the pursuit of these studies is to equip men for thinking.

It should be noted that this training to think—Plato's formal discipline—is based upon a system of philosophy which must have approached closely to reality in his own thoughts about it. The training may be described by saying that any universal truth was by definition capable of giving form to shapeless substance. If, therefore, a student mastered any idea or universal he had by the adoption of the idea or universal increased his ability to subsume not only many particulars but also substance in general.

Plato has been accused of misleading or subjugating the world for a thousand years or more after his day, but there are several matters which quite exonerate Plato of this crime. In the first place, it may properly be admitted that Plato did invent a very comprehensive and elaborate scheme for education and philosophy. Then, as a part of this scheme he must be commended for having made the most thorough and logical review of the needs of the young and the materials of instruction that had ever been recorded. In the second place, he chastened educators who used, for ethical training, literary materials of a sort which no critic of Plato can defend.

It is significant that in the matters which Plato treated thus—moral and religious instruction materials—American educators have only within the last decade advanced to the position taken by Plato. In the third place, even though Plato took high ground, there is no valid reason for accepting his conclusions without a retesting of them. This point, in the technique of dealing with critics, is one which may be applied again to Aristotle and also to more recent critics. That is, if one critic makes an important advance, there is no valid excuse for centuries of complacent acceptance of his position or belief or scheme of things. The critic's procedure must first be used by himself and then in turn used by men who live afterward in making still greater advances. The only reason why a critic is sometimes ten centuries instead of only ten years ahead of his time is that he is succeeded by sterile, docile fellows who find tradition easier than thought! One should always practice Butler's suggestion in regard to the technique of dealing with critics: "Books (of critics) should be tried by a judge and jury as though they were crimes, and counsel should be heard on both sides".

8. *Aristotle*. Aristotle's criticism of life and education was developed from his views upon three grades or levels of living. One type of life is, according to Aristotle, the life of enjoyment—that of the vulgar man who seeks mere happiness; another type is the complacently good life—the life of the politically honorable man who may be, despite his honor, good for nothing in particular; and, finally, there is the speculative type of life—the life of the philosopher whose mental activity is conducted in accordance with that form of goodness which is the best and most complete. The criticisms which lie in this classification of types of life were aimed at the merely practical man who may be either immoral or nonmoral, of little or no volue to the state, and lacking in rationality and justice.

To the extent that the artisan's work, which can only increase man's comfort, causes bodily deterioration and requires attention to physical matters, such work prevents the artisan from leading a life of excellence and is therefore illiberal. To the extent that the philosopher's speculation, which can make a rationalizing man more rational, determines the highest good, such speculation is ennobling and liberal. The practical life of the artisan deals with the passing, the changing, the inconsequential; the speculative life of the philosopher deals with the permanent, the self-sufficing, the universal.

While there must be "business for the sake of leisure, things useful and necessary for the sake of things honorable," one should subordinate the mechanical or illiberal to the speculative or liberal; that is, the single and passing experiences of life should be coordinated in such a way as to enable the thinker to bring them under a universal principle. Experience with things—sensory experience—is permanently valuable only insofar as it so coordinated. Unfortunately, Greek society was so organized as to provide little incentive for the improvement of manual activities, and Aristotle refrained from showing how the menial work of the artisan can be liberalized and made rational by science. Instead, he advocated universal education partially as a selective device for separating those who can perform only the common tasks of life from those who can be fitted for rational living. Common tasks are, he asserted, like the striving of politically honorable men because both are dependent upon fortunate circumstances rather than upon rational plans. Both are opportunistic, illiberal, and nonprogressive.

Therefore, since opportunism is unprogressive and only begets more opportunism, so irrational living should be minimized or eliminated: since, however, speculative activity, as can be shown in an analogous way, rationalizes life, gives meaning to experience, reduces error, and provides a guide to thought, so rational living should be encouraged and increased. Directly from this reasoning comes the conclusion that rationalized experience is a guide to life. One should, therefore, study that which has been rationalized and them advance by rationalizing the new or uncoordinated. Here lies the basis for the studies, 'mathemata', as distinguished from arts such as cookery, mensuration, professional athletic, and cheap oratory.

The studies might be based upon observation, as indeed Aristotle the biologist advocated, but the purpose of the observation must be that of rationalizing life. In somewhat more modern phraseology, this portion of Aristotle's criticisms of life as presented in the 'Ethics' and the 'Politics advocated an indirect and rational approach to the problems of living instead of a direct and opportunistic approach. Still further translated into academic terms, this view favored foundational studies composed of practice and sound theory instead of immediately useful studies composed entirely of practice.

Although Aristotle never completed the program which he began in the *Politics*, it is perfectly clear that this consistent logician was a precursor of the modern schoolman who tries (1) to develop a social conscience in pupils by providing various social activities and later coordinates the results of these experiences by means of a systematic treatment of civics; (2) to develop a knowledge of agriculture by providing first-hand experience with things agricultural—soils, animals, and plants—and later coordinates the results of these experiences by means of a systematic treatment of biology; or (3) to develop a knowledge of "business" English by means of projects which involve business situations and later coordinates the results of the projects by means of a thoroughly systematized course in English in general. He was clearly a nonbeliever in "short, practical" courses and was also a nonbeliever in purely theoretical training.

9. *Present-day values of Greek criticisms.* Each of these early adventurers in educational criticism, Thales, Anaxagoras, Protagoras, Socrates, Plato, and Aristotle, based his criticisms upon such reasons as those stated previously : the vital importance of adolescent training, the need for conformity of education with changing times, and the recognition of individual differences. Their criticisms as they affect the curriculum are in number :

(1) In the interest of the state, universal education must be provided according to the nature and station of the learners.

(2) The judgment of enlightened man is superior to traditions, superstitions, and myths.

(3) Science, if systematized, can overcome certain fears that interfere with progress.

(4) Opinion must be examined and where incorrect it must be superseded by science.

(5) Activities which are pursued without a view to rationality are illiberal and degrading.

(6) The pursuit of systematic studies is elevating morally, spiritually, and intellectually.

(7) Education must be planned in the light of a rationalized view of needs and aims – comprehensive, liberal values of the serious student are preferable to narrow illiberal values of the shallow, practical worker.

(8) Curricula should be so ordered that the succeeding years leave behind the fragmentary work of children and assume a systematic and rational character.

While it is not here maintained that an early acceptance of the criticisms of the Greeks would have solved educational problems centuries ago, it is maintained that a critical study and acceptance of certain of these criticisms would, even to-day, improve the curriculum thinking of the great mass of teachers and principals who guide the training of American boys and girls.

Criticism during the Middle Ages

Although there were differences of opinion during the Middle Ages, few, if any, of these differences assumed the form of free criticism such as that developed by the Greeks. Some of these differences of opinions took the form of literary and philosophical attacks upon superstition. The critics of superstition were apparently aware of inconsistencies among beliefs, but they were unable to extricate either their contemporaries or themselves, As Thorndike says of certain Roman skeptics, mediaeval critics also, when they attempted to avoid traditional superstitions, ended by plunging themselves into others almost equally enslaving. Near the close of the mediaeval era, the established church and state entertained many notions contracted from the Arabs and through them from the Greeks. These notions served a double purpose : from the Greeks. These notions served a double purpose : they increased criticism and, by their soundness, they clarified thought. The power of institutional censorship is shown, however, in the works of Adelard of Bath (d. 1142). Adelard did a considerable amount of original and advanced thinking, but he attempted to avoid adverse criticism by attributing certain modern discoveries to writers of earlier times. Adelard, in pleading for reason and for experimental science, accused many writers of the past of being "captivated by the appearance of authority" and being led about "by a halter." With regard to himself, however, he announced, "if you want to hear anything more from me, give and take reason." Criticism of contemporary educational practices, if present in the work of Adelard, was, however, cautiously guarded, as it was also in the writings of his young contemporary, the scholarly John of Salisbury (d. 1180).

Criticism of venerable authorities grew during the following century, particularly under the leadership of Robert of Grosseteste (d. 1153). "Even Aristotle does not escape criticism. We are told that we should not accept his statement concerning the number of movers of the heavenly spheres, for, as Avicenna and Rabbi Moses have pointed out, the science of astronomy was little developed in his time. Nor are the Arabian commentators upon Aristotle left uncensured."

Robert's famous pupil, Roger Bacon (d. *c.* 1292), although a mediaevalist in much of his thinking and writing, has the credit of launching more criticisms against the learning of his criticisms were neither unique nor sound. Temporarily encouraged by the Pope, Bacon made four vital criticisms. First, he alleged that the state of learning was higher in the days of his youth than forty years later, but Thorndike shows that Bacon was unacquainted with the most advanced learning of his day and could have referred to only two countries—France and England, and two universities—Oxford and Paris. As a part criticism, Bacon included the tendency of many of his brethren to rush into theology without having adequate preparation in "the common sciences, such as Latin, grammar, logic, and a part of natural philosophy, and a little metaphysics." Second, he complained of the waste of time in teaching only the elements of certain subjects.

He believed that he could teach more useful geometry in a fortnight than the young friars did in ten or twenty years; "the ordinary mathematician does not consider that he knows anything unless he demonstrates it, and so he takes from thirty to forty years' to master the subject, and that the 'text-books and the teachers of mathematics delight in multiplying conclusions to such an extent that one has to give years of unnecessary time to extracting the essentials,' and 'this is one reason why there are so few students of a science which is a prerequisite to all knowledge.' " Third, while overlooking the work of the eminent astrologer Bonatti and the scholarly student of optics, Witelo, Bacon deplored the contemporary lack of interest in science. In a similar omission, he ovelooked half a dozen diligent experimental scientists such as Albertus Magnus and Bartholomew of England, the encyclopedist.

These criticisms of science slighted the best work of his day. Fourth, Bacon repeats the criticism announced by Adelard and a hundred years later by Grosseteste in regard to authority and experimental science. As a criterion of truth, " 'all sciences except this either merely employ arguments to prove their conclusions, like the purely speculative sciences, or have universal and imperfect experiences'; whlle 'It alone, in truth, has the means of finding out to perfection what can be done by nature, what by the industry of art, what by fraud'; for it alone can distinguish what is true from what is false in 'incantations, conjurations, invocations, deprecations, and sacrifices."

The frequent repetition of criticisms such as these by the greatest scholars of their centuries enabled Adelard, Aquinas, Grosseteste, Albertus Magnus, and Bacon to make an impress upon tradition-bound mediaevalism. All these reformers were men of their times, yet all looked at least a short distance beyond their times : Adelard, Albertus, Grosseteste, and Bacon saw the approach of experimental science, or rather its growth from the works of their own day; Aquinas (d. 1274) saw an approaching tolerance of scientific research—"Christians who deny as contrary to their faith the philosophical solutions of problems which are really indifferent so far as the faith is concerned, simply bring Christianity, in Aquinas' opinion, into disrepute among the wise men of the world."

Although criticism is not the sole cause of progress, the comment of the scholars named in this section can be credited with much of the impetus given to learning in their own centuries and those which immediately followed. Science itself is by definition critical. Likewise, whatever aids science aids criticism. Arabian works translated by Gerard of Cremona, the scientific researches of Albert the Great, and the outspoken criticisms of Roger Bacon united in producing the greatest science of the sixteenth and seventeenth centuries.

Early modern critics

The men of mediaeval Europe—Adelard, Grosseteste, Albert, Bacon—would have lived in vain had not their union of curiosity and criticism brought forth a progeny of early modern critics. To these later critics fell the task of furthering progress by continued thought and criticism. All the mediaeval forts—tradition, authority, superstition, and fear - were still well fortified by three commanders or knights of intolerance. For early modern intolerance was, like ancient Gaul, "divided into three parts : the intolerance of laziness, the intolerance of ignorance, and the intolerance of self-interest."

1. *Petrarch.* It was the function of the "first modern scholar," Petrarch (1304-1374), to rescue classical literature from inaccurate, technical grammarians. His devotion to the classics and his lack of interest in science led him, however, to overleok the value of knowing the facts of science. "Even if all these things (facts of science) were true, they help in no way toward a happy life, for what does it advantage us to be familiar with the nature of animals, birds, fishes, and reptiles, while we are ignorant of the nature of the race of man to which we belong ?" By this passage Petrarch eliminates science from his problems of life as he eliminates his vernacular by the following comment on the popularization of literature : "I can only give voice to my irritation, when I hear the common herd

befouling with their stupid mouths the noble beauty of his Dante's Italian) lines."

It was partly to avoid this "befouling" of literature and partly because of his complete engrossment in Latin that Petrarch early abandoned the Italian language in his fine writing. Of scarcely less importance for the renascence of the classical spirit was Petrarch's criticism of academic dialectics or logic. Of this subject, he said that the dialecticians "waste their whole lives" in contentions. Such persons, he continued, think that because a road is proper to traverse, it immediately follows that we should linger on it forever.

But he himself held instead that, "Dialectics may form a portion of our road, but certainly not its end : it belongs to the morning of life, not to its evening." This devout churchman criticized also the narrowness of those scholars who could not remain in the church and at the same time enjoy the beauty and strength of the classics.

These four criticisms – of devotion to science, of using the vernacular in literary works, of wasting time at dialectics, and of narrowness in religion were, except for the aversion to science, requisite for literary progress. For literary progress seems in the fourteenth century to have required a return to the path which had been trodden by the ancients and lost by the mediaevalists as an aid to men in finding this path; it was probably fortunate that a great leader should exhibit both engrossment in and single-mindedness toward the classics. It was unfortunate that science had no equally influential servant. The retarding effect of the Renaissance upon science seems in no small part to have been due to a continued blindness to the fact that scientific as well as literary pursuits can purify and ennoble man.

2. *Valla.* A form of criticism which was neglected during the Middle Ages was advanced by Valla (1407-1457), one of Vittorino's pupils and styled the founder of critical scholarship. Besides criticizing the inaccurate texts of his day, Valla valiantly continued the age-long battle of reason *versus* authority. The

second criticism—that of following authority—is here mentioned to show the continued realization of the need for such a comment. The former criticism aided education by leading directly to a revision of textbooks.

3. *Erasmus.* Three fundamental criticisms of the subject matter of his times were made by Erasmus (1466-1536). All three were made also by his less notable contemporaries. The first criticism dealt with a problem which existed before the days of written history and continues to the present time. The scholarly treatment which Erasmus gave to this matter is pertinent to present-day difficulties. This criticism concerns the relation between secular learning and religion. As already shown, the issue had arisen in disputes about the most non-religious matters, such as arithmetic, as well as in subjects like philosophy which are closely related to theology. In the time of Erasmus this problem took form in this question : Can the Christian safely study the classics ?

In view of the fact that certain admirers of the classics went to the extreme of applying pagan nomenclature to the persons of the Trinity, a defense and criticisms were demanded. Erasmus was singularly well prepared for rendering authoritative criticisms of the view suggested by the question. He had tasted the simple faith of the Christian and had been charmed by the beauty of Greek literature. He had arrived at the full maturity of a man of well-balanced judgment when the issue confronted him.

He was a faithful churchman and also a classical scholar of international repute. Erasmus replied to the question, first, that the Scriptures did not and were not intended to give a complete account of the experience and wisdom which any generation may need. He agreed with Melanchthon that the question, instead of implying an antagonism between Christianity and the classics, should be so phrased as to ask how the Christian could advance spiritually and morally as well as intellectually without the classics.

The reply to this question would have been that such an advance was impossible. Next, therefore, he pointed out the dependence of Christian scholars upon Greek and Roman thought for an understanding of the *New Testament* and the writings of the early Fathers. Third, he showed that many early Fathers were classicists and were not contaminated by evil. Finally, he showed the moral value of carefully selected classical works.

A second fundamental issue with which Erasmus grappled was Ciceronianism. This issue had arisen among the pedantic satellites of Petrarch, Vittorino, and Valla. Indeed, Valla was in part, though innocently, the cause of this decadent humanism because his literary criticism had incited scholars to the attainment of a perfect classical Latin style of writing and speaking. Cicero was accepted as the touchstone of purity. Formalism developed so that certain scholars dared not speak lest they use words or forms which Cicero had never used. This stylistic degeneracy drew from Erasmus a satire entitled *Ciceronianus.* This satire tells of one Nosoponus who was once hale and happy. By continued craving for Ciceronian purity of diction. Nosoponus broke his health and became downcast. His Ciceronian labors had, however, included the spending of seven years with never a line of any writer save Cicero ; never was a portrait of anyone else allowed to take his mind from his noble exemplar. His dreams, like his walking moments, were given wholly to the Roman stylist. He compiled from Cicero three ponderous lexicons : the first was the complete Ciceronian vocabulary with comments on usage ; the second was a phrase book with all of Cicero's figures of speech ; the third contained all the examples of metrical expression in Cicero. By following these lexicons in another seven years of "imitation" of Cicero, Nosoponus became so facile that he could complete a Ciceronian sentence in a single night ! By holding up this picture of Nosoponus to ridicule, Erasmus soundly chastened the preudo-scholars of his day for their lack of appreciation of virility of expression and of the content of the classics.

Third, Erasmus criticized the incorrect Latin grammars

and methods of teaching grammar in his day. As an example of accuracy he praised the Latinity of Valla and the grammar of Valla's friend, Perotti. On teaching grammar, Erasmus censured teachers for their pedantry :

> But I must make my conviction clear that, whilst a knowledge of the rules of accidence and syntax is most necessary to every student, still they should be as few, as simple, and as carefully framed as possible. I have no patience with the stupidity of the average teacher of grammar who wastes precious years in hammering rules into children's heads. For it is not by learning rules that we acquire the power of speaking a language, but by daily intercourse with those accustomed to express themselves with exactness and refinement, and by the copious reading of the best authors.

That Erasmus avoided the error of believing that grammar could be acquired entirely incidentally is indicated in other passages in the discourse from which the above quotation was taken. He does, however, make clear that the purpose of study is not simply the mastery of grammar ; the student even in the beginning of his studies should attend to the content of what is read. The emphasis with which Erasmus discussed this matter indicates that many of his contemporaries, like many present-day classicists, failed to distinguish between language study and literature study and that they, like their pedantic descendants, seldom taught literature at all.

4. *Rabelais*. Although the waste of children's time and energy upon useless disputations and rules of grammar was ably treated by Erasmus and his contemporary More, still another contemporary, Rabelais (c. 1483—1553), added a satire which should have put an end to pedantry. In this interesting account of the "Lives, Heroick Deeds, and Sayings of Gargantua and his sonne Pantagruel," Rabelais records that Gargantua was carefully trained for "thirteen years, six months, and two weeks" in Latin grammar.

Thereafter he spent about nineteen years studying the commentaries of pedants upon the classics, and then sixteen years and two months in finding out "the age of the moon, the seasons of the year, and the tides of the sea," and then his preceptor died ! As Gargantua's education was still incomplete, "he got an old coughing fellow to teach him" still other "meally stuff, by reading whereof he became as wise as any weever since baked in an oven." Later, Gargantua forsook this old "muzzled dolt" and went to Ponocrates, who, after purging him thoroughly of all that he had already learned, began a systematic, economical, and beneficial course of study wherein Gargantua speedily mastered all the liberal arts of his day.

5. *Ramus.* Peter Ramus (1515—1572), who is remembered chiefly for his opposition to Aristotelianism and schlastic dialectics, entered his professional career as a curriculum reconstructionist immediately after having successfully defended as his master's thesis the statement that, "All that Aristotle has said is false." Upon the basis of three fundamental principles, which were products of his critical attitude, he attempted to reconstruct language studies, mathematics, and science. These principles were, that the reconstruction should be based, first, upon the results of the observation of nature : second, upon an adequate system ; and third, upon practical considerations or use. By "system," following the discredited Aristotle, he signified :

(1) the law of justice—that every principle must be true in all cases,

(2) the law of fitness—that every item must be relevant to the given subject ; and

(3) the law of wisdom—that all which applies to an entire subject should be stated once and for all at the outset.

By applying these principles of criticism to instructional materials, his works gained the attention of Descartes. Roger

Ascham, John Milton. and Francis Bacon. Few critics have had as important an influence throughout Western Europe as Ramus.

6. *Francis Bacon.* Early modern times produced no more valuable critic of learning than Francis Bacon (1561—1626). Whatever may have been Bacon's defects in experimental science, he formulated the most thorough criticism of learning that had ever been made, if, indeed, it has yet been excelled. The purpose of these criticisms was to find out "that which is good and sound, and to deliver that from the aspersion of the other." The "phantoms," "peccant humours," and "diseases" of learning which affect secondary-school curricula will be discussed in the following paragraphs.

First, there are three diseases of learning. One of these, Ciceronianism, is treated from the point of view of Erasmus. The second is fruitless learning—the learning of novel, subtle, or obsolete matter. This disease attacks both method and content. As applied to present-day content, it can be illustrated by much of the matter which had already been eliminated from histories and algebras. The third disease is "delight in deceiving and aptness to be deceived." In Bacon's time as in ours this disease can be illustrated by courses in the social and biological sciences.

Second, there are eleven peccant humours of learning:

(1) the uncritical veneration of either antiquity or novelty ;

(2) the distrust of new discoveries ;

(3) the belief that all possible opinions have been thoroughly tested and that only the best have prevailed ;

(4) premature reduction of knowledge to arts and methods and a consequent stereotyping of wrong beliefs as already cited among primitive peoples ;

(5) neglect of universalizing the knowledge drawn from particulars—the principle already cited from Aristotle ;

(6) too great a reverence for speculation combined with a neglect of observations and experience ;

(7) a tendency to mix knowledge and men's inclnations—to find what one looks for ;

(8) impatience of doubt, and haste to conclusions and assertions without due and mature suspension of judgment ;

(9) dogmatic delivery of knowledge ;

(10) the tendency to become commendators rather than original discoverers ; and

(11) mistaking the aim or "furthest end of knowledge."

Third, there are four types of phantoms each of which affects the curriculum. The first phantoms, those of the tribe, lead to the judgment of educational affairs with preconceived notions and with a narrowness of mind which prevents a thorough trial of the particular cases which are observed. Second, the phantoms of the den are characterized by an enslaving love for particular sciences and subjects of thought and by a failure to see the whole of the problem or science which is contemplated. Third, the phantoms of the market-place, which lead men into error by means of the words or phrases used in attempting to classify knowledge or speculative matters. Fourth, the phantoms of the theatre lead men to accept all kinds of unproved theories and to base practices upon them as though a given problem had been thoroughly tested by experimentation.

7. *Descartes*. Rene Descartes (1590—1650) charged the schools of his day with the neglect of the real values of algebra, geometry, and logic. He found geometry and algebra highly abstract ; "the former is so exclusively restricted to the consideration of figures, that it can exercise the Understanding

only on condition of greatly fatiguing the Imagination (the representative capacity) ; and, in the latter, there is so complete a subjection to certain rules and formulas, that there results an art full of confusion and obscurity calculated to embarrass, instead of a science fitted to cultivate the mind." Logic was found to be so full of error that the "severance of the true from the false" was quite as difficult "as it is to extract a Diana or a Minerva from a rough block of Marble." Instigated by these views, Descartes attempted to "borrow all that was best both in Geometrical Analysis and in Algebra, and correct all the defects of the one by the help of the other." The result was analytic geometry for higher education, but the effect upon secondary-school mathematics has only recently reached America. In the natural science Descartes continued the criticisms of Aristotelianism and greatly aided the cause of experimental science. It was this interest in science which insured its introduction into the curriculum of the French schools of his day.

8. *The encyclopedists.* Lord Herbert of Cherbury (1581—1648), whose views on the curriculum have already been cited, John Amos Comenius (1592—1671), John Dury (1596—1680), John Milton (1608—1674), and John Locke (1632—1704) criticized the narrowness of the contemporary courses of study and also the sterility which follows Ciceronian procedures in teaching. For example, Comenius held that the secondary school should enable pupils to become versed in the seven liberal arts of the Middle Ages and furthermore to be :

> Physicists, who know the composition of the earth, the force of the elements, the different species of animals, the powers of plants and of minerals, and the structure of the human body, and who, besides knowing these things, can apply them to the various uses of life. Under this head is thus comprised a part of medicine, of agriculture, and of other mechanical arts.
>
> Geographers, who are well acquainted with the external features of the earth, and know the seas, the islands that are in them, the rivers, and the various kingdoms.

Chronologers, who can fix periods of time, and trace the course of the centuries from the beginning of the world.

Historians, who possess a fair knowledge of the history of the human race, of the chief empires, and of the Church, and who know the various customs and fortunes of races and of men.

Moralists, who can draw fine distinctions between the various kinds of virtue and of vice, and who can follow the one and avoid the other. This knowledge they should possess both in its general form and in its special application to the life of the family, of the state and of the Church.

Finally, we wish them to be theologians, who, besides understanding the principles of their faith, can also prove them from the Scriptures.

When this course is finished, the youths, even if they have not a perfect knowledge of all these subjects (indeed at their age perfection is impossible, since experience is necessary to complete the theoretical knowledge that they have acquired, and the sea of learning cannot be exhausted in six years), should, at any rate, have laid a solid foundation for any more advanced instruction that they may receive in the future.

In addition to his constructive criticism of the curriculum in general, Comenius attacked the organization of instructional materials in Latin and finally reorganized them into a well-graded series of lessons. This series which revolutionized the teaching of Latin was accompanied by an attempt to compose a *Gate of Phenomena or Doorway to Wisdom*. This "outline of universal wisdom," although continuing a plan which had been carried out in part by Aristotle, Isidore of Seville (d. 635), and Vincent of Beauvais (1264) and strongly favored by contemporaries of Comenius, was never completed. It had, however, the great value of calling to the attention of scholars the need for a systematization and unification of all the knowledge then extant.

John Dury in his *Reformed School* (c. 1649) divided the branches of learning into two large groups:

> First, "the profitable Arts and Sciences," that is, "all matters of knowledge which direct man to the right use of all Creatures, and the ordering of his owne Faculties about them." Secondly, the Tongues which are most useful to enlarge the knowledge thereof, namely, Latin, Greek, Hebrew, and the Oriental affinities of the last. But in prescribing these ancient languages he is not urged by the literary motive, by the desire for culture, or by scorn of the "useful." Quite the contrary : "Tongues are no further finally useful then to enlarge Traditional Learning : and without their subordination unto Arts and Sciences, they are worth nothing towards the advancement of our happiness. The Immediate Use of Tongues is only to Understand what others say to us, according to their custome of speaking ; and to express our minds unto them significantly according to our custome."

As Adamson points out, the general plan of Dury, if it had been adopted, "would have revolutionized the schools of the time." Arts and sciences would have been taught first in the mother tongue, and languages postponed to a later period of study :

> The teaching of words is no further Usefull then the things signified thereby are familiar to the Imagination, and that the teaching of Rules before the Materiall Sense of the words is known, or before the formall coherence of things which their construction is to represent in a Sentence, can be apprehended, is wholly preposterous and unprofitable to the Memory.
>
> "So farre as children are capable of Traditional knowledge ; so farre in every degree of Science they may be

> taught the Tongues which serve for that Use ; but till they be fitted for the one, the other is Useless to them.
>
> Whatsoever in the teaching of Tongues doth not tend to make them to help upto Traditionall knowledge, by the manifestation of Real Truths in Sciences, is superfluous, and not to be insisted on, especially towards Children, whence followeth that the Curious study of Criticismes, and observation of Styles in Authors, and of straines of wit, which speak nothing of Reality in Sciences, are to be left to such as delight in vanityes more then in Truths.

9. *Defoe*. Daniel Defoe (1661—1731), to whome reference has already been made, criticized the customs which produced an ignorant gentry and proposed a solution for the difficulty. The solution was in part a curriculum problem. The schools were, Defoe alleged, designed by and for pedants and were not suitable for the boy who was to become a gentleman :

> "Shall my son," exclaims the incensed but gentle mother, "be sent to school to sit bare-headed and say a lesson to such a sorry diminutive rascall as that ; be brow beaten and hector'd and threaten'd with his authority and stand in fear of his hand ! *my son* ! that a few yeares after he will be glad to cringe to, cap in hand, for a dinner ! no, indeed, *my son* shall not go near him. Let the Latin and Greek go to the D—l. *My son* is a *Gentleman*, he shan't be under such a scoundrel as that."

This deplorable attitude toward schools was caused largely, Defoe believed, by the impractical program of studies and could be remedied by revising the program as suggested above, and as recommended also by John Dury.

8

Activities for Realization of Purposes

Later modern critics and their proposals for educational reform

Eight principal lines of criticism characterize later modern discussions of desirable educational reform. As a basis for the first line of criticism, the quality of Defoe's criticism of curriculum practices has continued to the present time and still colors much of present-day curriculum thinking. This quality may be called the conflict between humanism and realism. With many scholarly thinkers this conflict has changed to a reconciliation of humanism and realism and a consequent advocacy of a "liberal" education.

A second form of criticism and one which has continued from ancient times is that involved in the disciplinary conception of education. A third form of criticism and one which is closely related to the disciplinary variety is also an outgrowth of psychological issues. This critism has called attention to failure of schools to consider adequately the nature and the need of .the educand. A fourth form of criticism, although vagugly raised by mediaevalists, came into prominence in later modern times in connection with the philanthropic movement. Out of the philanthropic and realistic movements came a heightened interest in the nonprofessioal vocations.

When, in the latter part of the nineteenth century, this directly practical vocational tendency united with an attempt to rationalize the practical arts, there came criticisms of the narrow scope of secondary education and a plea for curricula which would train artisans in theroy and practice. There additional forms of criticism have left their impress upon modern secondary education. One of these forms of criticism has accompained the age-old interest in moral and religious instruction. Out of this latter interest has come of late a pronounced tendency to criticize the schools for their failure to provide adequate training for the general and specific duties of an efficient citizen.

Finally, the modern period has brought to notice such overwhelming amounts of subject matter and has uncovered so many needs for training that the program of studies has been unable to carry to each pupil even a bare sketch of many fields of knowledge, Consequently, much criticism has arisen since the beginning of the nineteenth century of the organization of the curricula, and, during the early years of the twentieth century, of the organization of the subject matter within each course of the curricula. This form of criticism, although older than Aristotle, has recently become popularized and has many advocates.

This section is devoted to the eight broad types of modern criticism just named :

(1) criticism of the relative importance of humanism and realism;

(2) criticism of the disciplinary values of studies;

(3) criticism of the neglect of child psychology;

(4) criticism of the facilities for educating the masses;

(5) criticism of the vocational values of education;

(6) criticism of the aesthetic elements of education;

(7) criticism of the social values of education as shown in moral, religious, and civic activities in schools; and

(8) criticisffi of the internal organization of curricula and of individual studies and activities.

Although these criticisms are in the general emphasized chiefly each in given period, it would be wide of the truth to attempt to confine any one of these or the reforms connected therewith entirely to any single decade or half century. Indeed, many of the ablest critics of modern times have thrust their shafts against several of thsee objects of criticism. Despite this fact, an attempt will be made in the subsequent discussions of this chapter to treat recent criticisms by movements instead of by men. This procedure will involve recurring references to certain critics, but will, it is hoped, give a simple and manageable grasp of the main lines of criticism. No attempt will be made to include all modern reformers in this discussion; only a few the most important names will be included in the text.

Critical discussions of humanistic, realistic, and libral studies

An unbroken line of criticism accompanies the modern expansion of the program of studies. In Chepter 5, the first modern schoolmaster, Vittorino, was portrayed as offering curricula which were liberal and inclusive in the later modern sense of the term *liberal*. The same chapter described other schools which were liberal ; but it showed also that the prevailing type of secondary school, the school which prepared boys for college, was a school of classical languages and, in some cases, of classical literature. A third type of school, that in which the classics were either subordinated or omitted, was also in existence from mediaeval times. As these three types of schools persisted, there were, naturally, advocates for each type.

The comments of Defoe, like those of his contemporary Swift, were called forth in connection with the controversy over the merits of ancient and modern learning. The significance of the educational controversy of that period has been indicated by its influence upon Franklin and other leaders in the academy movement. That further criticism was needed during Franklin's time has also been shown by the fact that has even in his own academy a modern curriculum experienced no little difficulty.

Such criticism was made by influential writers and publicists of many countries. In France, Diderot. the encyclopedist, criticized contemporary schools and advocated the dropping of useless studies and the providing of what he called a balanced program of studies. Instead of mere language schools in which not a word of biology, or geography and little of physics was heard, he proposed schools in which the first five years were to be devoted to science and mathematics and only the last three years to grammar and the classics.

In England, Adam Smith and Jeremy Bentham were important reformers. In 1776, Smith in *An Inequiry into the Nature and Causes of the Wealth of Nations* asserted that "The greater part of what is taught in schools and universities, however, does not seem to be the most proper preparation for the business" of living in a modern world. The narrow scope of education was criticized similarly by Bentham in his *Cherlstomania* (1816) in which he advocated giving prominence to physical science and reducing the attention devoted to the classics. A few years later Carlyle, apparently fired by Geoth's 'Wilhelm Meister', began his series of attacks upon the gerund-grinding of the schools. Instead of the deadening formalism of which he accuses the schools, Carlyle points the way to liberal training : "Here are Books, and we have brains to read them ; here is a whole Earth and a whole Heaven, and we have eyes to look on them."

From 1800 to 1875 a group of scientists preached realism, sometimes with moderation and at other times with the fervor of enthusiasts. Of the group of Englishmen who were especially important in this matter, George Combe (1788-1858) was one of the most active and influential. As a result of the existing schemes of education which had been devised by men learned in the Greek and Latin languages, in an age when extremely little of physical and biological nature was known and when linguistics constituted the staples of instruction, England, in 1850, had, according to Combe, little save antiquated curricula in here schools. Look at the schools over the kingdom, says he and see what is taught; the subjects are "Reading, writing, arithmetic, geography, and, in some, a little algebra and mathematics, and the catechism.

But in not one of those branches of knowledge is there one iota of causation ; and yet on our knowledge and judicious application of causes. depends our well-being or misery in this life." In order to correct this educational disorder, Combe proposed a "ground reform" which he believed could be achieved by teaching :

(1) things that exist;

(2) their modes of action;

(3) the nature of man;

(4) certain important relationships between man and nature; and

(5) social, aesthetic, and religious matters.

Combe, like his American contemporary, Caldwell, collected the opinions of other distinguished men such as Milton, Locke, Watt, Arkwrit, Franklin, Gibbon, and Adam Smith to show that, as taught, the classics were of little value. He closed his own account of the matter by saying that "The greatest evils attending a purely classical eduction appear to me to be the ignorance in which it leaves the pupil of the objects, agents, and relations existing in nature and social life, and the extent to which, in consequence, his mind is exposed to the influence of prejudice and superstition. A thorough education in knewledge, on the other hand, enlarges, invigorates, and humanizes, the whole mental powers, wherever they possess native aptitude for improvement." Combe's central theory was, in brief, "We should train to do more than to know." In pressing this point, however, Combe failed either to admit possible improvements in the teaching of the subjects which he condemns or to show how his favorite subjects could be effectively presented. He did, however, give many examples of how to present the sciences and social studies, but singularly enough, these examples show extreme reliance upon verbal experiences to which, in the case of the classics, he took exception.

Of greater influence as preaches of science were Spencer and Huxley. Spencer, in the essays on education which he wrote between 1854 and 1859, attempted to answer the question, "What knowledge is of most worth?" After canvassing modern life and its needs, he found that five tests would enable one to answer his question. These tests consist of determining whether knowledge is valuable for direct self-preservation, acequiring a livelihood, discharging of parental functions, regulating civic conduct, and participating in art in all its forms. He found that one subject, science, was of greatest value in each of these matters : "Necessary and eternal as are its truths, all Science concerns all mankind for all time . . . Though to the progress of science we owe it, that millions find support where once there was food only for thousands," yet, "Science is the household drudge, who, in obscurity, hides unrecognized perfections." While science was, therefore, accorded the highest place, there were at the opposite end of the scale the studies which received the greatest attention in the schools—those studies which are based upon the miscellaneous leisure activities. The whom this preeminent subject of science is most worth, and what parts of science are of greatest worth, Spencer does not say. Neither does he attempt to organize science into suitable units for teaching in different years of school. Of this last alleged fault he may be absolved, because he was attempting only to establish general principles. While the same excuse may be offered for his failure to discriminate among the recipients and benefits of science, his high purpose of popularizing science should have been fortified by at least a few rough specifications as to the administering of science to pupils.

In his 'Science and Education,' Huxley outlined an educational philosophy and a program of studies which should deal constructively with both classics and sciences. His criticisms have the great advantage of attacking not only the failure of schools to provide instruction in science. but also their failure to find humanishism in the classics. He contended that the gerund-grinding schools were language, but not literature, schools. The term 'humanism' as he defined it escaped the limitations of the classics and included literature in general, science, social studies, and art. The program of studies which he proposed consisted, therefore, of English literature. translations of the greatest works in all languages, English composition, natural science, history, civics, geography, music, and art.

Huxley give five reasons for his faith in science as a school subject. First, children should learn science in connection with their own spontaneous activities. If they are encouraged in suitable activities, they will become familiar with nature; then through curiosity and observance they will learn about nature. Second, youth should learn from science the place of man and the earth in the universe. From such knowledge should come a wholesome respect for life and a desire to know, by investsgation, more about man. Third, science exemplifies the idea of causation. Concrete cases of causation, as observed in science. should give practice in the application of a basic principle in human life and thought. Fourth, the study of natural science is the study of human life itself : that science is, based upon the universal method of life.

> The life, the fortune, and the happinesss of every one of us, and, more or less, of those who are connected with us, depend upon our knowing of the rules of a game infinitely more difficult and complicated than chess..... The chess-board (in this game) is the world, the pieces are the phenomena of the universe, the rules of the game are what we call the laws of nature. The player on the other side is hidden from us. We know that his play is always just and fair and patient. But we also know, to our

> cost, that he never overlooks a mistake or makes the smallest allowance for ignorance. To the man who plays well the highest stakes are paid with that sort of overflowing generosity with which the strong shows delight in strength. And one who plays ill is checkmated—without haste but without remorse........Well, what I mean by Education is learning the rules of that mighty game.

To this point, we shall return in the discussion of the disciplinary conception of education. Fifth, the capacity to conduct independent research is at the base of progress and depends for its development upon scientific training. The first four of these aims are directly connected with secondary education. Taken together, they give science a place among the humanities, and they give at the same time a basis for analogous claims for other school subjects. An earlier use of the same arguments for other science and language is that of Sidgwick in his essay on 'The Theory of Classical Education (1867). Although Huxley's arguments have been of great worth to the development of scientific teaching, they have been of hardly less value to literature teaching.

Up to this point, this section has given place to men who were chiefly interested in the sciences, Other scholars, such as Sidgwick, Mill, and Arnold, of the nineteenth century were in the classics as well as in science. Sidgwick assembled the reasons for studying Latin—linguistic, disciplinary, and literary – and maintained that in none of these respects was Latin unique in providing training. In purely linguistic matters, he maintained that, although Greek and Latin most certainly gave important elements to the English language, nevertheless they gave only a part, and that, for the professional man as well as for the general student, the philological values could be got by direct teaching of English as in general language courses.

In disciplinary matters, he asserted that, although there might be value in turning an idea from one language to another, the translations actually rendered often failed to give as clear discipline as classical advocates supposed. For example, the want of resourcefulness of pupils compels the schoolmaster to "sacrifice accurary or style, and he, as a rule, wisely determines to sacrifice style for the time." In literary matters he contended that few pupils carried the classical language to the point at which classical literature is thrown open; and, at anyrate, he held that many nations and many eras had created worthy literature, so that it was no longer "a point of capital importance that any particular literature should be so thrown open." Finally, he cited the instance of Plato who wrote over the door of his school of life, "Let no one who is without geometry enter here," and asked thoughtful men what the inscription over the door of the school of life should be in the nineteenth century of the Christian era.

In the same vein as Sidgwick's own answer to this question, John Stuart Mill answered :

> This question, whether one should be taught the classics or the sciences, seems to me, I confess, very like a dispute whether painters should cultivate drawing or colouring, or, to use a more homely illustration, whether a tailor should make coats or trousers, I can only reply by the question, why not both ? Can anything deserve the name of education which does not include literature and science too ? If there were no more to be said than that scientific education teaches us to think and literary education to express our thoughts, do we not require both ? And is not anyone a poor maimed, lopsided fragment of humanity who is deficient in either ? We are not obliged to ask ourselves whether it is more important to know the languages or the sciences... I am amazed at the limited conception which many educational reformers have formed to themselves of a human being's power of acquisition.... How absurd, they say, that the whole of boyhood should be taken up in acquiring an imperfect knowledge of two dead languages. I should prefer to see these reformers pointing their attacks against the shameful inefficiency of the schools, public and private, which pretend to teach these two languages and do not.

No less able was the plea of Matthew Arnold for literary study, but, like Mill, he contended for both science and the classics. Even among literary studies he would include knowledge of great scientific discoveries and methods. The literary study of science was not, however, accorded as high a place as that given to strictly literary studies. That is, human nature, according to Arnold, is strengthened and enriched by "the power of conduct, the power of intellect and knowledge, the power of beauty, and the power of social life and manners," and science serves to develop the power of intellect and knowledge, while fine literature serves the higher purpose of developing beauty and conduct.

A more recent group of educational reformers and critics includes Eliot, Flexner, Shory, Dewey, Cubberly, and Bobbitt. Eliot attacked compulsory Latin by pointing out, first, the recent conception of education and, second, the inutility of school Latin. These conceptions were :

1. that education now includes knowledge of the science of nature, economics, and society ;
2. that science is now the gateway to efficiency citizenship and material rewards ; and
3. that other subjects than languages provide training in such desirable matters as observation, recording, and reasoning.

The reasons for placing Latin upon an elective basis were :

1. that Latin is no longer necessary for the study of the world's most vaiuable literature;
2. that Lain litertnre does not provide indispensable discussions of society;
3. that Latin is not utilitarian even for professional men;
4. that love for Latin seldom follows compulsion:

5. that Latin is superfluous in the understanding of Roman life and thought; and
6. that Latin as a literary subject is a deadend subject because it is dropped before proficiency is attained.

Flexner continued the attack upon Latin in 'A Modern School." This pamphlet was mainly a description of a realistic treatment of the subjects which should, in Flexner's opinion, be offered in a modern school. These subjects are science, industry civics, and aesthetics—literature, language, art, and music. The lack of realism in present practices in certain of these subjects was soundly criiticized : science, including mathematics, as prematurely abstract and verbal literature as antquated in subject matter, ill-timed, and unappealing, foreign language as being taught as though the language itself were an end instead of an end. Undesirable traditional attitudes were blamed for both content and method in much of mathematics and English and foreign literatures. The following paragraph indicates the boldness with which this critic would eliminate the subjects which he regards as useless :

> Neither Latin nor Greek would be contained in the curriculum of the Modern School—not, of course, because their literatures are less wonderful than they are reputed to be, but because their present position in the curriculum rests upon tradition and assumption. A positive case can be made out for neither. The literary argument fails, because stumbling and blundering through a few patches of Latin classics do not establish a contact with Latin literature. Nor does present-day teaching result in a practical mastery of Latin useful for other purposes. Mature students who studied Latin through the high school, and perhaps to some extent in college, find it difficult or impossible to understand a Latin document encountered in, say a course in history. If practical mastery is desired, more Latin can be learned in enormously less time by postponing the study until the student needs the language or wants it. At that stage he can learn more Latin in a few months than he would have

succeeded in acquiring through four or five years of reluctant effort in youth. Finally, the disciplinary argument fails, becuse mental discipline is not a real purpose; moreover, it would in any event constitute an argument against rather than for the study of Latin I have quoted figures to show how egregiously we fail to teach Latin. These figures mean that instead of getting orderly training by solving difficulties in Latin translation, pupils guess, fumble, receive surreptitious assistance or accept on faith the injunctions of teacher and grammar. The only discipline that most students could get from their classical studies is a discipline in doing things as they should not be done.

Classicists were very properly aroused by these assaults upon the ancient languages. Promptly to the defense came Shorey. He contended eloquently that the classics should be retained because those subjects even now represent the survival, in a small class of educated leaders, of the true conception of linguistic, literary, and critical discipline. He held further, as did certain nineteenth-century English writers, that if the classics be eliminated, their place will probably be filled by less well-organized subjects of questionable value. West continued the controversy by assembling witnesses who professed that no negligible amounts of their powers were due to their profitable years of Latin study. The importance of this controversy lies partially in its influence upon the Classical League and the investigation conducted by the League.

The criticisms of the classics as cited have shown two tendencies : the first is that of beginning any consideration of school subjects with the apparent purpose of finding sufficient reasons for continuing the use of what is already provided in curricula; the second tendency consist of examining society to determine what needs the curricula should meet. The second tendency characterizes such analyses as those of Castiglione and Defoe. It is much more fully exemplified in critical works of Bobbitt and other modern writers. As applied to Latin, for example, this procedure leads Bobbitt to examine the five uses of a language as a form of expression :

1. in speaking or hearing language ;
2. in writing or reading communications ;
3. in finding out the learning of the world ;
4. in reading as a leisure occupation ;
5. in one's own thinking. In none of these activities does Bobbitt find Latin useful.

This leads to the criticism that Latin, as a means of expression, is therefore, not a legitimate subject for general education. The indirect functions of Latin are next canvassed, first, to discern whether Latin helps English to function better, and, second, to find out whether Latin possesses disciplinary values.

As a result of his conclusions upon these points, Bobbitt formulated objectives, guiding principles and assumptions which if properly carried out will, he believes, lead teachers of Latin to produce a maximum of benefit from their subject. In thus treating Latin, and by launching his criticism against both the content and the methods of Latin courses, Bobbitt goes beyond his predecessors in the extent of his analysis of reasons why this or any other subject should be admitted to a program of studies. His final challenge is united with the notion that pervades his treatment of other subjects; namely, the elements of any curriculum are effeective in proportion to the zest and self activity of the pupils who are studying. To obtain the disciplinary values, teachers of Latin are required, therefore, to arouse zest and pupil activity as at least partial guaranties of attaining these values.

Critical discussions of the disciplinary values of studies

From the time when Plato required that students come to him only after their minds had been whetted by geometry, disciplinary values of studies have been recognized. During the later modern period; discussions of such values have gained in refinement as a result of greater speculative analysis and experimental study. Two principal disciplinary theories, each with numerous modifications, have been held. According to the first theory, the mind consists of various parts or faculties, as judgment ; memory, discrimination, each and all of which can, by systematic training, be improved, singly or severally, in both facility and power. As this theory has been discarded by experimental psychologists, it has little if any value as a source of educational reform. According to the second theory, the mind consists of highly integrated tendencies or potentialities, and is under the domination of ideas or configurations which result from natural endowment, experiences, and interests, and which can be changed, broadened, or dwarfed by further experiences and interests. The mind is thus a correlated mass of active tendencies whose activity is influenced (1) by native capacity, (2) by interest or attitude, and (3) by content or stock of facts and skill. Education can affect the second and third of these items; special abilities may be due to any or all three items. As the acceptance of some form of this second principle of the mind has accompanied moderen educational reform, the following discussion centers about this theory.

Building in part upon Kant's psychology, Herbart asserted that every avenue to the pupil's mind should be thrown open to produce harmonious develpoment. In order to obtain an effective presentation of content to the pupil, he held that knowledge must be correlated about two main branch—the historical including literature and the scientific including mathematics, the first based upon social intercourse and the second upon experiences with nature. Disregarding the subject which Herbart happened to emphasize, there is here a departure from faculty psychology and a constructive account of how children can equip their minds for adulthood.

Here the discipline consist of opening the "windows of the soul" so that the ideas and attitudes of the child can be acted upon by the ideas which are pressing from without. The more perfect the windows, that is, the better the subject matter, the more effective the discipline. This form of discipline differs from faculty psychology in emphasizing the value of acquired content and of interest as a common denominator instead of emphasizing the development of powers such as memory and judgment. The influence of Herbartian philosophy was greatest near the close of the nineteenth century, and it was manifested by criticism of all curricula in which correlation was wanting within any subject or between different subjects.

Equally strong emphasis upon the organization and presentation of subject matter as determinants of disciplinary values can be found in the other nineteenth-century writings, Matthew Arnold, for example, criticized the sciences as taught in 1870, but predicted that when the sciences were as well organized for teaching as were the languages, the sciences would be as valuable as the languages in disciplinary effects. Again, Henry Sidgwick, in his essay entitled, *The Theory of Classical Education,* lays down criteria for judging the volue of linguistic training, and concludes that such training, to be effective, must be superior in both quantity and quality if desirable disciplinary effects are to be achieved.

He alleges that the pupil who is exhausted with linguistic struggles is not in a state to receive delicate literary impressions or their accompaniments; instead, such a pupil is filled to the brim with linguistic husks which from a literary standpoint are no more valuable to a modern youth than they were to the Ciceronian of the time of Erasmus. From a disciplinary standpoint, however, Sidgwick maintained that such formal linguistic drill was valuable, but that when followed exclusively, it led to a neglect of the disciplines which should be got from the world of objective phenomena. Substantially the same were the contentions of the scientists, Huxley and Spencer, although the latter seems at times to give little disciplinar credet of any profitable sort to linguistics.

Recent discussions of disciplinary values contain criticisms of the notion that all subjects will of themselves cultivate equally the capacities of all pupils, and of the related opinion that all pupils will profit equally, quantitatively, by pursuing any given subject. Dewey, for example, asserts that any subjecs, such as mathematics, may be used as aa instrument for the attainment of desired values, but that it does not of itself possess any miraculous powers. Instead, he says, mathematics has values only when it accomplishes certain results and not otherwise. The values depend, therefore, upon other matter than the nature of the subject itself; that is, upon the character of the teaching which includes the organization of the subject matter for purposes of teaching. To this criticism, Chapman and Counts add two very trenchant comments: first, that no subject is ever defended largely for its disciplinary value until after its more obvious social values begin to wane; and, second, that the amount of transfer is dependent upon the development of intelligence of the learner.

Critical discussions of the relationship between studies and child life

Modern reformers have built upon works of the numerous educators who, beginning with Quintilian, had emphasized child study as basic in planning curricula. The main line of this criticism runs through Rousseau, Pestalozzi, Herbart, Froebel, Colonel Parker, Dewey, and Bobbitt. While it is obviously impossible to teach without considering the person who is to be taught, Rousseau alleged in *Emile* that a mania for instruction obsessed the teachers of his day. This mania, he maintained, magnified the place of the teacher and the importance of content at the expense of the pupil's nature and needs. This neglect of the child's disposition, interests, and stage of maturity, was appreciated by Pestalozzi, who as he read Rosseau and practiced the art of teaching became convinced that "all educative instruction must be drawn out of children themselves, and be born within them." This principle which Pestalozzi applied in discussing contemporary schools was applied by him to both methods and curricula. Scientific and philosophical bases were given for the principle by Herbart and Froebel. The belief held by Froebel that education consists of accepting each pupil as he is and providing means and causing activities which will facilitate normal growth was further elaborated by Colonel Parker. Instead of attending to the "dead forms of thought," Parker asserted that educators should take advantage of the child's spontaneous activities which naturally lead the child voluntarily to begin "all subjects known in the curriculum of the university." Dewey, Bobbitt, O'Shea, and others have continued the criticism of curricular activities which do not conform with or naturally grow out of children's needs and interests. As Part IV of this treatise is devoted to this problem, further discussion of it will be omitted in this chapter.

Critical discussions of the relationship between sociological conditions and curricula

Stimulated by the work already accomplished by Francke and by the critical writings of Rousseau, Basedow led a sociological movement in education in which such men as Kant, Lessing, Campe, and Von Rochow were participants. The movement grew directly out of the criticisms of educational systems which were prejudiced against the provisions. Besides the schools which Basedow and his followers established, there are the Pestalozzi-Fellenberg schools, which also developed as a part of the same movement. The sociological criticisms which accompanied this European development were reported to American readers in John Griscom's *A Year in Europe* (1823) and Alexander D. Bache's *Report in Education in Europe* (1839). From Griscom's report it is apparent that Fellenberg, Pestalozzi's disciple, did not hold a point of view which is now acceptable, although in 1833 it was far in advance of the beliefs and practices of many American communities. Fellenberg, Griscom wrote, "considers society as divisible into three distinct parts; the higher (comprehending the noble and wealthy), the middling, and the poor. The greatest defects of education he supposes to exist in the two extreme classes, and that these distinctions or classes among men would always prevail in every civilized country he believed to be incontrovertible; and, of course, and attempt to break down the distinction would be fruitless." Consequently, a cosmopolitan but stratified school was advocated as the best form of educational institution for all classes. In Part V discussions of the modern versions of the sociological point of view of Small, Dewey, and Chapman and Counts will be continued.

Critical discussions of the subject of nonprofessional vocational education

From the Athenian Age to modern times, vocational training has been provided for professional workers. Throughout the same period, the vocational training of nonprofessional workers has been neglected. It was inevitable that this condition should change; three elements or forces contributed directly to critical discussions of the situation :

(1) the development of knowledge about nonprofessional vocations;

(2) the failure of apprenticeship educational to meet industrial needs after the rise of the factory system; and

(3) the reinforced interest in mankind in general which accompanied eighteenth-century philan thropinism. In the extension of industrial or nonprofessional vocational education in European countries as well as in America, the third of these forces seems to have played a role comparable with that implied in the passage from Griscom cited above.

One of the foremost English critics, George Combe, will serve as an example of the nineteenth-century reformers who were bent upon the establishment of education for industrial workers. Combe held that since "the working-classes are God's creatures," they are as

> well entitled to justice as the higher ranks. Our opinions of the kind of education which the industrious classes should receive, will depend on the objects which we assign to their lives. If they have been created by Providence merely to toil and pay taxes, to eat, and transmit existence to future generations, a limited education may suffice. But if they have been born with the full faculties of moral, intellectual, and religious beings;... in short, if they are

> rational beings, capable of all the duties, and susceptible of all the enjoyments, which belong to the rational character : then no education is sufficient for them which leaves any portion of their highest powers waste and unproductive.

Later, in 1851, in an address to workmen, Combe maintained that the "human laborer learn to do something which these (modern machines) cannot accomplish; he must acquire skill to form more intricate combinations, and taste to produce finer results than they."

These somewhat general notions had only to be combined with the practices of Pestalozzi and Fellenberg or with the practices suggested by J. A. Froude to produce modern industrial education. "Every occupation," said Froude, in one of his critical addresses.

> even the meanest—I don't say the scavengers or the chimney sweeps—but every productive occupation which adds anything to the capital of mankind, if followed assiduously with a desire to understand everything connected with it, is an ascending stairway whose summit is nowhere, and from the successive steps of which the horison of knowledge perpetually enlarges. Take the lowest and most unskilled labor of all, that of the peasant in the field. The peasant's business is to make the earth grow food; the elementary rudiments of his art are the simplest, and the rude practice of it the easiest; yet between the worst agriculture and the best lies agricultural chemistry, the application of machinery, the laws of the economy of force, and the most curious problems of physiology. Each step of knowledge gained in these things can be immediately applied and realized. Each point of the science which the laborer masters will make him not only a wiser man but a better workman; and will either lift him, if he is ambitious, to a higher position, or make him more intelligent and more valuable if he remains where he is. ... The millions must ever be condemned to

> toil with their hands, or the race will cease to exist. The beneficent light when it comes, will be a light which will make labor more productive by being more scientific; which will make the humblest drudgery not unworthy of a human being, by making it at the same time an exercise to his mind.

Recent years have brought additional critics who contend that training is most effective when educalion is planned to enable pupils to do better the things which they are doing or will later do anyway. This Comenian principle has been given a thorough philosophical treatment in Dewey's *Democracy and Educatton* where integrity of developmental processes is emphasized and the artificiality of trying to make the school unlike normal life is criticized, where he criticizes narrowing forms of industrial education, but contends that a necessary relation exists between the support of thorough-going mentioned education and realization of democratic ideals and aims. A direct application of this principle to curriculum reconstruction is contained in Briggs's discussion where is asserted the the

> first duty of the school is to teach pupils to do better the desirable things that they will do anyway. This assumes that the school man can decide, as inevitably someone must do, which of the activities of life are desirable. Lacking any authoritative list of such activities, which will, of course, differ to some extent from one community to another and even from one individual to another, the school man must take the responsibility for making tentative decisions and for modifying his list as new factors are discovered. Then he must ascertain the ways in which each of the most important desirable activities may be performed better.

Although the criticisms which have here been cited do not cover the period under discussion, they do indicate the main line of argument and present-day thought. There has been no attempt to treat adequately the voluminous discussions since

1876 of the values of the practical arts courses for both boys and girls.

Critical discussions of aesthetic, moral, and religious values and of the internal organization of subject matter. As the remaining types of critical discussions lie either outside the province of this treatise or of this chapter, only brief reference will be made to them. The two main lines of criticism which have aided the development of aesthetics in education are those (1) of Schiller, who in *The Esthetic Education of Man* advocated art as a contributor to civilization by the free spontaneous activity which it induces, and (2) of Ruskin, who in many scattered passages, as in *Fors*, pleaded for art as contributing to both the individual and the social aspects of the manufacture of souls of good quality. Throughout historical times the lack of adequate provision for moral and religious values in schools has been criticized.

As modern examples, William Cowper in *Tirocium* and *The Task* indicts the schools for their lack of moral control and and moral training; Dickens in many novels deplored the evil social effects of contemporary education; Ruskin, Carlyle, and many other publicists in addresses and writings criticized the lack of adequate moral training in schools, and advocated training which should be both adequate in amount and adapted to children's nature. The internal organization of subject matter has been the target of critics particularly from the time of Comenius. An excellent example of the advocacy of such reform is contained in Fifteen (1895). These recommendations represent the views of many leaders in the correlation movement which grew out of nineteenth-century German educational philosophy. (1) Topics and branches should be sequentially organized so "that each branch develops in an order suited to the natural and easy progress of the child, and so that each step is taken at the proper time to help him advance to the next step in other related branches of the course of study." (2) The branches studied should be so adjusted that, so far as possible at the pupil's stage of maturity, the whole course of study shall represent all the great divisions of human learning. (3) The selection and organization of subject matter within each branch should provide the best possible psychological sequence of subject matter. (4) The course of study should be correlated with the spiritual and natural environment within which the pupil lives.

The importance of the critic as an educational prophet and the problems raised by critics will be discussed in Chapter 8. Still further consideration of the reconstruction of subject matter and the problems which lead thereto will be found in Part VI.

9

Selection of Subject Matter

Critics as educational pioneers

A canvass was made in the two preceding chapters of the work of certain eritics whose comments apply to secondary-school curricula. Each of these critics expressed variation from the thought and practice of his time. It should now be possible to discover the extent to which departures from undesirable traditional restrictions have been due to criticisms have been due to criticisms, and particularly to ascertain whether or not, in general. recent desirable reforms have resulted from the application of constructive criticism to curriculum problems.

These critics may be thought of also as social diagnosticians; if they have located and defined curriculum problems, their services in locating and defining problems are of the utmost importance whether or no t their plans for the solution of the problems have been practicable. This chapter will treat, first, of the value of certain representative criticisms; second, the generl tenor of the criticisms; and, third, it will present an outline of a more complete account, which is to be given in later chapters, of how to meet these criticisms and of what is now being done to meet them. Chapters 6 and 7 on constructive criticism form, therefore, a matrix from which issues a progeny of ideas generated by frontier minds.

These ideas are the bases for the subsequent chapters of this book.

The Value of representative critical discussions of curricula

It has often been asserted that one of the distinguishing traits of man's superiority over the lower animals in his ability to forecast the results of real or proposed actions. Greatest amongst the forecasters are the critics; their prevision is often based upon a more adequate understanding of contemporary conditions than that possessed by most men, and to this understanding is added is vision, which, in breadth and distance, exceeds the range of that of their fellows.

Great periods of history are the result of the acceptance of constructive criticism just as stagnant periods of history are the result of stereotyped ignorance. Just as progress is the result of change, so arrested development is the result of premature stereotyping of systems of thought. But all change does not lead to progress any more than all systematize thought leads to arrested development. It is true, however, that all progress is accompanied by change, as all arrested development is accompanied by stereotyping.

What human beings must seek is, therefore, progressive alteration; that is, they must seek guidance during change. Critics offer such guidance not only for their own times, but also for subsequent periods. In other words, if men can examine the proposals of critics and derive therefrom sound principals and adopt those principles, then the acceptance of criticism becomes equivalent to the acceptance of progressive variation in thought.

The way of the critic in proposing sound principles is, however, beset with obstructions. The obstructions comprise the thought and practice of his times. Much of this thought and practice has been, in all periods of his history, a consequence of earlier constructive criticism and experimentation; a part of this thought and practice is of proved worth. The critic has always been forced to discriminate between the worthy and the unworthy. To this difficult task of discrimination there has been added task of breaking through the folkways which have not proved their worth, and of showing the defects of such undesirable folkways. For the best thought of all periods of history has been unknown to smung contemporaries, and advancement has been thwarted by the ignorance of the masses.

Within the group of smung contemporaries who have stood as barriers to advancement, certain educators have played a major role. By assuming an uncritical veneration for tradition and authority, these educators have connived with the most ignorant minds of their times in suppressing both change and the consideration of change. Almost equally culpable have been those educators who have uncritically championed the alleged merits of certain novel cultural or practical usages. When, for example, Socrates or Adelard or Roger Bacon pointed out high purposes of society and more direct means of attaining those purposes, other educators rose as champions of unworthy folkways. When Isocrates, Plato, and Quintilian pleaded for thoroughness in the academic preparation of youth, other educators advocated superficial training in directly practical curricula. When Gerbert, Petrarch, Erasmus, and Huxley proclaimed the moral worth of modern learning, contemporary educators frightened timid and ignorant fellows by insisting that knowledge is inimical to religion and morality. When Comenius, Descartes, and Ramus advocated the reconstruction of Latin, mathematics, and logic, other educators showed grave concern about the vanishing of mental discipline. The moral of this account is that many educators exhibit an ignorant fear when critics show sound methods for shortening man's apprenticeship.

The unrecorded and forgotten history of most of the censors of the critics just named, together with the evident soundness of the views of critics, gives hope for educational progress. History shows that critics often present new views which lead to reforms of educational thought and practice.

That is, if enlightened men can formulate their views so as to show the superiority of their views to outgrown folkways, the way to progress will thus be cleared. The duty of the curriculum maker seems, therefore, to be that of finding out how to test criticism and how to apply the desirable elements of criticism. Such a policy will lead the curriculum maker to accept the judgment of the enlightened man as superior to traditions, to examine current opinions in the iight of criticism, and to displace deficient opinions by sound principles. In short, this policy will lead to a manly facing of issues and to an honest attempt to derive adequate criteria for measuring educational values. Preparatory for the employing of this policy are :

1. an examination of traditional practices, social conditions, and the traits of pupils, and
2. the development of methods of controlling ill-founded criticisms.

Bases for such a preparatory discussion have been laid in the foregoing pages.

The relation of critical thought to curriculum making for secondary schools should be clear. Secondary education is of vital importance to all pupils. The practices of secondary schools should, therefore, be governed by the best thought of the times. In the determination of these practices, criticism is invaluable, because critics subject educational needs and objectives to a searching analysis, and then estimate the value of actnal practices in the attainment of objectives. Even though the critic lacks a complete policy or program, as did Socrates, his searching analysis may have great value in diagnosing educational problems. The critic may, and often does, as did Plato and Aristotle, suggest or collect vast ranges of materials for the training of adolescents. In the periods of progress in secondary education, criticism had led educators to examine the subject matter of secondary education and to see its worth for enjoyment, for futile objectives, or for real and valid ends.

Such a procedure has often led to trenchant and most unpleasant comments upon education. These comments have indeed been at times so unwelcome to the ears of powerful reactionary educators, that critics such as Adelard have assigned their comments to unmentioned or earlier men. More frequently critics have proceeded directly, as did Roger Bacon, in their attempts to unshackle the schools from vested interests. Erasmus, for example, criticized teachers of Latin soundly for teaching language only, while they pretended to teach both language and literature. In a similar mood, Rabelais ridiculed the pedantry of self-styled educators.

Later in the same century, Descrates exposed the failure of teachers of mathematics to grasp the meaning of their own subject, and. in the following century, Dury challenged the classical approach to the study of natural science. Few if any critics of any period have diagnosed more clearly than Francis Bacon the ills of educational practice. His discussion of the diseases, peccant humor, and phantoms of learning is still the basis for some of the most apt criticisms of secondary-school curricula.

The need for the recurreence of such criticisms as those of Francis Bacon is shown by the fact that his criticisms are still applicable. That is, just as fifeeenth-century educators required chastrning by Valla in the same terms employed in the thirteenth century by Grosseteste, so modern educators still require counsel and chastisement similar to that delivered by Francis Bacon to educators of the seventeenth century. Other criticisms which recur and which have perennial value are those of Aristotle upon liberal and illiberal values. In contending that ill-organized materials and practices lead to irrational results and that subject matter to be effective must be integrated, Aristotle anticipated the work of Herbart, Arnold, Harris, and Dewey.

Out of such criticism have sprung the attempts of recent educators such as Dewey and Cubberley to avoid confusion of the terms liberal or cultural and illiberal or practical and to attempts to organize curricula and individual subjects to yield both liberal and practical values. Still later, such criticism has led Bobbitt and Charters to activity analysis to discover the liberal and practical values which pupils need to attain.

A somewhat different development of criticism of the same sort led during the nineteenth century to a series of attempts to estimate the relative values of single subjects, of different curricula, of different forms of organization of subjects, and the validity of different immediate and remote results as educational objectives. These attempts have led in turn to the dropping of rigid prescription of courses and to a defense of the elective system.

In this section the value of critical discussions of curricula has been shown by pointing out :

1. that critics are seers;
2. that the acceptance of constructive criticism has accompanied and apparently led to the great periods of educational advancement;
3. that the vital importance of secondary education requires the guidance of competent critics in planning progressive changes;
4. that significant modern issues have been envisaged, analyzed, and, in some cases, solved by critics; and
5. that progress depends upon recurrent consideration of sound criticism.

Additional modern issues which have been analyzed by critics will next be cited.

Educational Attitudes and Conditions which Provoke Criticism

At least five purposes or forms of desire appear to have instigated criticism of secondary-school curricula. First, there is the desire to adhere to the old—the tested and somewhat satisfactory formulae. This desire is exemplified abundantly in the later Greek and the later Roman periods and in each succeding period. Certain characteristics give this desire great strength : it usually exists in combination with other tendencies and attitudes which indicate the stability of its defenders; it is fused with vested interests in subject matter—and element in the thinking of many teachers of well-established subject matter; institutional life is usually organized in conformity with the old; reverence for the old · the stable; it is cherished by respectable persons; and it often indicates a high degree of affluence.

The contributions of this desire have been varied and numerous : it seems to have hastened the death of two great martyr-teachers among the Greeks and the Hebrews; it checked Greek learning in Rome; it retarded development during the Middle Ages; it has prompted the burning of many scientific manuscripts; it prevented the interrelationship of the labors of advancing workers of the Middle Ages; it prolonged absurdly the period of adherence to Aristotle; it blocked experimental study and teaching for centuries: it has perpetuated much subject matter long after the need for it passed; and it has perpetuated much desirable subject matter.

Second, there is the desire to make education practical. This desire has led to many later innovations since the days when it prompted Korax to invent the art of rhetoric and Gerbert to use Arabic numerals. It has been characterized by a spirit of utility; by an emphasis upon ready-made answers and processes rather than upon underlying basic principles; by impatience with subject matter that is alleged to be mainly cultural; by arguments designed to show the cultural values of the practical; and by a lack of fundamental philosophical principles such as Dewey has supplied. The contributions of this desire include the encouragement, since the later Greek period of the immediately practical at the expense of broad training; the popularization of education; the adoption of Arabic notation; the development of new subjects throughout modern times; the connection of schools with current life;

and the development of the functional attitude toward all subject matter.

Third. there is the desire to make education cultural. Plato, Erasmus, Milton, Herbart, Jebb, Huxley, Arnold, and Bryce are notable adherents to this cause. Among the characteristics of this type of thought are frequent confusion about the meaning of the term *culture* and valiant efforts to define it; periodical defenses of certain studies for their cultural values; impracticality—as viewed by the "practical"-minded; attempts to measure cultural values by measuring the concomitants of such values; and a dignified, leisure-class attitude. The contributions of this desire include attempts to teach subjects for certain "higher" values; the encouragement of fine writing on educational subjects; the preservation of fine literature; an excessive emphasis upon literary values; a heightened tone of instruction; and an interest in well-organised subject matter. The last-named contribution is sometimes accompanied by a naive belief that new subject matter lacks cultural possibilities because it lacks good organization.

Fourth, there is the desire to cultivate certain traits of character, such as morality, religious attitude, courage, patriotism, and strong mental fiber. This age-old desire has, at times, been accompanied by such undesirable characteristics as an extreme tendency toward didacticism; a failure to recognize pupils, equipment, iterests, and needs, and a consequent intrusion of an overmature, adult point of view in the selection of subject matter; an overemphasis upon the views of certain leaders; and a consequent distortion of subject matter by misguided partisans.

The eontription of this desire, when it is aceompanied by recognition of the nature of the learning process, include whatever of worth there is in the employment of wholesome subject matter. Under the guidance of untrained partisans, this desite has contributed to the neglect, for centuries, of important bodies of knowledge; to the development of overmature, moralizing from of subject matter; and to a retroactive tendency toward mental discipilinary values and the attendent verbalism of that tendency.

Fifth, there is the desire to improve the subjects pursued at any given time. This desire assumes many forms by including attempts to improve the methods of teaching, the organization of subject matter, and the planning of suitable pupil-activities. The noblest educators of all times have been impelled by this motive : Isocrates, Plato, Aristotle, Quintilian, Comenius, Descrates, Eliot, and a host of modern reconstructionists. This desire has been characterized by an attempt to find the roads of the past and leave the ruts; by wholesome conservatism; by intelligent leadership; by the application of progressive philosophy, psychology, and sociology to education; by attempts to improve teachers systematically; and by using the best available means for measuring educational values and results.

The positive contributions of this desire are the stabilization of content—not always a desirable result; a heightened value of subjects by virtue of vital organization; an improvement of the technique of teaching; the gradual elimination of undesirable subject matter; an emphasis upon individual needs; the attempts to extend educational opportunity to larger and larger groups of persons; and a realization that each age must provide its own organization of education and that subject matter must be winnowed anew for each new set of conditions.

Educational reforms proposed by critics

Out of these five types of reasons for criticizing curricula constructively, have developed five principal types of educational reforms. The following account provides a brief historical summary of these reforms.

Owing to the tendency to adhere to the old, Socrates and Isocrate attempted to show the youth of Greece that the short and superfical courses offered by other teachers were based not upon facts and sound judgments but upon opinions and that such courses could lead only to specious results. These critics alleged that departure from a solid body of knowledge which required years for its matery could not safely be undertaken by any youth who was destined to lead his people.

The same tendency reappears at times in the proposals of critics and at times in workers who only imply their attitudes by attempting to make scholarly compilations of established subject matter. In these forms, the tendency is exemplified by by Seneca's reverence for the older learning when he thought of it in comparison with the new learning of his later years, by Quintilin's account of what he believed to be an adequate curriculum, by Varro, St. Augustine, Capella, Donatus, Priscian, and others who formulated the subject matter of the Middle Ages, by mediaeval translators of early manuscripts, by Petrarch and other humanists, by Comenius, and by scores of protagonists of ancient learning and established curricula in modern times. At times, this tendency has encouraged progress by showing the soundness and applicability of the old to the present. At other times, it has stifled progress by allowing ancient lore to monopolize the time of scholars. The history of education provides an ample defense for a temperate use of this tendency and also ample evidence against overindulgence of it.

Owing to the tendency to make education immediately practical, the superficial teachers of Greece came near overthrowing the ancient learning of the old Greek period. Again in Rome same superficial critics prevailed to the same end. In the Middle Ages the commercial teachers advanced their cause by proclaiming the unwisdom of the scholars and by advertising courses which would yield great returns after short study. Out of the same tendency grew the advocacy of practical schools for worldly men in early modern France and Germany. Later, Fngland and, under Franklin's leadership, America advanced practical reasons for reducing the amounts of certain types of content and increasing the amounts of other types.

During the nineteenth and twentieth centuries Combe, Spencer, Eliot, and Dewey have advocated practical subjects and have rationalized the arguments for the thorough study of subjects. It is to be understood that the subject matter of practical courses have developed into large, rational bodies of content and that modern advocacy of such content is very unlike the advocacy of ancient and mediaeval practical courses. Concomitiants of the tendency to criticize curricula for their neglect of practical-content have been the development of rhetoric, public speaking, commercial subjects, science, mathematics, and the teaching of modern languages. While all these branches have been benefited by practical demands, other demands and tendencies have, of course, been operative. It should, however, be clear that many subjects which are at present pursued by many pupils for their cultural value were in earlier times championed chiefly by persons whom scholars rated as illiberal.

Owing to the tendency to emphasize cultural aspects of education, many formalities have been fostered and many values which modern men regard as cultural have, as just stated, been rated as lacking in cultural qualites. Instead of agreeing with the saying of Matthew Arnold that culture is an acquaintance with "the best that has been known and said," many defenders of culture have restricted this term to the best that has been known or said about only certain matters or by only certain persons. Dewey's account of the broadened scope of the term culture shows that its earlier restricted use grew out of ancient social conditions, the lack of organized content in certain departments of thought, and the force of tradition in maintaining a *status quo*.

If one examines the works referred to above in the discussion of humanism and realism, one finds that the modern works on education emphasize the three aspects of culture named by Mathew Arnold :

(1) a richness of dynamic mental attitude instead of dependence upon external and mechanical appliances.

(2) an harmonious mental perspective instead of a narrow view limited to a single pursuit or mental set; and

(3) a dynamic social perspective which leads general social advancement instead of only selfish purposes.

This attitude, when compared with the literary humanist's attempt, to confine culture to 'belles lettres' as Arnold himself seems to have done in certain passages, discloses many of the reasons for misunderstanding the meaning of the term 'culture' : different writers have limited the term to different aspects of culture. Modern writers, in accepting Arnol'd broad tripartite conception, are able to show the cultural value of all substantial and well-organized content. By accepting this conception, the old distinction between the terms paractical and cultural disappears.

Out of the desire to cultivate moral traits by education has grown criticism of content from primitive times to the present day. Crises in tribal or national life seem to have led to curriculum revision to improve the moral fiber of youth. Comopolitan Athens, for example, like modern America, had to choose from many available sources the content which should be taught to adolescents. Isocrates urged the moral values of his broad curriculum, while Plato classified different items of content as to their moral values. St. Augustine and many other of his mediaeval successors made moral and religious valus the chief consideration in their discussions of curricula. In modern times, the founders of great school system – Strum, Colet, Erasmus, and Franklin—attended critically to character education. Nineteenth-century writers, such as Dickens, Carlyle, Ruskins, and Herbart, formulated principles of moral training which were identified at the close of that century with the agitation for the correlation of subject matter. The last decade has witnessed an extension of the term moral education to include social or civic education. The alleged failure of schools provide adequate training of this kind has led to a deluge of criticism by such educatiors as Adler, Sadler, Bobbitt, Charters, O'Shea, Dewey, Sharp, Sisson, and Judd. As a dlrect result of this criticism, an inventory of social education has been made and this training has been increased and systematized. Paralleling the attempts to cultivate desirable traits of character, there have been attempts to analyze pupils to discover their capacities, interests, and needs. Plato and Aristotle conducted extended philosophical investigations upon this point, as did Vives, Comenius, Dury, and also the scores of modern students of child psychology during the last century. Criticism of subject matter for its failure to conform with its failure to conform with child nature have played an important role in the reconstruction of curricula.

Out of the desire to improve the traditional subjects have come criticisms thoughout history. The avowed aim of critics who would improve existing subjects is to utilize the best available knowledge in the respcctive departments of learning. The constant implication of this branch of criticism is that the critic is ages ahead of the masses and that the masses jointly or severally are sworn to thwart him. This group of critics seem originally to have been inspired by the battle of intelligent realism against superstition and traditional lore.

Certainly from the time that Thales called upon his people to use the revelations of science and turn their backs upon outgrown beliefs and practices, tradition and advanced knowledge have been at war. Protagoras and Socrates pleaded with their contemporaries to abandon mere opinion and follow reason. Plato pleaded for the abandonment of unworthy literature and music and the cultivation of literary and musical activities which might advace the learner. Aristotle pleaded for real experience as the touchstone of beliefs and practices. Like Roger Bacon, Aristotle urged the abandonment of opinionated arguments after scientific data has been assembled. Adelard would have had students pursue existing bodies of knowledge, but still would not have had them led as by a halter in the pursuit of learning. In turn, as knowledge grew, criticis turned upon one another as Grosseteste and Ramu did upon Aristotle, and thereafter reached a new level of curriculum making; for there has been a continuous need to break down complacency and bigtory whether it has applied to superstition or to early science itself. In this attack upon complacency, it is significant that although many conservatists have been fortified by allying themselves with powerful institutions, critics have not entirely lacked the fortifying encouragement of the church ; as examples, Aquinas, tolerant of research, and Bacon, a research worker of the thirteenth century, were, during their most productive periods, encouraged and protected by the church.

It is by this branch of critism that the modern era was brought forth, and by it also that the modern era has continued to progress. Later mediaeval and early modern scientists sought not to wreck exlsting systems of knowledge, but instead to extend these systems. By so conducting their campaign, they slowly built the basis for modern science. Petrach and Boccaccio were not destroyers of existing subjects of study, but instead they enriched such subjects. As rapidly as the advances made by one generation or era of workers are either surpassed or formalized by latter workers, the diagnostic criticism of Francis Bacon has to be applied. For example, before Bacon's time, Frasmus and Comenius proposed substitutes for the diseases of the learning of their day. To science, modern crities, such as Spencer, Huxley, Eliot, Bode, and Flexner, have again applied criticisms of the diseases, humors, and phantoms of modern learning. All criticisms of this type aim at the preservation of the good elements in the old materials, and more effective organization of an entire department of learning.

Always, however, there has arisen an insuperable obstacle to immediate and full success in the improvement of existing subjects of study. This is the obstacle which Robinson has emphasized. Our curricula are, he says, "an unconscious avoidance of the responsiblility which would be involved in stock notions and habits. 'We are not yet in a position so to revise our education that a new type of mind will be cultivated appropriate to our present knowledge and circumstances."

The reasons for this inability to conduct a complete revision of subject matter are :

(1) that ancient, tested knowledge to, many persons, preferable to new knowledge, and

(2) that new knowledge is sometimes upsetting if applied to established usages.

This antagonism between reconstructionists and conservatives sometimes applies either to a reorganization of the old, as in many of the revivals of the classics, or to the entrance of new materials into old departments. Upon this point the curriculum maker must decide whether knowledge will gain or lose by attempts to take any given progressive step ; he must recall that the critic is a frontier thinker and that a reaction to certain critical views is still as inevitable as it was in the days of Socrates or of Galieo. He must recall that social attitudes as well as advancements in research are elements which may thwart or foster progressive tendencies.

Ultimately, each reform that is carried to fruition gains the sanction of "respectable" persons. If such sanction can precede the introduction of new knowledge into the curriculum, there is an obvious advantage for the elements of knowledge in question. If, however, sanction must wait upon the adoption of new knowledge by curriculum makers, it is equally obvious that curriculum makers must in this case have the courage to face martyrdom.

How to meet the problems raised by critics

Up to this point this treatise has attempted to present many of the important and fundamental curriculum problem of the present day and to provide a background for discussions of these problems. The five subsequent sections of this book present discussions of attempts to meet such problems :

(1) educational objectives and curricula;

(2) pupils' equipment, interests, and needs in relation to curricula;

(3) curricula and local conditions ;

(4) the reconstruction of curricula to provide for the best possible pupil activities in the mastery of subject matter ; and

(5) a study of present-day practices as final guide in formulating standards for constructing and administering curricula.

10

Grade Placement and Time Allotment

The Place of Objectives in a System of Education

The educational issues raised in the preceding surveys of historical development and constructive criticism challenge serious thought. Only when one recalls the fact that from the beginning of time scores of traditions have withstood each proposal for change, that millions of dissenters from progressive thought have risen to confound each critic of his times—only then can one apprehend the tremendous need for standards which point out the truth. If at last in modern times these standards or criteria can be arranged and then reduced to order, our generation of men may yet hope to solve problems which have persisted through the ages. Without such guiding principles, America's schools are bound nowhere ; they will drift asea like a mutineers' ship. For Plato described accurately the condition of American education in the story of an artless captain and his men :

> Imagine then a fleet or a ship in which there is a captain who is taller and stronger than any of the crew, but he is a little deaf and has a similar infirmity in sight, and his knowledge of navigation is not much better. The sailors

are quarrelling with one another about the steering—every one is of opinion that he has a right to steer, though he has never learned the art of navigation and cannot tell who taught him or when he learned, and will further assert that it cannot be taught, and they are ready to cut in pieces and one who says the contrary. They throng about the captain, begging and praying him to commit the helm to them ; and if at any time they do not prevail, but others are preferred to them, they kill the others or throw them overboard, and having first chained up the noble captain's senses with drink or some narcotic drug, they mutiny and take possession of the ship and make free with the stories ; thus, eating and drinking, they proceed on their voyage in such manner as might be expected of them. Him who is their partisan and cleverly aids them in their plot for getting the ship out of the captain's hands into their own whether by force or persuasion, they compliment with the name of sailor, pilot, able seaman, and abuse the other sort of man, whom they call a good-for-nothing ; but that the true pilot must pay attention to the year and seasons and sky and stars and winds, and whatever else belongs to his art, if he intends to be really qualified for the command of a ship. and that he must and will be the steerer, whether other people like it or not—the possibility of this union of authority with the steerer's art has never seriously entered into their thoughts or been made a part of their calling.

The pilot of our schools may not assume command, "whether other people like or not," but that this "true pilot must pay attention to the year and seasons and sky and stars and winds, and whatever else belongs to his art, if he intends to be really qualified for the command of a ship," is indisputable.

No less discerning of the true place of clear objectives in the system of education was Erasmus when he exclaimed :

> Tell me, can a man run his best in the dark? Or, can a gladiator conquer if he be blindfolded? The precepts of philosophy—which is knowledge applied to life—are, as it were, the eyes of the mind, and lighten up to the consciousness of what we may do and may not do. A long and manifold experience is beyond doubt. of great profit, but only to such as by the wisdom of learning have acquired an intelligent and informed judgment. Besides, philosophy teaches us more in one year than our own individual experience can teach us in thirty, and its teaching carries none of the risks which the method of learning by experience of necessity brings with it.

The results of running in the dark, battling while hoodwinked, acquiring experience while neglecting theory, are nowhere better set forth than in Judd's discussion of the American experiment in secondary education. There, Judd cites the indifference of the American people to a real "insight into the essentials of their democracy." And, as this writer shows, even a well-planned school may fail unless the "true pilot" share his art and his philosophy with the "other people." For:

> What education is, and how the young should be educated, are questions that require discussion. At present there is a difference of opinion as to the subjects which should be taught; for men are by no means in accord as to what the young should learn, whether they aim at virtue or at getting the best out of life. Neither is it clear whether education is more concerned with intellect or character. And the question is brought no nearer solution by reference to the actual practice of contemporary education. Therefore no one knows whether the young should exercise themselves in those studies which are useful in life, or in those which tend towards virtue, or in those of essentially theoretical interest. All these opinions have found supporters. Furthermore, there is no agreement as to the means of cultivating virtue; for different people, starting from different conceptions of the

virtue which all respect, naturally differ as to how the practice of it should be cultivated.

The purpose of Part III of this treatise is to canvass and classify the literature of educational objectives with a view to relating these objectives to curriculum practices. Before the derivation or the types of objectives are discussed, it is essential that certain distinctions of terms be made.

Important distinctions to be observed in the discussion of educational objectives

The philosophy of education is often confused by the cloudy connotations of certain terms and by a failure to recognize the interrelationships of certain complex processes.

1. *Value*. The term *value* signifies an observed or imagined condition which is either useful or leads to or produces something useful. By *useful*

> is meant that property in any object, whereby it tends to produce benefit, advantage, pleasure, good, or happiness, (all this in the present case comes to the same thing) or (what again comes to the same thing) to prevent the happening of mischief, pain, evil, or unhappiness to the party whose interest is considered : if that party be the community in general, then the happiness of the community : if a particular individual, then the happiness of that individual.

The term may, therefore, indicate a condition which will become for community or an individual, a standard of value. As such, an object of value possesses regulative characteristics which influence but do not necessarily determine conduct. Before an object of value can become an element in the production of action, it must all itself with certain forces. For example, an efficient automobile is an object of value to most pedestrians ; still, one does not therefore immediately obtain an automobile unless certain forces ally themselves with the notion of value in such a way as to produce desire. Of the forces involved in this particular case, the economic forces are often the most difficult to manage. Other forces, such as physical and psychological, are readily directed toward the possession of an automobile. In other instances, moral forces are necessary for action with reference to an object of value : in the case of one who resists any form of temptation, there is an appreciation of the value of the tempting object, but there is a higher appeciation of an object which lies in a direction indicated by moral forces. These forces—economic, physical, psychological, and moral—serve as allies in giving motive power to values ; every object of value, if attained, must have its parallel cause or force which leads to action.

The great importance of this point is illustrated in secondary education by the "cardinal principles" which were secondary education in 1918. These principles were largely names of values, and consequently they could not become causes of action until they were given motive power by association with forces which lead to action. "Worthy home-membership" and "ethical character" are among the values there set up, but these terms cannot stand for compelling forces or causes of action. They are merely names of abstract values drawn from instead of associated with the objects and activities which one performs and thinks about. Only after these values were supplemented by further analysis and then allied with economic, physical, psychological, or moral forces could they become causes of action.

2. *Ideal*. The term *ideal* signifies a value which is accepted as desirable of attainment. The conscious action of acceptance of the notion of desirable attainability distinguishes an ideal from a value. The worth of an object of value is here realized and to that realization is added the element of desire or wishing. An ideal has, therefore, power to cause action on account of the element of desire as a moving force.

This desire is of course dependent for its fruition upon the four types of forces named above in the discussion of value. Owing, however, to a possible conflict of tendencies or wishes, an ideal is not a certain cause of action – knowing or even wishing does not always lead to performance. There are on record many cases of both individuals and communities in which holy ideals have run amuck because of the greater power of counter and baser ideals. Educators may not, therefore, be satisfied by the acceptance of such ideals as universal education or of command of fundamental processes of school subjects. Instead, they must further require that counteracting ideals be subordinated to the attainment of ideals which are believed to be socially justifiable. Every ideal, to be effective, must possess a dominant, parallel cause for action throughout the period of its supremacy.

In educational matters an accepted proficiency in purposes and performances may be adopted as a practical or attainable ideal. Character in general, as well as specific performance traits, stands within the scope of ideals. It is to be expected that certain standards of proficiency in purposes or performances lie far beyond the field of distinct vision and are, therefore, only dimly envisaged ideals. It is believed that by referring to ideals as definite proficiencies a much closer union of ideals and their attainments can be formed than is probable if ideals are referred to as indefinite, dimly apprehended, general traits.

3. *Objective.* The term *objective* signifies a value or an element of a value which is set up for attainment together with plans for appropriate activities for the attainment of the value. An objective thus serves as both guide and prompter to action. With reference to any given value there may be one objective or many integrated objectives. When many objectives are integrated, the basis of integration is a recognized social or individual good of too complex a character to be attained as a single simple objective. For example, the ability to spell can be set up as a worthy attainment.

But until this ability was analyzed with reference to social needs and individual pupil capacities, no useful working objective was derived. Recently, however, analysis of this ability has led educators to envisage social demands for spelling and the separate activities which pertain to proficiency in spelling. The results of thus objectifying this fundamental process are to be found in the reconstructed methods and materials of spelling in a modern school. Similar instances could be cited in the case of other school subjects.

The term will be used in this treatise as generally synonymous with the terms aim, end, or goal. As ideals result from the acceptance of values as desirable of attainment, so objectives result from definitely setting up ideals as objects of attainment together with plans for this attainment.

How the objectives of education can be derived

The objectives of education are derived by observation and analysis of and speculation upon human activities, interests, needs, and capacities. Plato, Erasmus, Rousseau, and Spencer as well as more recent educationists, have followed this procedure. The differences among their ultimate objectives are due usually to differences in the character of the observation, analysis, and speculation employed and the amounts of attention given to activities, interests, and capacities rather than to differences in the activities, interests, and capacities considered. In order to illustrate different procedures in the derivation of objectives, a brief survey will next be made of the use of seven different approaches to the formulation objectives. In this survey certain characteristics or predominant points of departure in the work of different men will be employed as examples.

1. *The derivation of objectives from an ideal form of society*. It will be recalled that Plato wished his philosopher or educated man to be so trained that three characteristics of the soul should be properly tempered and nurtured. His speculation upon and analysis of this matter led him to complete his objectives by examining existing subject matter and making suggestions for its use. The values and ideals which underlie his objectives were hypothetical rather than real, and, consequently, his plans for accomplishment were also marked by their indefiniteness. It is plain that Plato's objectives of education grew out of the

discrepancy which he observed between society as he thought it should be and society as it was in his day. Since the picture which he drew in his *Republic* of this hypothetical society provided the general basis of his plans, Plato's objective lacked the close relationship to actual performances and conditions that is possessed by later formulations.

2. *The derivation of objectives by analysis of "good character."* Erasmus attempted in his *De Civilitate Morum* to derive an integrated system of objectives looking toward organized life in a civilized, enlightened community. His general objective of education was social efficiency which included piety, scholarship, or love for and proficiency in liberal studies, the general duties of life, and skill in civic affairs. These four aspects of social life were distinguished from one another only for purposes of discussion and curriculum planning. In actual life they are, as Erasmus saw, inseparable. With reference to each of his four subordinate aims, he examined life : religious institutions, the family, the community, and certain vocations—the Church, land-ownership and diplomacy. In this examination, he found certain characteristics many of which, in his opinion, necessitated formal training of the young. As the individuals about whom Erasmus showed most educational concern were of the sort whom Plato expected to develop into "philosophers," the plan of Erasmus has serious limitations in an age of universal education.

Although he analyzed subject matter with considerable care, he suffered serious limitations in this also because he confined his curriculum entirely to classical literature. A superficial survey of a state or a community with the present-day point of view would have yielded numerous items, such as training for everyone who was engaged in many of the activities which Erasmus quite overlooked. His assumption was that the world had changed so little since the classical days of Greece and Rome that all educational nurture could be derived from the works of those days with the addition of the materials of religious education.

3. *The derivation of objectives by analysis of one class of individuals.* Castiglione derived the essential objectives for a liberal education by observing and analyzing the lives of men who succeeded in the court life of his day. So well did Castiglione analyze the life of his day that his book, *The Courtier*, has been cited as the fullest account in any single volume of "the chief moral and social ideas of the age." As a result of his analysis, he included objectives in conversation, arms, literature, music, drawing, painting, sculpture, and manners.

Other subjects, such as manual arts and science, he quite neglected. If this omission of certain subject matter is charged as a limitation of Castiglione's book, one should charge the limitation to the scope of his analysis rather than to his treatment of the courtier's needs. For the scope of this analysis was limited by the scope of this writer's notion of a liberal life. As his notion of a liberal life excluded the greater part of human beings, his work has little general application in a democracy.

4. *The derivation of objectives by analysis of the nature of children.* Rousseau, while setting up as objectives the attainment of both social and individual values, looked to the nature of children rather than to the nature of society as a source of educational objectives. His hope was that society might become adjusted to nature.

When parents and teachers learned "the art of forming men" according to the child's nature, then, he believed, there could be developed a society which was also natural. By challenging the emphasis in education upon adult standards and by setting up instead the nature of the child, Rousseau called the attention of educators to objectives which have influenced and still are influencing the organization of teaching materials. Despite the notable contribution of Rousseau's procedure, it led to a search for objectives in a place where they can not be found. Children's tendencies and interests, unless largely formed or guided with reference to adult standards, lead only to primitive savagery. Rousseau failed to outline a satisfactory system of objectives because the elements of his analysis remained unreconciled. Had he analyzed the child and society and then united into a consistent system the results of his analysis, he might have reconciled the two conflicting elements, child nature and adult society. Instead of reconciling these elements, he decided in favor of child nature, and as a consequence involved himself in confusion regarding the basic conditions of education.

5. *The derivation of objectives by special reference to a certain branch of knowledge.* Although Herbert Spencer set up "complete living" as the objective of enlightened man and seems in the *Data of Ethics* and a portion of his first essay on education to be analyzing educational problems with that objective in view, classicists have been certain that Spencer's real motive for writting his essay entitled "What Knowledge Is of Most Worth ?" was that of proving the superiority of science over letters. By most readers it will be granted that Spencer was an ardent protagonist of science and that he was an almost equally ardent denouncer of the practice of exalting literary studies above the sciences. Unfortunately, Spencer analyzed the values of science only partially and left much undone with respect to certain social studies which he also favored.

A more complete analysis of science would have shown Spencer that the different elements of science are very uneven in value to one who is living a reasonably complete life. His failure in this respect to distinguish between the items of knowledge which are indispensable to the specialist and of slight value to the layman is perhaps as great a fault as any in his analysis. His lack of success in deriving objectives which are adapted to the complete living of persons with literary or artistic knowledge is a serious reflection upon his own great scientific powers.

6. *The derivation of objectives by analysis of sociological values.* Although many writers since the time of Plato have emphasized social and political needs as determinants of education, recent emphasis upon a new social determinant and found an early advocate in Small. This new social objective is characterized by an attempt to connect all education with democracy. Small insists that both society and culture have

changed since "the old aristocratic ideal of culture" was adopted, and that the change requires that less time be given to the old literary humanities and more weight placed "upon preparation for efficiency and service. The scientific method, broad concepts, and higher appreciations must," he continues, "ever be the foundations of citizenship and of practical activities; but a larger proportion of time must be given to the vocational aims." That is, education must enable man not only to be familiar with his environment as reflected in science and letters, but also to "develop original power to change the environment and to cope with whatever problems of efficiency and ethical conditions a given period may present."

In elaborating upon the attainment of sociological progress, Smith analyzed four aims of education – the development of physical vitality, of cultural attainment, of vocational efficiency, and of social service. He found sound reasons for bringing about a realization of all four of these aims by society in general as well as by a few individuals selected upon an economic basis; and he also showed the need for social hygiene as well as for individual health, "for social aesthetics, social self-control, and social ethics as well as for individual artists, individual self-control, and personal morals, the value of vocational responsiveness and idealism as well as of vocational efficiency, and the superiority of organized social service inspired by group loyalty over egocentric social service inspired by individual impulse and ambition."

7. *The derivation of objectives by activity analysis.* The derivation of the objectives of education by a detailed analysis of the activities required by contemporary society is examplified by the work of Bobbitt and Charters. This procedure in the determination of objectives looks rather to the needs for certain item of knowledge, skill, and attitudes, in everyday life than to the assembled bodies of traditional subject matter. Among these needs are found many specific types of objectives which can be classified into more general types. Bobbitt, for example, finds that ten general objectives subsume the specific objectives which he has discovered. These ten objectives are :

1. Language activities or social intercommunication.
2. Health activities.
3. Citizenship activities.
4. General social activities.
5. Spare-time activities.
6. Keeping one's self mentally fit.
7. Religious activities.
8. Parental activities.
9. Unspecialized or nonvocational practical activities.
10. Vocational activities.

Unlike the general objectives of earlier philosophers of education, these objectives grow out of the hundreds of specific objectives which are to be employed in the application of these ten larger objectives. Earlier philosophers, it is true, analyzed society, but they failed to recognize the need for more than a general view of society. Also in contrast with such a general approach, Charters has employed investigators to engage in occupations for the purpose of determining the details of abilities needed by those occupations.

When this method is used in such a manner as to indicate in detail the demands which are to be made upon the products of the school and the possibilities for further developments in occupational and nonoccupational activities, and when all this material is interpreted from the sociological point of view, this method seems to bear a close analogy to that of the manufacturer who, before deciding upon what and how much to produce, first surveys carefully the marketing conditions for his commodity. In thus canvassing each important life activity, one who follows this method closely resembles the biologist who collects and analyzes one after another of the members of each important biological category. Another elaboration of this procedure in the case of the social studies is found in the work of Rugg and Hockett. This elaboration consists of a comprehensive examination of society through the writings of specialists

—frontier thinkers—in the major activities of human life and in children's interests and capacities.

The fact that one may, by this plan, discover a multitude of important gross activities which can be analyzed into an even greater multitude of specific activities has been a source of grave annoyance to many educators. Owing to a lack either of careful attention to the real character of these specific objectives or else of the ability to classify data as all scientists have classified their own data, these educators are disturbed lest major objectives be lost among minor specific objectives. Surely this situation must be full of humor to one who has followed the history of sciencel. Imagine, for example, Linnaeus in an analogous situation. Would he have decided, since there was such a multitude of uhnumbered and unclassified plant specimens, that distinctions between plants were, after all, of no consequence ? As a matter of fact, science has not progressed by becoming disturbed in the presence of facts, whcther few or many, whether neatly classified or in an apparently hopeless jumble. Instead, science has even welcomed the discovery of elements. It matters not one white whether the field of a scientist is that of botany or that of education, he must at times avail himself of the power to magnify, study, classify, and interpret small, significant matters.

The foregoing survey of procedures of deriving educational objectives discloses seven approaches to the matter :

(1) by way of an ideal form of society—the procedure of Plato;

(2) by way of generally recognized good character—the procedure of Erasmus;

(3) by way of one class of individuals—the procedure of Castiglione;

(4) by way of the nature of children—the procedure of Rousseau;

(5) by way of a certain branch of knowledge—the procedure of Spencer;

(6) by way of sociological values—the procedure of Small and Smith;

(7) by way of activity analysis—the procedure of Bobbitt, Charters, and Rugg and Hockett.

It is, of course, to be understood that none of these philosophers of education have worked upon the sole basis of the procedure attributed to them. Although many of them have employed more than one of the seven bases, they can, nevertheless, be fairly characterized as exhibiting a predominant tendency, respectively, to employ the procedures named.

To one who seeks a procedure for deriving the educational objectives of a democracy, the shortcomings of certain procedures indicate the need for an eclectic policy. No one should, like Plato, pursue an ideal policy for his state so far as to lose sight of the immediate practical needs of the state and her people; still, one may at times cast a wistful eye towards conditions which are far different from these about one.

One should not, like Erasmus, be content with a general analysis of society and derive therefrom only such aims as are so general that they neither specify nor demand certain entities; still, the highly analytical specialist must not forget that a superabundance of trees sometimes obscures a greater vision of the forest as a whole.

One should not, like Castiglione, confine one's objectives to the needs of a certain stratum of society; still, it should be be recorded that this writer did one thing very well for his times

One should not, like Rousseau, attempt too largely to derive objectives from the nature of the person to be educated; still, there is hardly a department of knowledge which either has been or could profitably be recorganized with a view to meeting Rousseau's demands.

One should not, like Spencer, be too deferential toward a given branch of knowledge; still, one must, at times, champion with the partisan's zeal a subject which organized societies of teachers ignore.

Out of the seven procedures for deriving educational objectives, there have come three principal types of objectives. First, there are general objectives like those of Erasmus which are integrated by an unanalyzed, alleged greatest good. Second there are cardinal objectives like those of Spencer which grow out of a very general analysis of human life. Third, there are hierarchies of aims like those of Bobbitt and Charters which grow out of an analysis of human life into specific activities.

These three types of objectives are, as has already been shown, the direct out-growth of different approaches to an analysis of human life. The first and second of these types of objectives have been employed in behalf of theological views, encyclopedism, general utilitarianism, and other special or general postulates. Such objectives are, therefore, to education as the philosophical postulates of ancient scientists are to science. But science no longer opens an investigation by setting up an alleged "essence" of the object to be investigated; instead science looks to the object itself to discover its character. True it is, that science adopts hypotheses as guides and then proceeds to an evaluation of them in terms of the data derived from an investigation. But if the hypotheses disagree with or fail to embrace the findings of observation and experimentation, the hypotheses are discarded or enlarged. By following this practice for four hundred years, science has discovered and systematized more than was accomplished in the preceding four thousand years.

Education can profit by the example of science. By adopting the pattern of science, education need not be deprived of the guidance of any fundamental principles which point out the goal or goals of human existence. But education must not permit such goals to blind students to the necessity of analyzing life realistically and at first-hand. If after such an analysis the data obtained can be systematized into hierarchies and subsumed by such terms as Bobbitt uses, the data can them be readily employed in formulating practical objectives.

Education must abandon the practice, long obsolete in science, of relying soley upon easily found traditional values as guides in the educational process. Like scientific progress in general, educational progress grows out of experimental study combined with sound principles of scientific procedure. That is a science of education can develop only from (1) analytical and accurate observations of the elements which are related to education, (2) logical formulation of the results of such observations, and (3) interpretation and integration of the results so as to show the meaning and significance of such formulations of results. This scientific procedure opens to educational investigation the method of other sciences and, in the process of interpreting and integrating the results of investigation, makes use of all valuable philosophy of education.

In short, the modern philosopher of education must envisage society, men's activities, human interests, human capacities, growing departments of knowledge, and facilities for guiding adolescents toward the world of modern man. As a result of their attempts so to view modern life, contemporary students have already revealed educational problems which cry out for such perseverance, subtlety, intensity of effort, and command of investigative resources as can be found only in the most heroic professional efforts of technicians.

Here are required soundness of logic, breadth of experience, and thorough investigations of society, schools, and subject matter. When this program is followed, the derivation of objectives will consist of :

1. an investigation of human society which is conducted specifically and comprehensively enough to cover definitely all important aspects of society ;

2. a classification of the results of such an investigation so as to facilitate thought about and discussion of them ; and

3. interpretation of these results in terms of the philosophy of human life, subject matter, and all the educactional facilities required for the attainment of the objectives so derived. Only by following such a program can curriculum makers derive adequate educational objectives.

A Comprehnensive formulation of objectives of education

Up to this point, our survey of the objeceives of education has shown that values can be or have been derived by following any of the seven procedures which have been discussed. Fundamental reasons require, however, that certain of these procedures be abandoned and that certain others be employed as far as present-day knowledge of human society will permit. That is, if the discussions of the methodology of deriving objectives are valid, further progress in the derivation of objectives can be made only by analysis of society. Such analysis can be made with reference to social activities and individual capacities, tendencies, and interests. The analyses which have already been made of these activities and conditions, insofar as they influence objective, will, therefore, be eanvassed.

1. *Analyses of social activities.* Activities which have social significance have been analyzed from five fairly distinct points of view. Some of these analyses have been attempted with reference to society as a whole, others with reference only to certain communities or occupations.

(*a*) Analysis of Social Activities with Special Reference to Certain Communities. Two surverys conducted by the United States Bureau of Education illustrate analyses of social activities with special reference to certain communities. The Elyria survey was conducted so as to discover (1) the occupations of parents of children in the Elyria high school, (2) the occupations which the pupils of that school plan to follow and the schools which they expect to enter, (3) the occupations pursued by older brothers and sisters of the pupils then in school, and (4) general industrial, civic, and recreational conditions of the city. The Wilmington survey included a somewhat more detailed analysis of the local industries. The special occupational needs of workers were obtained in statements from the workers and employers in certain industries. It appeared from the statements of workers that :

> more drill in the common brancher is desired for the boy before he leaves school and after he begins working at his trade both as apprentice and journeyman. Drafting and blueprint and plan-reading are demanded by a large number of the workers. Many other courses are suggested. Sanitation, cleanliness, and courtesy are suggested by several. A study of the industries and practical shopwork along a number of lines are suggested.

The suggestions obtained from employers closely resemble those obtained from the workers. With this information in mind, the surveyors next analyzed the existing outline of objectives of the school courses with a view to relating the courses more closely "to the life and experiences of the childern".

(*b*) Analysis of Social Activities with Reference to the Major Lines of Human Experience. Bobbitt, who has analyzed social activities with reference to the major lines of human experience, begins by analyzing and conditions, then proceeds to group the results into the broad range of experience within the ten large units previously named, and next breaks these units into smaller ones. This process of analyzing, dividing, and subdividing is continued until the data of experience are reduced to manageable specific items.

This procedure is adopted with the assumption that the term health activities, for example, represents too gross and unwieldy a portion of experience for use in curriculum planning. To say merely that health should be an objective of education is analogous to a traveler's saying, if he wishes to go to Waco, that Texas is his objective. Such a traveler may by chance arrive at El Paso and then be directed therefrom; he may even by chance arrive at San Marcos. In any given case, however; the traveler who is so indefinite in his itinerary is unlikely to be economical or efficient - a more efficient traveler would limit his objective and would also chart definitely a route thereto. Likewise, if health is desired one must not merely wave one's arms twelve times a day, but instead must chart definitely one's route to health by way, according to Bobbitt, of thirty-nine objectives of physical education, forty-two guiding principles, and an unnumbered throng of pupil activities and experiences of which twelve are catalogued.

The derivation of these guide posts to health education were derived from an analysis of the activities, habits, and standards of physical behavior (1) of men and women who have been preeminent in their development and maintenance of a desirable physical condition, and (2) of persons who exhibit physical weakness, defects, and ailments. From these analyses of successes and failures, Bobbitt derives health objectives which he states in terms of the following abilities :

1. The controlling of one's dietary so that one's food contributes in maximum measure to physical well-being
2. The keeping of one's body properly oxygenated
3. The utilizing of physical exercise as a lifelong means of maintaining physical vitality.

The relation of these specific objectives to the curriculcm is clear : adequate physical education consists of developing correctly through appropriate physical activities and experiences. For example, this objective includes training in the right kinds of food activities during the growing years. As the ultimate performance of these correct food activities must be self-directed, it is necessary that the training for their performance consist as completely as possible of impressive activities which will lead to permanent and satisfying habits. As food habits are variable and complex, the individual needs also technical information about foods. Three constituents of training—habits, attitudes, and technical information—enter, therefore, into the statement of this health objective. The same fundamental constitituents are required for all other health objectives.

This program which demands training in the classroom and everywhere else in the community demands changes from the usual activities of physical education, A platform of guiding principles and assumptions is, therefore, formulated : training in physical activities is necessary for every-one; children have a long period of infancy in order that they may play; to become permanent, training activities must be enjoyable; the development of permanent habits is facilitated by activities and conditions similar to those habits which should operate in later life; and extensive reading of gripping materials will aid in the adequate understanding and visualizing of the conditions of healthful living.

Furthermore, Bobbitt continues, there should probably be separate pupil activities planned for each separate health objective. As a beginning of such planning, general types of activities are suggested : the observation of examples—directly and by readings and pictures of desirable physical activities and qualities; the analysis of his own health conditions as a basis for individual improvement: and opportunity for a continuance of desirable habits. Finally, after the formulation of general types of pupil activity has been completed, the objectives are to be taken one by one and reduced to specific activities. A similar procedure is to be followed in the formulation of the specific objectives of each of the other nine major lines of experience and provision made for each objective in pupil activities.

(*c*) Analysis of Social Activities with Reference to Certain Institutional Organizations. The value of local institutional analyses in curriculum planning is emphasized in reports of such analyses as those of Lull. By the term 'institutions,' Lull refers to typical local business organizations, factories, public service companies, civic organizations, and so forth. The uses which are to be made of such analyses are tentatively stated as follows :

1. To develop and "round out" the experience gained by the pupils in their community contacts and participations.

2. To furnish a basis for the pupil's point of departure into the more remote experiences to be gained from the curriculum.

3. To give a practical answer to the question, "What ought the pupils of the junior high school to know about the community in which they live ?"

4. To furnish the groundwork of experience necessary in the development of citizenship.

5. To furnish the information requisite for vocational guidance.

6. To furnish materials essential to the attainment of other objectives, such as health efficienty, leisure time efficiency, moral efficiency, home-making efficiency, etc.

It is recognized that such analyses will not indicate the entire program of studies of schools and that three other limitations condition the usefulness of this procedure :

1. the classes of institutions representions in the community,

2. the objectives set for the entire curriculum,

3. the adaptability of the institutional materials to the abilities of the pupils.

Although, the analyses which Lull reports were undertaken primarily to discover usable items of instructional content, the availability of the results of such analyses has an obvious relation to the formulation of specific objectives, provided, of course, that any of the pupils are likely either to live permanently in the community or to be employed in any of the institutions analyzed. For example, an analysis of a number and building materials company reveals facts under the following heads :

Purpose of the business.
Origin and development of the business.
Extent and kinds of service rendered by the business.
Financing the business.
The bookkeeping system.
Legal knowledge required by the business.
The demand for labor in the business.
Sources of labor supply in this business.
Different types of jobs in this business.
Training needed for the different types of work.
Standard of health required of an employe.
Personnel of employes.

When these results are itemized and appropriate matter is placed in the course of study, specific objectives such as acquaintance with local industries and welfare associations are provided for. For example, Analysis No. 5 dealt with an automobile sales agency and garage; the appropriate items of this analysis are used for purposes of illustration and application in seven subjects which the pupils are pursuing in Grade VII.

d. Analysis of Social Activities Occupations. If detailed lists of duties of workers in various occupations were catalogued together with the proficiency demanded of workers in each task, such lists could be used in the formulation of the objectives of vocational courses leading to those occupations. A valuable analysis by Charters of secretarial duties and traits provides the beginning of such lists. Fortunately for the timid persons who fear that a large number of specific objectives will upset their somewhat unstable skills, Charters explains the possible uses of his long lists : the materials may be of use, he believes, to employers, secretaries, vocational counsellors, and to teachers.

The commercial teacher will find this material of use in several ways:

1. The traits serve as standards of performance to be demanded of the students. For instance, since accuracy is so important it is obvious that teachers must demand accuracy in everything that the student does. In like manner, they must see that the student develops dependability in all assignments that are made to her, and they must demand the use of intelligence in such tasks and situations as clearly call for this trait. It is definitely the duty of expert teachers to determine specifically what traits need to be considered in connection with each duty that is performed, and to so train the pupils by holding them to the proper standards that the trait will actually be developed in connection with those duties.

2. The sympathetic commercial teacher can make a direct attack upon the traits by leading the students to see their importance and by helping them to develop those traits in which they are weak. For instance, he may strongly emphasize the importance of dependability and through these trait-actions and others, help the pupil to develop dependability. Obviously, it would be necessary for the careful teacher to add to the professional trait-actions which we have listed, those which are found as an expression of the trait in the school environment.

It cannot be too strongly urged upon commercial teachers that the success of their students is as dependant upon traits of personality as upon efficiency in technical performance. Many excellent students in typewriting, stenography, bookkeeping, and filing, make egregious failure as stenographers and secretaries because of the lack of certain traits which are necessary in the position. Personality is of so mueh importance that its development cannot

> be left to chance, and it responds with such reasonable ease to treatment that the development of secretarial traits ought to be included in the curriculum of secretarial schools, both by indirect attack through all duties performed, and by direct attack upon specific weaknesses which are discovered.

Charters made his analysis of secretarial duties and traits by employing three investigators to interview one hundred twenty-five expert secretaries employed by men representing the major professions and types of business. These secretaries were asked a prepared list of questions, and, as a result of this inquiry, 871 duties of such workers were catalogued. A list of the 871 duties was then printed and sent to 1845 secretaries whose names had previously been obtained from the schools of which they were graduates. Seven hundred fifteen of the responses to this questionnaire were in such form as to admit of tabulation.

> Compilation revealed 871 differentiated duties. The median number of duties performed by an individual was about 130, with three-fourths of the secretaries performing less than 210 duties each . .The duties from each occupation and from all occupations together were next ranked in order of frequency of citation. These 871 duties arranged in order of frequency were then divided into ten groups, each group containing about 87 duties. In the third place, the duties were divided roughly into twelve classes, according to the type of duty—mailing duties; taking dictation; transcription; typewriting; filing; duties connected with filing, indexing, etc.; telephones, etc.; editorial duties; duties involved in meeting and handling people, and financial, bookkeeping duties; clerical duties, and miscellaneous duties and personal services for employer. Some of these duties are, of course, those which do not require especial skill and can be learned during service; other duties require preparatory training. It was found that the amount of training which

the secretaries had received was not so good an index of the character of work required of them as was the kind of job. High schools can, therefore, use the Charters list as a guide in curriculum planning as well as can business colleges or university schools of commerce. Although variations in the relative frequencies of citations of duties were found among the fifteen occupational classes investigated, there were very few variations in the highest ten per cent of frequencies.

Besides the names of specific duties which Charters catalogued, he found, by interviewing employers, forty-seven traits which are believed to accompany success in secretarial work. While all the forty-seven traits are important, "the traits which head the list are clearly those which distinguish the successful secretaries. Among these, accuracy is given first place, and of almost equal value are the traits of responsibleness, dependability, and intelligence. The mere naming of such traits as these and others like initiative, judgment, tact, personal pleasantness, and personal appearance, gives us a picture of the expert secretary, who stands at the head of her profession.

Insofar as traits are acquired by academic activities, they may be regarded as curriculum objectives. By keeping in close touch with such analyses as this as they are reported from time to time, directors of vocational education "Can elevate the acquirement of vocational skill from the plane of wasteful undirecting learning to that of effective directed activity which is the ideal of the modern demand for the scientific study of education."

e. Analysis of Social Activities with Reference to Certain Subjects of the Curriculum. The social objectives of high-school English as held by teachers of that subject have been collected by Pendleton. His investigation consisted of (1) the cataloguing of the objectives which have recently been stated by teachers as the desirable outcomes—668 sources besides all the articles published in eleven important education periodicals in five years;

(2) a verification of these aims by checking them against the linguistic abilities of 2759 mature leaders in many communities; and (3) an appraisal according to their relative importance by eighty instructors in English of established competency. As a result of this survey, 1581 objectives were found. As Pendleton explains in discussing his procedure,

> in the accumulating and the appraising of the goals of school English, the investigation depends upon personal judgments. It does not set up an impersonal, objective scheme for ascertaining the facts. The judgments are, however, not mere *obiter dicta*, but the careful utterances of expert teachers representative of those whose influence is today formative regarding school English. The decisions are subjected to a scrutiny which shows them worthy of respect. Furthermore, the check afforded by the study of linguistic abilities of adults operates toward securing objective validity for the catalogue. The study, therefore, does not present merely arbitrary, unverified opinions. Nevertheless, it does not assume to effect an establishment of the ideal, wholly objective social goals for instruction in English which possibly will some day be determined by an exhaustive examination of society itself, rather than of the usages and ideals of teachers.

Several other limitations of the inquiry are also important to note. First, it deals with social outcomes only. These are the linguistic and quasi-linguistic abilities in vernacular intercourse, spoken and written, which are deemed worth while in the world of business and pleasure, beyond the school, into which boys and girls will ultimately go. There are other, non-social endeavors prevailing in some schools—such as, for instance, satisfaction of formal college-entrance, or technical trade, requirements—with which this investigation is not concerned.

The study is also strictly limited to the typical public school, elementary and high. It does not aim to include the special endeavors prevalent in private or parochial schools, in technical institutions, or in colleges.

Furthermore, it does not undertake to determine just where in the school course (that is, in what grades) certain abilities shall be most directly emphasized. The specific arrangement of the curriculum is quite another problem.

Nor does it assume that every objective aimed at can be quite attained during any child's institutional schooling. On the contrary, it recognizes the fact that many desirable ultimate outcomes can be only remotely approached during this short period and in the pupil's necessarily immature experience of life. But the school may accomplish at least preliminary instruction, so that the education to be had in full only in later stages of development will be delimited and, in large measure, predetermined. An objective is a goal aimed at, not necessarily a goal completely attained.

Perhaps nothing more overwhelming could be announced to a complacent superintendent of schools or teacher of English than that 1581 objectives had to be attained at some time in his pupils' linguistic experiences. It is, therefore, comforting to find that many of these objectives can be attained outside the school. Sufficient numbers of objectives are, however, left to the school and are gathered into one or another of six practical categories :

Fundamental language facts	Oral reading
Written compositions	Conversation
Silent reading (including literature)	Public speaking

Inasmuch as these objectives have already been in the minds of educators for years, the Pendleton list provides an opportunity for the scrutinizing of current practices in the light of these more of less conventional aims and of any other criteria that may be set up. The next step is that of deciding in what grades and by what activities the valid specific aims shall be set up for attainment.

A second example of analysis of social activities with reference to certain subjects of the curriculum is that of the American Classical League, which attempted first to set up and then to evaluate a list of twenty-one ultimate objectives of high-school Latin. The objectives which were derived by an examination of the literature of the subject were first evaluated means of opinions obtained in three ways :

(1) A comprehensive general questionnaire filled out by 1150 experienced secondary teachers of Latin and covering the entire field of objectives, content, and method for the secondary course as a whole.

(2) A special score card for the relative evaluation of objectives year by year filled out by over three hundred teachers in various parts of the country.

(3) A symposium on the disciplinary aims of Latin to which nearly seventy leading professors of education and psychology contributed.

On the basis of evidence secured from objective data and from analyses of opinion we have sought to answer the following questions about each objective in the list :

1. For what Latin pupils, and for what proportion of Latin pupils is this objective of value, if attained ?

2. To what extent are there elements common to the study of Latin and to the more general field or fields with which this objective is concerned ?

3. To what extent is this objective attained or attainable through the study of Latin ?

4. What content and methods are found to be most effective in attaining this objective ?

5. What constructive measures should be taken in reorganizing content and method to insure a fuller attainment of this objective ?

The objective data referred to in the passage just quoted were obtained by many collaborating investigators. The data consist of the results (1) of numerous tests of several thousand Latin and non-Latin pupils; (2) of vocabulary studies; and (3) of questionnaires to tens of thousands of students or former students of Latin and to psychologists.

After investigating and obtaining expert opinions upon the problems of Latin, the investigators formulated the objectives of Latin for four-, five-, and six-year secondary-school courses. The objectives agreed upon for a six-year course are as follows :

I. IMMEDIATE OBJECTIVES

The indispensable primary immediate objective which underlies the entire process for each year of the course is progressive development of power to read and understand Latin. This involves an increasing mastery of the elements of the language, namely, vocabulary, forms, and syntax. The relative emphasis to be attached to these elements year by year will depend upon the contribution which they may make to the ability to read and understand Latin or to the attainment of certain of the ultimate objectives. The application of this principle will be discussed in detail in the chapters on content and method.

II. ULTIMATE OBJECTIVES

The following lists give the ultimate objectives we regard as valid for each successive year of the six-year course. The relative emphasis ordinarily to be attached to these ultimate objectives is indicated by the order in which they are given.

First year

1. Increased understanding of those elements in English which are related to Latin.

2. Development of an historical and cultural background.

3. Development of correct mental habits.

4. Development of right attitudes toward social situations.

Second year

1. Increased understanding of those elements in English which are related to Latin.

2. Increased ability to read, speak, and write English.

3. Development of an historical and cultural background.

4. Development of correct mental habits.

5. Development of right attitudes toward social situations.

Third year

1. Increased understanding of those elements in English which are related to Latin.

2. Increased ability to read, speak, and write English.

3. Development of an historical and cultural background.

4. Development of correct mental habits.

5. Development of right attitudes towards social situation.

6. Increased ability to learn other foreign languages.

7. Elemantary knowledge of the simpler general principles of language structure.

Forth year

1. Increased understanding of those elements in English which are related to Latin.

2. Increased ability to read, speak, and write English.

3. Development of an historical and cultural background.

4. Development of correct mental habits.

5. Development of right attitudes toward social situations.

6. Increased ability to learn other foreign languages.

7. Elementary knowledge of the simpler general principles of language structure.

Fifth year

1. Increased ability to read, speak, and write English.

2. Development of an historical and cultural background.

3. Development of correct mental habits.

4. Increased understanding to those elements in English which are related to Latin.

5. Development of right attitudes toward social situations.

6. Development of literary appreciation.

7. Increased ability to learn other foreign languages.

Sixth year

1. Increased ability to read, speak, and write English.

2. Development of an historical and cultural background.

3. Development of correct mental habits.

4. Development of literary appreciation.

5. Development of right attitudes toward social situations.

6. Increased understanding of those elements in English which are related to Latin.

7. Improvement in the literary style of the pupil's written English.

The objectives of algebra have also been derived by the same methods as those employed in English and Latin. In addition to employing these subjective methods for discovering the objectives of algebra, Thorndike turned to the school textbooks in subjects for which algebra is alleged to be preparatory and to liberal samples of the *Encyclopedia Britannica.* It was assumed that, if algebraic skill or information is needed in the study of these books, the character of their contents would indicate that fact. Although one may not be able to show full justification for the pursuit of one subject by pointing out its value to a pupil who is to pursue other subjects of unknown or questionable worth, yet this method may not be contested so long as such other subjects actually are pursued.

The results of the investigation can be stated briefly. The canvass of forty-four high-school textbooks in social sciences, physical and biological sciences, and practical arts showed, out of a total of 98,630 linear inches of textbook material, a per cent of 2.1 of linear inches in which algebra is useful. Although Thorndike suggests possible enrichments of other subjects by means of which algebra might advantageously be more widely applied, he finds that, for the books examined, the use of algebra are chiefly as follows :

(1) The most important objective algebra should be that of teaching pupils to read statistical graphs.

(2) For use in physics, the chief objective is the mastery of the formulae, especially in "the transformation known as 'changing the subject of the formula".

(3) Physics raises also the objective ability in choosing appropriate formulae, making substitutions, and solving equations—that is, ' skill in clearing of fractions (chiefly in proportions), transposing, combining, and taking numerical square root.

(4) Chemistery raises the objective of ability to form proportions, as in problems which deal with proportion mixtures and alloy.

The same objectives—skill in the reading of graphs and formulae combined with a demand for somewhat less skill in computing formulae - are derived from the examination of the 'Encyclopedia'. In short, "(1) for utilitarian values in the first year of algebra one must pay much attention to the formula and to the statistical graph," and "(2) the student whose aptitudes and capacities will probably lead him into any one of a large number of fields of advanced (technical) study...... should have preparatory work not merely in algebra but in many other branches of mathematics to which rigorous algebra is the necessary antecedent and tool."

2. *Classification of the results of investigation of human society.* The results of the five types of investigation of human society can, of course, acquire significance only when classified and interpreted in terms of life - life as conditioned by certain communities, life as an enterprise which comprises certain major lines of experience, life as constituting the activities which, in turn, compose the child's academic experiences. Furthermore, if our classification of human activities and needs is to be comprehensive, it should be compared with other classifications of a different nature ; that is, with the classifications of speculative philosophers.

Our next problems are, therefore, first, that of classifying such results as have been obtained by the five types of analysis of human activities and, second, that of finding out whether the legitimate and real values as set up by other philosophers of education can be classified under the terms which are used by educational philosophers whose investigations of human society have just been canvassed. If, for example, it can be shown that the recent analysis of society yield results which admit of systematization, and if the somewhat more manageable terms used by Bobbitt can be interpreted so as to comprise the more general philosopher's terms, then, and only then, can the newer terms be adopted.

a. Classification of the Results Obtained by Analyses of Human Activities. Local analyses such as city or community surveys or the "institutional" analysis of Lull are attempts to discover in detail what one must encounter and indeed what one must do to be successful in a given locality or business oganization. As far as such analyses go, they show that certain vocational requirements together with other more or less specialized duties exist in a community. They show also that certain specialized duties require highly specialized skill or information, while certain more general duties require somewhat indefinite amounts of general skill and information. When this type of analysis is pressed further to find out the characteristics of specified occupations. as it has been by Charters, it reveals also a large number of traits which characterize successful workers. These traits, like the duties discovered in other local analyses, are divisible into those which are fairly specific and those which are very general, so far as the required skills and information are concerned.

Analyses which are conducted to discover the values possessed by certain bodies of knowledge show that any subject, such as English, Latin, or algebra, can make contributions of which men may profitably avail themselves in technical vocations, in unspecialized activities, in individual pastime pursuits, and so on. Some of these contributory values are very definite, as learning the uses of capital letters, periods, and important word roots; other contributory values are very general—in some cases even indefinite—such as the appreciation of approved or standard literature, the development of right attitudes toward social situations, or, the understanding of the function concept.

In other words, a subject such as English, Latin, or algebra can be shown to have outcomes which contribute to both utilitarian and inspiration values, to both general and specific situations, to both community and personal needs, and to both real and imagined situations. Furthermore, analysts believe that these diverse outcomes can be achieved in any well-conduct pursuit of these subjects.

The analyses in which human activities are viewed as a whole consider examples of both successes and failures in meeting life situations. Such analyses show that the most successful persons are those who continue to improve after successive tentative goals are attained. They show that the efficient citizen is one whose interests are diverse, whose skills are specific and general, and whose aspirations are numerous. Such analyses admit of the formulation of objectives in terms of each specific human activity. They inculded all activities for which any branch of training or subject matter can prepare, inspire, or direct any person and also all the specific objectives of persons who employ in their activites any such training or subject matter. For example, all the 1581 objectives of English can be classified as readily as to many botanical specimens by means of the general or major objectives of Bobbitt : the ability to spell, to comprehened the meanings of common foreign words and phrases, to identify the leading English and American writers, to appraise the degree of authority with whith an author writes – these objectives, as examples, may in different individuals fall under any or all the following general objectives of Bobbitt—activities which involve language, citizenship, general social life, spare time pursuits, or vocations. Similarly, each of the objectives set up by the Classical League may, for different persons, fall under the same five general objectives, Likewise, it seems that, for purposes of classification, all objectives of education can be subsumed under the ten names of general objectives of Bobbitt.

b. Classification of the Findings of General Philosophers of Education into Ten Major Objectives. An examination of the terms used by speculative philosophers of education to denote objectives reveals these terms : intellect, knowledge, character, virtue, piety, happiness, individual or group perfection, culture, intrinsic value, instrumental value, utility, and so on. Life, one finds, is, according to philosophers in general, concerned with body, soul, intellect, morality, utility and leisure, because life is material, moral, social, and religious.

> For we assume as our fundamental principle that man is spiritually free, and yet determined by the spiritual life he has lived and is living, and by the spiritual environment in which he has lived it ; that the ultimate aim of life is, therefore, spiritual and not material ; that spiritual growth is advance in spiritual capacity both to receive and to impart spiritual strength ; that this implies that man's spiritual life is derived from, dependent on, and substained by, spiritual agencies which are supernatural in the sense that they are above and beyond the material. In brief and plain terms, that man's life is not only material but moral and social, and yet more, religious. Consequently, the theory of education we are attempting to set forth is one which assumes that the activities of life should be evaluated according to a spiritual standard which finds the heighest good of man in the perfection of his spiritual nature—in nobility of heart and mind, in reverence and awe in the contemplation of the divine perfection, in love of all this is great and good, in hearty acceptance of duty, in strenuous endeavor, in earnest longing for truth, in appreciation of beauty, in an estimate of the things of life consistent with the view that what man is far outweighs what he has, whether of material or of intellectal possessions.

As all objectives named or implied by either the speculative analysis of society or the analysts of concrete activities can be classified within the ten major objectives of education, that formulation can be agreed upon as meeting the requirements seated on page 280. This formation will, therefore, be referred to in the succeeding ehapters of this book as a representative and workable inventory of present-day objectives. In those later chapters these objectives will be treated in connection with the topics of the respective sections. The next chapter will relate these objectives to secondary-school curricula.

11

Teaching Procedures

Should Objectives and Curricula be Divorced or Integrated ?

The objectives of education must be carried into subject matter and pupil activities. Indeed, subject matter and pupil activities, as means of instruction, constitute a large division of the objectives of education. For the accepted definition of the term *objective* includes the plans for the activities to be employed in attaining values as well as the values themselves. tAccording to this accepted meaning of the term objective, here are, consequently, as many specific items of subject matter and forms of pupil activities as there are specific objectives.

Naturally, the concept of the term objective has been restricted by many practitioners. These persons have attempted to set up objectives, but have instead only set up values. Alongside these values which usually denote crude, gross aspects of life, these practitioners have arrayed subject matter indiscriminately, if not blindly. They have lived in neither the philosophical age nor the scientific age of their more penetrating and enlightened contemporaries. Groping when the light of day shone all about them, self-styled educatiors have grasped at huge masses of subject matter as a drowning grasps at floating reeds. Living in an age of science, they seek man in linguistic syntax ; or, living in an age creative literary achievement, they seek man in the dismal fragments of unordered science. The meaning of science, of literature, of art, of life itself is hidden to these complacent, though often well-meaning and industrious, pedagogues. And here lies the fault : either practice has run amuck for lack of clear thinking, or thought has proved vain for lack of the touchstones of practical life.

In order to insure concreteness of these paragraphs three types of examples should be in the reader's mind :

(1) examples of educators who have attempted to formulate objectives without an adequate survey of subject matter ;

(2) examples of educators wh , have amassed subject matter without clear objectives ; and

(3) examples of educators who have attempted to formulate either objectives or subject matter or both without an adequate acquaintance with practical life.

Of the first type of examples—educators whose values lack definiteness in subject matter – Plato and Francis Bacon are excellent instances. True it is that each of these men said much about subject matter, but it is also true that each of them discussed values and then either dismissed the values or else failed to present a comprehensive system of subject matter for the attainment of them. To this type belong, as additional examples, all teachers of English who talk of enjoyment and broad literary contacts as values and then confine their pupil to a narrow range of unpleasant readings, and all teachers who essay to instruct pupils in science and then proceed as though the textbook itself were science. All such persons fail to analyze the values which they esteem and later to provide appropriate subject matter as one of the means of attaining such values.

Of the second type of examples—educators whose subject matter lacks systematizing influence of clear objectives—thousands of present-day teachers are illustrations. Teachers who drill pupils upon mathematical formulae without giving meaning to these formulae—such teachers as one often finds in charge of secondary school classes—all these know subject matter in a limited way, but are either ignorant or indifferent. Teachers of science, literature, language, and his history often ally themselves with this group of undesirable practitioners. School administrators who allow their elementary, secondary, and cellegiate English departments to drift so far apart that pupils can only with difficulty make the transition from one school to another, or those whose elementary courses overlap seriously their secondary courses—such administrators lack definite objectives in the sense in which the term objective is here employed. The strong tendency to conduct extensive commercial courses in rural high schools illustrates still further the tendency to allow subject matter to be used as the chief guide in school planning.

Of the third type of examples—educators whose objectives or subject matter or both lack a close relationship to practical life—all Ciceronians are instances. John Sturm, despite his notable work in the extension of secondary education in Germany, must be assigned to this group because of his failure to envisage life in its relationship to curricula with such completeness as Vittorino had envisaged it.

This limitation led Sturm and hundreds of his successors in the *Gymnasien* entirely to overlook as much of secondary school subject matter as they included. The fact that such impractical persons often gain control of schools and exert a blighting influence for centuries as they did in early modern English secondary and collegiate institutions, leads one to classify these educators as the most dangerous of all. These dangerous but fortified conservatives invade all ranks of teachers. Even vocational schools are infested with them : note, for example, the utter lack of appreciation that is shown for practical matters by vocational teachers who expect the acquisition of certain simple skills to equip a pupil for secretarial work.

In contrast with the educators just described as exemplars of maladjustments of values and subject matter, there are other educators who are able to integrate values and subject matter and thus see beyond the narrow interests of partisans. Such exemplars can be found among literary humanists, scientists, educational philosophers, and school administrators. Of literary humanists whose objectives were broad and clear, Matthew Arnold and Jebb may be cited ; of scientists who saw beyond narrow partisan interests, Huxley is an illustrious example ; of educational philosophers who have thought in terms also of subject matter, John Dewey is a striking figure ; of administrators who have integrated objectives, subject matter, and practical life, W.T. Harris is a notable example.

Aristotle provides a pertinent theory which by way of analogy can be used profitably in closing this introduction to the discussion of the relationship between formulation of objectives and the curriculum. It was Aristotle's belief, as stated previously, that an occupation which lacked order or rationality was illiberal and that the pursuit of such an occupation was consequently illiberalizing. Without unduly extending Aristotle's concept of illiberal or liberal activities, one may classify subject matter and curricula as liberal and the results of such subject matter and curricula as productive of both "culture" and utility only when they are planned with the guidance of sound objectives. All values must, therefore, be canvassed, and those which are feasible for attainment in secondary schools must be systematically provided for in the formulation of objectives. Historical examples have already warned educators against a belief that either values or methods of attaining them are permanent, unchanging entities.

Educational Values and Objectives are Main Guides in Curriculum Planning

Five ways in which values and objectives guide the modern curriculum maker will be discussed in this section. It is recognized, of course, that many variants of these five ways are encountered in actual curriculum planning.

1. *How subject matter grows out of success and failures.* In the earlier discussion of Bobbitt's procedure, reference was made to the derivation of health objectives by analyzing the characteristics of various persons who exemplify both physical superiority and physical inferiority. Insofar as means to fit the ends can be found, the detailed objectives thus derived indicate definitely the character of courses in physical or health education.

A similar plan has long been used by teachers of English, who have been able in this manner to discover the future needs of pupils and then to drill them upon elements of English in which they are found to be deficient. When so used this plan consists of three steps : first, of discovering the elements of successful living by analysis of the successes and failures of any or all groups of persons ; second, of organizing into a course all the desirable elements found in the analysis ; third, of arranging the teaching materials so that pupils are tested for proficiency in each unit of content, instructed in and drilled upon any elements in which deficiencies are discovered, and finally re-tested to determine whether sufficient drill has been administered. Whenever any important aspect of life is analyzed, the results of the analysis, whether in the form of deficiencies of the inferior or the merits of the strong, indicate socially valid subject matter.

2. *How the development and enrichment of knowledge leads to new values and then to new subject matter for schools.* All departments of knowledge are in a flux. At the present time new developments are rapidly affecting physical theories, great literary achievements are numerous, social studies are being enriched, many common activities, such as home-making and agriculture, are becoming systematized, and so on. Each advancement made outside the school should, in case the

advancement affects or should affect school subject matter, be reflected by an advancement inside the school. This principle has, however, been conceded reluctantly in the case of many new forms of subject matter. As the preceding historical sections have shown, the vested interests of educators have often formed a bulwark against valuable progress in subject matter. Educators are not always the first persons to pass favorable judgment upon new bodies of knowledge.

Often, it has happened, as in the case of Dr. William Harvey's profession, that the discovery of important facts is followed by the belief that the discoverer "was crackbrained," so that "all the physitians" have turned against him. Another example is found in the "crack-brained" individual, J.R. Mayer, who discovered the law of the conservation of energy ; he had also to undergo suffering at the hands of scholars for a principle which modern schoolboys are required to learn.

After some time, however, the world becomes reconciled to each new notion or fragment of knowledge ; next, the fragment of knowledge may becomes essential in scientific thought, and then there should be a demand for an expansion of the curriculum of the school. In guiding this cycle, modern educators have been quite as prone to retard as to accelerate curriculum reconstruction and expansion.

Three hundred years ago Harvey thrust new knowledge upon an ungrateful world. A century later Defoe concluded that for many persons, a better education might have been acquired if the existing curriculum could have been discarded and a new one comprising such subject matter as that developed by Harvey, Descartes, and other modern men adopted in its stead. The struggles of each modern European language for a place in the curriculum of the respective countries is a further series of reflections upon the world at large and upon educators in particular. At the present time, however, many teachers are attempting to show the values of newly discovered items of knowledge and are attempting to incorporate them into their courses. Curriculum progress follows the adoption, by educators of the values which grow out of new discoveries of knowledge.

3. *How new subject matter grows out of the basic concepts of an age.* Many educators, including Plato, have believed that concepts could be learned by youth and so applied to the world's issues as to bring order out of chaos. For example, Rugg, in elaborating this belief, has discovered in the writings of "frontier thinkers" in the social sciences a large number of basic generalizations and concepts. This procedure apprises the investigator of advanced critical thought upon the social studies and, when combined with the other steps of Rugg's procedure, leads directly to a reorganization of subject matter with the guidance of the most enlightened counsel of the present day. Fundamentally, this procedure is the same as that employed in the physical science departments ; in these departments "frontier thinkers" are laboratory investigators whose results are winnowed and interpreted and finally adopted as subject matter for teaching. In the social sciences, the "frontier thinkers" are obliged to work in laboratories which exist wherever society exists ; the results of their work are also winnowed, interpreted, and adopted by schools.

For example, up to the present time, Rugg's program has led (1) to the discovery of some three hundred important contemporary problems, such as "the problem of determining on what bases to admit immigrants," "the problem of providing continuous employment for all," and "the problem of correlating our rail. water, and motorized transportation" ; (2) the defining of basic generalizations of the social sciences, such as the following : "the problem of food supply underlies all other problems of industrial nations," and "as hand labor gives way to machine labor, the standard of living for the general population slowly rises" ; (3) the study of "cue concepts," such as "pressure of population," "democracy," and "nationalism" ; and (4) the collecting and organization for instructional purposes, "the great movements and themes underlying the development of American life, and of the focal persons, events, and facts of time and place."

4. *How theoretical or unmeasured values influence subject matter*, Despite the implication by experts in educational measurements that whatever exists at all can be measured, there are at present certain deficiencies in the measurement program. In discussing educational objectives one has to rely in part upon philosophers' terms, which stand for somewhat intangible traits or characteristics. That is, one may adopt activity analysis as the source of most if not all educational objectives and still be confronted with such terms as *responsibility*, *tact*, *judgment*, and *accuracy*. Indeed, it is only when one assumes that an activity requires solely automatic and mechanical responses that, in conducting activity analysis, one can state one's results in terms which stand for measurable entities. That is, the traits which distinguish successful secretaries were found by Charters to be accuracy, responsibleness, dependability, intelligence, initiative, judgment, and tact. Without debating the question as to whether attainments in these traits can ever be measured, one may assert that these terms now stand for qualities which have not yet been isolated sufficiently to make them readily measura ble.

One is, therefore, on the speculative philosopher's territory if one attempts to construct a curriculum to provide training in the traits which distinguish successful workers. The traits which are revealed by modern activity analyses are similar in general character to those which Isocrates, Plato, and Erasmus derived by their analyses of life. Only after further analyses of the operation of these traits and the various forms of content employed by one who possesses them have been made, can these traits become definite guides in formulating curricula. Until that time arrives, curriculum makers may assume either that since traditional subject matter has been pursued by many persons who possess these traits, the subject matter must have engendered these qualities, or that these traits develop somewhat independently of the subject matter by which one is nurtured. In either case, the matter will be settled by speculation and interpretation and not by strictly objective data.

The importance of the traits in question leaves no choice about facing the issues involved, and the lack of knowledge about the traits makes speculation necessary. These two conditions, the importance of the traits and present-day ignorance about them, may lead one to justify any subject of a curriculum; and no one else can prove, save by equally speculative arguments, that the first person is incorrect. If, however, the consideration of these traits leads the curriculum maker into speculative philosophy, it may be urged that he seek counsel in his speculation from experts in this matter.

This will lead him to consider the principles of Aristotle, Herbart, and Arnold (1) that well-organized subject matter is an essential of a good curriculum, (2) that subject matter should be selected and organized so as to facilitate desirable self-activity of the pupil, and (3) that both literary and scientific studies are necessary parts of a complete education, and so on. It may be suggested that friends of any of the traditional subjects which have fared ill in their attempt to stand upon objective grounds now have recourse to arguments drawn from the most objective procedures ever used in curriculum construction.

5. *How preparatory values influence subject matter*. Prerequisites for certain subjects or curricula have existed since Plato's time. The implication of these requirements has been that certain subject matter must have been mastered by a student in order to equip him for the specific tasks of an advanced subject. It is alleged, however, that many preparatory values are only apparent. It appears, therefore, that the curriculum maker can organize sequences of subjects with reference to preparatory values only after he has analyzed each subject in the sequence. Such an analysis should reveal the specific skill and knowledge required by an advanced subject, and perhaps, as in Charters' activity analysis, the traits which accompany the the successful pursuit of advanced subjects.

Thorndike's analysis of algebra indicates that such an analysis has not generally been made in the planning of sequences of subjects. He found instead that possible preparatory values of elementary subjects are overlooked in the planning of advanced subjects, so that possible values are missed, and also that elementary subjects sometimes lack the type of enrichment which is needed to ensure their having preparatory values for certain later studies. That is, an elementary and prerequisite subject can be so pursued as to yield little preparatory value for an advanced subject. Thorndike's findings indicate that there should be not only extraschool activity analyses to find out what subjects should be pursued in schools, but that analyses should also be conducted to show what items should compose elementary subjects in order to provide preparatory training for pupils who are to pursue advanced courses.

The attainment of educational objectives as a measure of curriculum values

Curricula are judged mainly in terms of the attainment of educational objectives. When objectives are attained through the agency of curricula and curricular activities, one or more of the four following types of contacts can be designated as the generator of desirable results. First, contact with subject matter; this type of contact implies only the subject matter to be presented in some fashion to pupils. As far as this contact is sufficient, any teacher or any book in a given field may present any subject matter within a desirable field and achieve desirable results. Second, effective contact with subject matter; this type implies that subject matter must be presented in certain ways in order to attain objectives. Third, contact with teachers; this type of contact implies that the teacher's equipment may be an effective factor of the teaching-learning process. Fourth, contact with the social life of the community of pupils, this type of contact emphasizes the inspiration and reinforcement received by each pupil from the other pupils of his group. Since the actual curriculum which a pupil masters is the only effective curriculum for him, and since the effectiveness of a curriculum may depend largely upon the type of contacts employed during the learning process, the selection and organization of subject matter with reference to these contacts is a fundamental curriculum problem.

Although one can seldom discover even by diligent investigation, the extent to which each type of contact has been effective in a given curriculum or subject, one can discover the effects of certain types of emphasis upon the attainment of objectives. Some of the investigations of pupils' attainments show only that the types of contacts employed were inadequate, while others show that the attainments which follow certain miscellaneous contacts are sometimes adequate. A few samples of the results of inquiry into the effectiveness of subject matter will be reviewed in the following paragraphs.

1. *Investigations of attainments in certain subjects.* Crow conducted an investigation in which he evaluated English literature in terms of the objectives of the course in literature. The objectives which Crow employed as criteria were derived from a canvass of authorities on the teaching of literature and are as follows :

(1) to "interest and entertain the pupil in his English literature reading and study so that he will form the purpose and habit of reading books of a like high type during his leisure time";

(2) to "inspire the pupil with high ideals of character, loyalty, love, service, etc., which, as purposes and standards, ought to give needed direction and control to his life";

(3) to "give the pupil an appreciation of the classics as works of art through emphasizing elements of beauty in both thought and form of expression":

(4) to "lead the pupil to recognize the permanent value of books." Crow proceeded in his evaluation by obtaining the judgments of 1999 juniors and seniors of twenty-nine high schools upon literature which they had read.

As a measure of the attainment of each of the four objectives, pupils were requested to rate each literary selection upon a seven-point scale, ranging from −3 to +3. By obtaining in this way the "educational record" of each of seventy-four literary selections, Crow was able to judge its relative value in attaining each objective; its value for girls and for boys; its effectiveness when studied either in class or out of class; the effect of its relative difficulty and the relation of pupils' academic expectations to its effectiveness. Table VI shows for each of the four objectives the six selections which stand highest and those which stand lowest.

This table can be used to indicate the character of Crow's results in regard to the relevant variables which he studies. The relative values of different selections for attaining each objective indicate, for example, that as presented in schools, Chaucer's *Prologue* is one of the poorest choices possible, and that, for three objectives, Van Dyke's *The Story of the Other Wise Man* is one of the best choices which teachers could make.

TABLE VI

The Literary Selections which Stand Highest and those which Stand Lowest in Pupiles' Judgments

1. As to leisure time value

a. Selections Which Stand Highest

Daddy Long-Legs	The Call of the Wild
Freckles	The Virginian
The Crisis	Little Women

b. Selections Which Stand Lowest

Emerson's Essays	Macaulay's Life of Johnson
Chaucer's Prologue	Bunker Hill Oration
Bunke's Conciliation	Il Penseroso

2. As to moral value

a. Selections Which Stand Highest

The Story of the Other Wise Man	Little Women
Helen Keller's Story of My Life	Peter Stirling
The Man without a Country	The Crisis

b. Selections Which Stand Lowest

Chaucer's Prologue	Twice-Told Tales
Rip Van Winkle	Jungle Books
The Odyssey	Poe's Tales and Poems

3. As to aesthetic value

a. Selections Which Stand Highest

The Story of the Other Wise Man	Thanatopsis
Evangeline	L'Allegro
To a Skylark	The Chambered Nautilus

b. Selections Which Stand Lowest

Dr. Jekyll and Mr. Hyde	Macaulay's Life of Johnson
Rip Van Winkle	Twice-Told Tales
De Coverley Papers	Chaucer's Prologue

4. As to permanent value

a. Selections Which Stand Highest

The Story of the Other Wise Man	Freckles
Helen Keller's Story of My Life	Ben Hur
Little Women	The Crisis

b. Selections Which Stand Lowest

Dr. Jekyll and Mr. Hyde	Macaulay's Life of Johnson
Rip Van Winkle	Twice-Told Tales
De Coverley Papers	Chaucer's Prologue

The relative values for either boys or girls were found to be much alike save in the case of the aesthetic objective. Girls were found, however, to read more extensively into these selections and to rate them higher than do boys. It was found that such selections as *The Call of the Wild*, *The Last of the Mohicans*, and the *Bunker Hill Oration* appeal more to boys than to girls, while the reverse is true of *Little Women*. *The Little Minister*, *The Bluebird*, and *Enoch Arden*. For certain selections, reading outside the class gave better results for leisure time values than did class study, while for other selections class study was found more beneficial Selections which produced better results by cursory reading are *Poe's Tales and Poems*. *The Man Without a Country*, *Lamb's Tales*, *The Princess*, *Midsummer Night's Dream*, *Burns' Poems*, and *Twice-Told Tales*. Selections which were more beneficial when studied in class are *A Tale of Two Cities*, *Silas Marner*, *Ivanhoe*, *Evangeline*, *Enouch Arden*, *The Courtship of Miles Standish*, *The Last of the Mohicans*, *The Lady of the Lake*, *The Vicar of Wakefield*, and *Idylls of the King*.

Similar findings were obtained for extraclass reading and class study in the case of each of the other three objectives. The effect of the relative difficulties of literary selections is obvious from Table VI. Considerably higher ratings were given to the seventy-four selections by pupils who expected to go to college. Crow concludes that, "such an evaluation of each of the seventy-four classics now commonly used in our high schools ought to center attention on definite social values to be sought through English literature as a means; ought to be influential in reorganizing our present course of study in English literature; and ought to be suggestive of aims and methods of teaching which will help to realize in a fuller way the peculiar social values of each one of the classics."

Corroborative evidence for Crow's conclusions has been found by investigating literature study in Wisconsin high schools. This investigation showed, however, that the attainments of Crow's juniors and seniors in leisure time values are little if any in advance of those already achieved by freshmen and sophomores. That is, *The Call of the Wild*, *Freckles*, *Little Women*, and *Daddy Long-Legs* along with others of similar difficulty and intrinsic appeal are the outstanding favorites of pupils of Grades IX and X as well as of older pupils. The fact that in the choice of reading matter, as in the naming of the desirable values of literature the pupils of many schools show little improvement from Grade IX to Grade XII indicates that the real problem of literature study consists of establishing different kinds of contacts in literature classes. Such contacts, if they are to lead to increased attainment of values throughout the course, must be accompanied by joyous, wholesome, and instructive experiences.

Several investigators have tried to discover the extent to which pupils' contacts with Latin lead to desirable results. In Part I of the report of The Classical Investigation, the objectives of Latin are presented and the present-day attainments in each objective are canvassed. This canvass showed that the achievements of pupils vary according to the type of contacts which are provided in the study of Latin. It was disclosed that many teachers proceed as though all their pupils were expecting to pursue Latin for four or more years, while only fourteen per cent of the pupils who begin Latin actually do pursue it for even four years. It was found also that although teachers generally agree that the study of Latin should heighten one's standard of English expression, many teachers employ methods which encourage slovenly translations. While teachers that the study of Latin should lead to the development of an appreciation of literary qualities of Latin literature, many teachers emphasize almost solely the linguistic elements of Latin language, and their pupils discontinue Latin study before the literature of Rome has become intelligible to them.

Similar discrepancies were found between objectives and practices in the case of many other valves which are believed to grow out of the study of Latin; the use of English derivatives as an aid in the study of Latin, although almost universally favored in discussions of the teaching of Latin, was found to be far from universal in practice. Parlleling this neglect of derivative study, was the failure of Latin pupils of a given initial ability to show outstanding superiority to non-Latin pupils of the same initial ability. The upshot of this portion of the Classical Investigation is that the

> automatic realization of the values implicit in Latin cannot be counted upon and that time must be found for the introduction of appropriate material and the use of appro-

priate methods in order to secure the satisfactory attainment of any of the ultimate objectives.

In a monograph which will be reviewed more fully in Chapter 15, Curtis found that, in general science, teachers agree upon the effectiveness of extensive reading in general science. In spite of this agreement of teachers, he found that few teachers provide for such reading. By experimentation, Curtis found, however; that carefully directed, extensive reading has demonstrable effectiveness in enabling pupils to attain the desirable objectives of general science.

These investigations of the relation between the attainment of objectives and the subject matter and contacts employed show that curricula can be evaluated in terms of the attainment of educational objectives. The investigations show, however, that one may err seriously in the employment of such a criterion for evaluating curricula. It apppears that many teachers believe that their subjects have implicit values which will automatically enter the lives of all pupils who pursue these subjects.

This obsession of teachers leads them to fail to establish proper contacts between their subjects and their pupils. Instead of choosing the best subject matter within their fields, teachers often choose much that is poor or indifferent. Instead of employing the best methods known, teachers often employ methods which cannot fail to interfere with the attainment of desirable objectives. That is, the first type of contact mentioned at the beginning of this section—any relevant subject matter with any form of procedure—is often established, and then the best of results are vainly hoped for. Instead of such systematic choice of subject matter and methods as will be illustrated later in Chapter 15, educational objectives are often forgotten and an opportunistic adoption of readily accessible subject matter and methods is made. Until that chapter is reached, one should postpone judgment upon curricula in terms of the attainment of objectives. As now organized, many schools indicate by their attainments only what can be done when there is a lack of knowledge of the relative effect of different subject matter and methods in a given field and also a lack of knowledge whether desirable values are the results of teaching or of general maturing.

Briefly, the formula of this section—the evaluation of curricula in terms of progress toward desirable objectives—can safely be applied only to schools whose curricular activities have actually been systematically planned with reference to sound objectives.

2. *Investigations of attainment in entire curricula.* The attainment of objectives as they are related to curricula can be measured in terms of entire curricula as well as in terms of individual subjects. Two investigations of this nature will be reported here.

In conducting an investigation of the junior high school, Bruner assembled representative theories about this institution and then, in view of these theories, organized the curricula and later examined the attainments of the Okmulgee, Oklahoma, junior high school. He found general agreement that (1) "the junior high school offer an enrisched curriculum, and (2) should assist in guiding pupils according to their interests, aptitudes, capacities, and abilities." Accordingly, "broadening and finding" courses were organized in different departmenes of the school. These seventh- and eighth-grade courses were organized with reference to three aims :

(1) the provision of opportunities to explore some of the important ramifications of each of the subjects pursued;

(2) to show some of the vocational possibilities which grow out of different subjects; and

(3) the presentation of material which is both worth while and pedagogically justifiable.

These courses have, within the first five years of their use, reduced the number of failures in difficult courses, they have led many pupils to engage happily and successfully in vocations discovered through the courses, and they seem to have led to an extraordinarily successful election of senior high school studies. That is, the organization of courses with reference to definite, comprehensive objectives has led to achievements which are not generally attained.

Mort and Devricks conducted an accounting of general values of the curricula of small high schools. The criteria used in this accounting are the aims of education as stated by Parker. One hundred eighty-three graduate of ten high schools were asked to rate the values of the curricular and non-curricular activities of the schools from which they had been graduated. Replies showed that the subjects as offered to and as estimated by these graduates vary widely in value for each of the five types of habits. Other judges or the same judges under different conditions might have rated each of the subjects differently.

Furthermore, the summary rating of total value should be understood as presenting only a summation of the estimated values for each type of habit; that is, the relative importance of the five types of habits is unknown. Consequently, a subject which is given a high rating in three of the habits and a low rating in the other two may or may not be as valuable as one which is given a low rating in two of the habits and a high rating in the others. So many subjective elements enter into such ratings of subjects that, like the ratings of the classics by various scholars, these judgments can be interpreted as only suggestive data. There are not at present objective results based upon a comparison of the attainments of schools whose curricula have been organized in response to detailed activity analyses with the attainments of schools whose curricula represent traditional practices.

How can Objectives be Attained ?

The curriculum maker may well ask at this point how the best formulation of objectives can be reflected in his program of studies. He may agree that a fuller and clearer statement of objectives than any now available is desirable. He may also agree that each item of subject matter should be included in a curriculum only after it has proved its value and its practicality for pupils in secondary schools. Even though one agrees to these and other implications of this and the preceding chapters, one has yet to set one's theories of education in operation : the necessity for a thoroughgoing coordination of curriculum values and practices is indicated by the investigations reviewed above.

The program for curriculum making begins with a survey of educational needs. This survey leads, by way of observation, analysis, and interpretation of life to the discovery of educational values. When these values are integrated with subject matter and pupil activities, they form the basis for educational objectives. Each subject of the program of studies must be developed upon this pattern. Obviously, then, present-day curriculum planning must be limited by the incomplete results of present-day observation, analysis, and interpretation of life and by available subject matter. Two additional limitations exist : first, curricula planned with sound objectives and justifiable subject matter must be submitted to experimental teaching before they can be generally adopted; and, second, changes in curricula must be tempered to the communities in which they are to be offered.

12

Evaluating the Outcomes of Instruction

There has been a decided tendency in recent curriculum programs to employ larger centers of organization for course of study materials than individual lessons. There larger centers are currently referred to as *units* or *units of work*. Organization of course of study materials in units implies, of course, that instructional organization will also be in units. Unit, consequently, is a term widely used in curriculum work at the present time.

LACK OF CLARITY IN USE OF THE TERM UNIT

Although the term unit is widely employed, there is a general lack of clarity or uniformity in its use. In many cases it is not defined at all and definitions that are available vary widely in fundamental respects. One element only appears to be common to most concepts. This element is the organization of instruction in such a way that the scope and time requirement are greater than in individual lessons or daily recitations. Concepts of the unit vary so widely in meaning that organization of instruction in units may imply fundamental reorganization of the curriculum or it may mean that an significant shuffling of subject matter has taken place. "The mere subdivision of a course into units," states Harap, "may have no further significanee than the subdivision of a course into sections, parts, topics, or lessons." Nor can the fundamental characteristics of a particular unit organization be determined without careful analysis of course of study materials and observation of instruction. The frequent requests of teachers and curriculum committees for titles of units indicate failure to grasp the basic concept of the particular type of unit being developed. The title of a unit indicates little if anything about its fundamental characteristics, for units involving opposite points of view and widely different content and activities may have the same title.

The result is confusion in discussion and treatment of units. Carey, Hanna, and Meriam, in preparing a list of units of work, activities and projects, found such diverse meanings of these terms that they were unable to set up generally applicable definitions by which their selection could be made. They state :

> These chaotic conditions became most obvious when the authors attempted to formulate definitions for "units of work," "activities," "projects," "themes," etc., which would serve as criteria for selecting or rejecting the materials they discovered in print. Indeed, they have found it impossible to select-and-reject .These "activities," "projects," "units of work," etc., have not yet been so defined as to command general acceptance by students of education.

Bruner points out the same condition :

> ...the term unit means different things to different writers. Units differ in form, in length, in completeness, in adaptability, in richness of suggestion, and in possibilities of integration, and express different meaning in respect to the use of content and activities.

Variations in meaning of the term unit probably account in part at least for the wide use of this basis of organizing instruction. Proponents of nearly any educational theory can find some kind of unit organization to which they can give approval. Because of this state of confusion and the popular use of the term, this chapter presents a brief analysis of various types of units.

UNITS AND SPECIAL PLANS FOR ORGANIZING INSTRUCTION

An effort is sometimes made to clarify concepts of the various types of units by identifying them with special plans for organizing instruction. Billett, for example, in dealing with the unit considers the contract plan, Dalton plan, individual instruction, laboratory plan, Morrison plan, problem method, project method, unit assignment, Winnetka plan, long unit assignment, and differentiated assignment. But after considering these plans be states that "if one sought merely to establish that no such thing exists as an orthodox problem method, differentiation of assignments, laboratory plan, system of long-unit assignments, contract plan, project method, or method of individualized instruction, be would need go no further than the literature of the field, where the evidence is written in letters so high tbat he who runs may read." Consequently, there appears to be little hope of clarifying the concept of units by identifying various types with specialized plans for organizing instruction. A more fundamental basis of classification must be sought.

CLASSIFCATION OF UNITS

The expression 'unit' implies unity or wholeness. It suggests that there is some central force or factor which binds together the particular phase of instruction to which reference is made. It is in the effectiveness of this unifying force that the made of a particular unit as a basis for organizing instruction depends. Consequently, 'source of unity' provides a basis for determining essential differences between various units.

All units may be classified under two major headings. In one case, the primary point of orientation may be a phase of the group culture or a segment of potential subject matter. The dominant purpose of the unit is to develop understanding of a particular body of content—expressed either in terms of facts to be mastered or generalizations to be understood—or of a given phase of the group culture, or of an aspect of the environment.

The point of view in approaching development of units of this general type is essentially as follows. Students in various subjects have found certain facts and principles in certain relationships to be especially significant in explaining individual and social development and life. It is assumed that these phases of potential subject matter possess inherent unity. Consequently, the source of unity for an instructional unit is to be found in relationships between items of potential subject matter.

This does not mean that in this type of unit the learner and his individual characteristics are ignored. After the unit has been selected he receives consideration. As the units are organized in form to be learned by the pupil, efforts are made to provide for individual differences. A variety of pupil activities is suggested that may achieve understanding of the unit. Means of motivation which will be especially effective with the particular group of children to be taught are canvassed. The unit is made as attractive as possible in all respects. But it is clear that the source of unity is external to the learner. The unit is a unit independent of the learner or any group of learners. Whether or not the learner profits from the unit depends on his mastery of it.

The second general group of units seek their primary point of orientation in the experience of the learner. It is held that subject matter that may possess unity for one person or group may be entirely lacking in this quality for other persons or groups. Needs, purposes, or interests are considered essential elements in determining whether a series of activities or body of content have real unity. Subject matter that possesses unity for a specialist or an adult student, it is contended, very probably cannot be brought to possess real unity for a child because of fundamental differences in interests, purposes, and needs. Consequently, units of this general type find their source of unity in the learner and the primary point of references the experience of the learner.

It does not follow, as is sometimes concluded, that subject matter is considered a non-essential in units of this type. It is recognized that a unit cannot be developed without subject matter and that the general significance and variety of subject matter required by a unit conditions materially the value of the unit. However, the initial point of orientation and the source of unity is sought in the experience of the learner and subject matter is selected to help realize ends the individual wishes to reach.

Examination of definitions of units shows how concepts of units tend to divide under these major headings. Consider the following definitions and notice the differences in emphasis on the environment, group culture, generalizations, and subject matter, on the one hand ; and child experience, interest and activities, on the other.

A unit is any division of subject matter, large or small, that, when mastered, gives an insight into, an appreciation of, or a mastery over, some aspect of life.

What is a teaching unit ? It is a meaningful body of subject matter so organized with appropriate learning activities as to lead to the mastery of a definite major understanding.

(A unit is) a comprehensive and significant aspect of the environment, of an organized science, of an art, or of conduct, which being learned results in adaptation in personality.

.. a unit is so organized that everything that is included in the way of content, the organization itself, and the method of presenting it to the class is for the purpose of making it possible for the child to grasp the big understanding or theme that is back of it.

Units of work...means the larger learning situations which will draw upon all phases of experience and make use of all kinds of subject matter.

By a unit of work we mean the various experiences and activities of a grade which center around some one interest.

A unit of work is a series of worth-while experience bound together around some central theme of child interest.

...a unit of work is a complete experience based upon a meaningful situation in child or adult life. The unit is a fusion of mental, emotional, and sensory experience; it proceeds in a physical and social setting that resembles life, as far as possible; and it is directed toward the accomplishment of a goal that results in some imporvement in life.

The unit of living has been variously called an activity, a complete act, and a unit of work. It seems more logical to use the term "unit of conduct" or "unit of life"... The unit of life or the unit of conduct, while it suggests that separateness of a part from its whole, at the same time provides for the notion of wholeness and coherence which is suggested by the term unit.

If these definitions of units are classified under the general headings described heretofore, it will be noted that those under the same heading emphasize somewhat different points of unity. This provides the basis for a more specific classification.

There are three kinds of relationships between the facts and principles in a given body of content which may be emphasized more specifically as sources of unity for subject matter units. Likewise there are three sources of unity for units that may be classified as experience units. These are shown in the following outline. Each is described in the succeeding discussion.

Types of Units

I. Subject Matter

   A. Topical unit
   B. Generalization unit
   C. Unit based on significant aspect of environment or culture

II. Experience
   A. Unit based on center of interest
   B. Unit based on pupil purpose
   C. Unit based on pupil need

TOPICAL UNIT

This type of unit differs only in degree from the customary topical organization of subject matter. Topics as frequently developed are short and more or less choppy. In marking a topical unit topics are simply broadened to cover a larager area than previously. The same sequential relationship is maintained between facts and the same point of view is held toward the learner. Frequently, the principal difference is that what previously might have been called a chapter or part is renamed a unit.

Two questions are raised by this type of unit. First, is the source of unity upon which the unit rests fundamental? Second, does the unit involve a significant reorganization of instruction? The answer to the first question will depend upon one's viewpoint concerning the importance of logically organized subject matter. If subject matter is considered an adequate basis of instructional organization, then the topical unit will be considered sound. If considered inadequate, the topical unit will be considered unsound. French clearly brings out the issue in a discussion of units.

> In what way will they (the students) now or in the future realize that failure in this unit made a real difference? How will society be recompensed by those who did succeed? What penalty will society pay because some were unable to master this unit? The answer is that the unit has none of these things in mind—it isn't intended to make any difference. The purpose of the unit is to teach pupils some things about botany that are needed by those who study more botany. Anything else learned during the study of the unit was purely accidental concomitant learning unconsciously included by the teacher and untes-

ted at the end of the study. Now we come to the crux of the issue. Is secondary education to be devoted to a study of units written for the purpose of getting students ready to study more units of that subject, or is secondary education to be a period in which adolescents undergo selected experiences which contribute to understandings and attitudes, skill and abilities of use and value in superior living under the conditions which a complexly organized social structure lays upon us all ?

Considering the second point, it is obvious that topical organization differs in no important way from the usual organization of instruction. Texts and courses of study are simply divided into units instead of chapters or parts. Many illustrations of this type of unit development may be found. For example, the following are typical of units in arithmentic :

Unit I—Learning More about Addition and Subtraction
Unit II—Learning More about Multiplication and Division
Unit III—Learning to Find Parts of a Nunmber
Unit IV—Learning to Use the Common Measure
Unit V—Learning to Multiply by Two and Three-Figure Numbers
Unit VI—Learning More about Solving Problems
Unit VII—Learning to Divide by a Two-Figure Number
Unit VIII—Learning More about Long Division
Unit IX—Learning More about Fractions
Unit X—Getting Ready for the Fifth Grade

The units in geography in a sixth-grade course of study follow :

Unit I—The British Isles
Unit II—France
Unit III—Germany
Unit IV—Three Small Countries
Unit V—Sdandinavia
Unit VI—Iberia

Unit VII—Italy, Switzerland, Austria

Unit VIII—Six New European Countries

Unit IX—Japn

Unit X—China

Unit XI—India

Unit XII—Southeastern Asia

Unit XIII—The Land of the Five Seas

Unit XIV—Bridge Lands of Southeastern Europe

Unit XV—Russia

Unit XVI—Eurasia

It is obvious that renaming the parts of a course of study or textbook can have no real significance except in that it meets the demand of the time for a book or course of study organized in units. When a new terminology arises, the term unit may be dropped as readily as chapter or part, since no fundamental reorganization of materials has occurred.

Unit organization on the topical basis has little if any significance. Perhaps upon occasion it does emphasize longer assignments and the need to see relationships from one recitation period to another. Even so, chapter or part or topic would seem to serve just as well. Consequently, unless the curriculum maker or textbook writer sees something more fundamental in unit organization than the concept underlying this type of unit, there appears to be no justification for departing from the customary topical organization of instruction.

GENERALIZATION UNIT

The generalization unit is organized to develop understanding of a particular generalization, principle, or law. The term "theme" is sometimes employed to designate the generalization which is selected as a basis for the unit. In developing such units, generalizations that seem to be most widely applicable in explaining contemporary life are usually selected. Content and activities are then chosen to illustrate the application of the generalization. For example, the generalization that men move from place to place in search of better living conditions might be chosen as a basis of a unit. In organizing the unit the teacher might select content from any period of the race's development which requires this generalization as a basis of explanation. Materials might be selected from the history of nomadic tribes, from the migration of people about Rome, from contemporary conditions in which various classes of labor move from place to place, and form other such sources. Materials in this was may be employed from a large number of the periods of history and from the histories of various peoples. Thus, instead of dealing with the history of a people chronologically or sequentially, the phase of their history which contributes to the particular generalization is employed in relation to similar materials in the histories of other peoples or periods.

This type of unit may be employed in any subject field. Special use has been made of it in the social studies. A social studies unit of this type involves an organization of subject matter quite different from the traditional one. Thus, history, which has tended to be organized chronologically, is recoganized completely round the basic generalization; geography, which has been organized largely by regions, likewise must be completely reorganized to develop units of this type.

On the other hand, there are some subjects in which the generalization type of organization is the traditional or logical type. For example, in physics the general tendency is to organize subject matter around basic principles or laws. Illustrative materials from all sources are brought together to demonstrate the general applicability of a particular physical law. The laws are cutomarily arranged in something of a sequential order. Consequently, organization of instruction around generalizations, principles, or laws is not a new basis of organization. It is new only in its application to the social studies.

Perhaps the contrast of this type of unit with other types of subject matter units may be made clearer if the various bases of so-called logical organization of subject matter are considered. The relationship which makes possible a logical organization of subject matter is not the same in all subject fields.

There are three types of relationships that are employed. The first is the chronological, that is, working from the beginning to the present or from the present to the past, taking up all materials in terms of their time relationships. This is the sequence traditionally used in history. The second is to work from the simple to the complex. This is employed, for example, in biology, were instruction starts with the simplest from of life and gradually approaches the most complex form. The third type is the sequence between a series of laws or principles around which the knowledge in the field is organized. This, as we have pointed out above, is the basis of organization in physics. Geometry is another subject which illustrates this type of organization.

The generalization unit, then, is in all respects subject to classification as a subject matter unit. From the standpoint of developing control of a particular subject field, the generalization unit may be quite valuable in some subjects, but very much less valuable in others. If a subject matter unit is to be employed, the extension of the generalization unit to the field of social science by curriculum makers is open to question, for an organization and sequence of subject matter is thus employed which is not considered sufficiently fundamental by subject matter specialists to be established by them. That is, it would appear that if the subject matter unit is to be employed the safest guide is to use the type of subject matter unit which subject matter specialists have indicated as establishing the most fundamental and significant relationships and sequences in the subject matter of a particular field. Consequently, the generalization unit, while being a wholly appropriate type of subject matter unit for physics, might be seriously questioned when extended to the field of history or geography.

UNIT BASED ON SIGNIFICANT ASPECT OF ENVIRONMENT OR CULTURE

The third type of subject matter unit is one which is organized around a widely significant aspect of the environment or culture. It is readily noted from observation of man's group and individual activities that there are certain aspects of the environment that are particularly significant. For example, the need for food, which forms a point of confluence for many activities, makes aspects of the environment, such as the markets and stores. the water supply, and the farm, of great significance to all persons. There are also certain significant forces or development which have exerted such profound influence on life that present living can be understood only as their influence is understood—for example, such forces and developments as the westward movement, the Industrial Revolution, the Reformation, and the scientific method. The type of unit here discussed employs these significant aspects of the environment or culture as the center of unit organization.

This type of unit has significant merits not possessed by the other types of subject matter units. The basis of organization is the significance of the material in exaplaining contemporary life. It well selected it is almost certain that the unit may be brought to have real meaning to a majority of learners. However, it must be emphasized that such units are selected because of their general significance, not because a particular group of children, in a particular school, at a particular time, would profit, in the judgment of the teacher, from such a unit. Thus, when this type of unit is employed, potential subject matter is the primary point of reference. Unit may be selected and organized in advance as they are to be taught and the same units may be taught again and again, thus permitting an inflexibility of instruction to develop unless carefully guarded against.

The greatest impetus to development of this type of unit has been afforded by the work of Henry C. Morrison. Morrison's definition of a unit is so broad as to include more than this one type of unit but much of the unit development encouraged by his work, especially in social science and general science, has been of this type. Morrison defines "the external things-to-be-learned" as *learning units*, and a serviceable learning unit as "a comprehensive and significant aspect of the environment, of an organized science, of an art, or of conduct, which being learned results in adaption in personality."

Four possible sources of unity of the "things-to-be-learned or potential subject matter are suggested by this definition. "The things-to-be-learned" may be related :

(*a*) because they are associated in the environment in a significant way, *e.g.* water mains, water supply, house connections, standpipe;

(*b*) because they are associated in a significant way in an organized science, *e.g.*, addition, subtraction, fractions ;

(*c*) because they represent a means of expression, *e.g.*, the novel, biography, sculpture ;

(*d*) because they are associated in a particular type of conduct, *e.g.*, sustained application, sense of duty, leadership. The first relationship or source of unity is the one that is the basis of the classification of units we are now discussing.

This type of unit organization is the most significant and forward looking of the three types classified under the subject mater heading. Reorganization of instruction on this basis has done much to vitalize teaching. Meaningless facts, useless information, and unimportant relationships tend to be eliminated. Learning by memory is thus reduced. There is little doubt that units of this type are a distinct advance over the traditional organization of instruction.

However, examination of the way such units are selected, organized, and taught shows that consideration of the learner is a secondary matter even in this unit. "The things-to be-learned still receive primary attention. The usual procedure is to select the units by examination and study of the environment and of given areas of culture. Those aspects considered sufficient significant are selected for units. The units are then arranged in courses. Having determined what to teach, the teacher then enters the classroom and turns attention to how to teach. In other words, when the teacher enters the classroom the problem becomes wholly one of method. No question is raised at this point concerning the interest or purpose of the child. It is, of course, better if he is interested, and the teacher will endeavor to find pleasant means of motivating the work, but in any event the unint is administered to the child. In fact, Morrison states that attention to subject matter which is intially unappealing is what is required. "Somebody," he states, "either parent or teacher, has to constrain and compel the pupil to the point at which this adaptation takes place."

Since the basis of this type of unit is found in potential subjeet matter, the units that fall within a given field tend to be the same, variations being due to inadequacy of techniques. This makes it possible to organize this type of unit in advance in all its details, to teach the same units again and again, and to assign a specific amount of time for the develoment of a unit. It follows that units are self-contained. They are good or poor solely because of relationships between the subject matter involved. They may be will or poorly taught but that in no way influences the intrinsic value and character of the unit.

Although this type of unit organization appears to the writers to be a distinct advance over the wholly logical and topical development of subject matter, there is one point inherent in the plan which, from the point of view presented in preceding chapters, is open to question. This relates to the source of unity of this type of unit.

The issue is this : Is it possible to find a real source of unity for organizing instruction outside the experience of the learner ? The fact that students of a subject matter field have found that a particular aspect of potential subject matter has general significance and involves essintial relationships does increase the chances that others, as they become students in the field, will find the material to be significant and to possess unity. But it does not necessarily follow that the aspect of the environment or of culture which is significant to a specialist or an adult will be significant to the non-specializiag student or to the immature individual. Neither does it follow necessarily that the unity which the special student sees in an aspect of the environment is brought to one's realization by direct consideration of the aspect.

In fact, it is entirely possible that direct consideration may be as barren in results as the piecemeal type of instructional organization which this type of unit supplants. Real unity enters when the individual or individuals dealing with the unit have an experiential background which makes the unit significant to them and causes them to hold a purpose or have a need which makes the subject matter used an integral part of experience. Lacking such a need or purpose the relationship or unity which is inevitable for the specialist in the field does not necessarily come to exist for the puil. In brief, unity cannot be determined without consideration of the learner. Go to use Morrison's terminology, what is a *comprehence and significant* aspect of the environment cannot be answered adequately unless considered in conjunction with the question, *for whom* ? It that aspect of the environment which is significant to the adult specializing student in a field significant to the immature student ? To illustrate, might not the chronological period 1800-1830 involve real unity for a graduate student in history, whereas it would be only a patchwork of facts for an undergaduate student ? Might not be Westward Movement involve real unity for a college student and not far a high-school student ? Might not Pushing Back the Frontier be a suitable unit for high-school pupils and not for elementary-school pupils ? But it may be said in answer to these questions, units are selected for students on particular levels.

This is true and a step in the right direction, but the situation is further complicated by differences in environment and the experiential backgrounds of children. No two groups of children on the same grade level may necessarilly be assumed to be equally prepared to undertake a particular unit. The result is that when teachers who are sensitive to pupil interest, needs, and abilities teach units with the same title, the content and organization in the different situations varies so greatly as to make them essentially different units. For example, the unit which Morrison outlines on the Water Supply is provided. But in a rural area this might or might not be a significant unit, and if it were significant it would be an entirely different unit from the one outlined.

Our conclusion is this. The aspects of the environment which the specialist or adult finds of general significance are suggestive areas in which units may be located, and hence provide valuable leads for units. Units may, in fact, frequently coincide with the areas thus indicated. But the type of unity which gives meaning to a series of activities cannot be found outside the experience of the learner and consequently, units even though within the same general area, will vary in organization and content as the experintial background, the purposes and needs, and the environment of learners vary.

UNIT BASED ON CENTER OF INTEREST

We know turn to the type of unit based on a center of interest. This type of unit falls under the general classifieation of experience units. Development of this type of unit may be largely attributed to Lincoln School of Teachers College, Columbia University. The account by the staff, published ten years after the opening of the school, of the procedures of curriculum making employed, gives a definition of units of work, criteria for selecting units of work, and a number of illustrative units. Units of work are defined as "the larger learning situations which will draw upon all phases of experience and make use of all kinds of subject matter. This definition, it will be noted, emphasizes the range of experience and subject matter involved as the determining characteristic of the unit. In *The Child-Central School*, however, published a year later, Rugg and Shumakar emphasize the point that difference in range of activities ....is only an obvious surface distinction between the unit of work and the school subject. The true difference," they state, "is found far deeper—in the realm of child interest." Definitions published at later dates by members of the Lincoln School staff also emphasize of child interest. Baxter, a member of the staff, in a discussion on selecting and teaching a unit of work, published in 1929, defined a unit of work as "the various experiences and activities of a grade which center around some on interest." Keelor and Sweet employ essentially the same definition in their publication of 1931. "A unit of work is a series of worth-while experiences bound together around some central theme of child interest." The dominating characteristic, then, of this type of unit appears to be the relationship of activities or experience to a central interest of the children.

Methods of selecting such units indicate how child interest is employed. Hopkings suggests three methods :

> First, the experiened teacher of a given grade recognizes certain areas in which the genuine interests of children of that age are usually located. She concludes that any unit of work within these areas will probably be developed wholeheartedly by the children. During the summer she selects tentatively and prepares herself to teach some unit which the believes will fall within the range of this interest. In this process of preparation, she lists all types of different possible activities to give breadth; she plans a number of orienting experiences as approaches ; she designates the subject matter most helpful in enriching the different activities ; she defines tentatives objectives to be achieved ; she indexes sources of materials for the pupils and for herself ; she anticipates the many questions which pupils will raise and plans means of helping them obtain materials with which to make intelligent answers ; she examines the unit with care to discover that richness so necessary to provide for differences in individual interests within the general unit and for individual abilities within those special interests ; she records all possible

opportunities for group drives and leads ; she acquires a knowlege of the subject matter so necessary to enable her to give intelligent guidance to pupils ; and finally, she examines the whole proposal with a most searching critical analysis to assure heself that the pupil learnings are socially and individually important both for the present and for the future, and are of greater value than some others which the unit replaces.

The teacher who uses the second method of selecting a unit may enter the classroom in the fall with no definite idea as to a unit of work for the year. She begins by accepting the interesting immediate and remote expriences of the children. The visit to the seashore during the summer suggests a study of sea life ; the trip to Europe calls for water transportation ; the vacation spent in the mountains creates some demand for a unit on science ; the summer on the farm leads toward farm life ; and, because of the already incipient tendency toward art, one individual student proposes a unit on murals. As these suggestions arise the teacher explores them to determine whether the interest of the group is genuine or cursory. She knows that her unit must be built upon incipient that interests that are or will develop into real, genuine, purposeful interests. She is skeptical of cursory, temporary, capricious interests. To distinguish between the two types she gives information about a suggested unit and arouses activity toward it through readings, excursions, motion pictures, and discussions. If the enthusiasm for water transportation subsides under the sunlight of information and activity, the teacher turns to another suggested unit and repeats the process of orientation. Through a period extending from two weeks to a month, there emerges a permanent interest which the teacher capaitalizes into a unit of work.

The third method of selecting a unit differs slightly from that of the other two. The teacher may examine the previous education of a group and decide that a certain unit is necessary to give richness, area, or breadth to their experience, or to fill in what appear to be important gaps. During the summer she will plan such a unit and begin the pupil orientation immediately after the opening of school. Such planning is always in relation to the interests and educational needs of the *particular group*, and is in no sense similar to a planned-in-advance curriculum to be followed by all teachers of a given grade in a large number of schools or school systems regardless of the previous educational experiences and present interest of the learners.

After the unit is selected, the children and the teacher decide what activities will be employed to satisfy their interest. As they carry out these activities new questions arise which require further activities. So long as each series of new activities leads to further questions and problems that fall in the general area of interest, the development of the unit continues. The variety and duration of activities which develop in this way are very great. Frequently the entire school year is required for one unit.

This method of development is well illustrated by Keelor and Sweet :

> . . . . suppose a group of children in interested in making toy sail-boats, an interest rather universally evident in younger children. As a group, they take a ride on a ferryboat and see various types of boats on the river. They increase their narrow sailboat interest to ask how each boat goes, where it goes, how the ships signal to each other. and many other questions connected with boat travel. One child decides to make a steamer ; another a tug. A third child makes a dock and a lighthouse. One becomes interested in the flags of various nations and their locaticn on the boats. The group sees a book called *The Story of the Ship* with pictures of boats of all ages. This fascinates them and they begin to draw

models of such historic ships as the "Santa Maria." They associate this experience with Columbus' voyage and the beliefs of his day concerning the shape of the earth. This leads to a score of other questions and stories until the interest in boats expands to include boats of all types and boats of all ages, and the people who built them. In this manner the children's first interest in making toy sailboats grows and grows with each fresh experience and each activity until in the end they have as a group gathered a most interesting fund of knowledge.

When new points cease to arise and the immediate desire for information is satisfied, summarizing activity is planned as a conclusion to the unit. The purpose of this activity is to organize the information gained into a related whole.

This type of instructional organization has probably stimulated, in recent years, more experimentation and advance in curriculum making than any other single development. New materials and varied activities have been brought into the instructional program. The needs and interests of children have been given more adequate consideration. The importance of environmental materials and of first-hand experience have been emphasized. Consequently, this is a type of instructional organization of outstanding significance. There are, however, a number of points about this type of unit which, from an analytical point of view, might be given critical consideration. The soundness of pupil interest as a basis for instructional organization and the disregard of subject organization are frequently questioned. These issues have already been considered in a general way in the preceding discussion, and, consequently, will not be treated here. The point, from the standpoint of organizing instruction, which requires special consideration is the source of unity of this type of unit.

The source of unity is the "central theme of child interest". Just what is this central theme of child interest ? Analysis of such units shows that it is an area or phase of culture within which there are activities and objects of interest to a given group of children. That is, the term "boats" suggests an area of culture which includes many objects and activities of interest to children, such as sailboats, ocean liners, taking boat rides, making boats, and stories of boats.

Now the question is this : Is there within such a culture area a dynamic unifying element which relates interests and activities in a fundamental way? The writers believe that there is not and that the mere fact that activities and content employed may be classified in this area in no way assures unity of experience. To be more specific, reading about boats, taking an excursion to see boats, and drawing pictures of boats are not necessarily related in a fundamental way in the learning situation merely because all of these activities deal with boats and the children are interested in each activity.

It should be recognized that good teachers, no matter what type of instructional organization is employed, tend to inject into learning situations, experiences which give real unity to learning. The development of many units of work of the type here discussed gives evidence of such unity. But the point we are considering is whether or not the real source of unity is in the classification of a variety of objects and activities of interests under a general heading which indicates an area of culture.

The conclusion stated above is based more upon observation of public school teachers who have attempted to develop units of this type than upon reports of such units as taught by artist teachers. As this type of unit is developed in general practice, one of two things frequently occurs. First, no thread runs through the unit that gives the activities vital relationship to each other and that makes one the inevitable outgrowth of the other.

The element is lacking that requires the constant integration of knowledge gained to carry the work forward, that indicates progress toward a desired end, and that gives the activities of one pupil a fundamental relationship to the activities of other pupils. Rather, the unit is apt to flow on and on more or less like the brook, activities being carried forward simply because a preceding activity has suggested them and the pupils think they would be interesting. There is frequently a tendency for aimless exploration of an area which has in it many interesting things. Like a Sunday visit to the museum, it is pleasant and worth while upon occasion, but is hardly the type of experience suitable for developing functional education. Critical consideration of the illustration presented previously from Keelor and Sweet will reveal this tendency even in it. The units of work presented in many courses of study have pronounced evidences of this characteristic.

Second, since immediate child interest tends to be emphasized, there is hardly any area of culture in which some activities of objects cannot be found in which children will not express at least a passing interest. This makes it relatively easy for a teacher to use the unit as a means of studying topics which, because of tradition, are considered good. That is, immediate child interest alone is not an adequate criterion for selection of units. The result is the development of many units that appear but little more functional than much study of logically organized subject matter. Units, for example, on Greek life, Roman life, Indians, Eskimos, Dutch life, and similar topics frequently have many of the earmarks of "well-motivated" instruction of the usual subject matter organization. Melvin emphasizes this point. He states of this types of unit as frebuently reported :

> . . . . one may often suspect that the units do not arise from a real life situation . . . . It seems hard to believe that small children can have the judgment, the knowledge, or the fixity of purpose to enable them to choose such a unit as Indian life and carry it through in its various implications through a month or two. One suspects, in such cases, that the work carried on is the teacher's opinion of what the children want, rather than the children's choice. Any skillful teacher may persuade a group of children, in a ten-minute talk, to embark on any

of half a dozen so-called units, from the study of the Eskimos to the building of a tunnel in the schoolyard. Is the unifying principle here the children's need and purpose, or is it the teacher's concept of some extensive unit of work ?

UNIT BASED ON PUPIL PURPOSE

In the unit based on pupil purpose a series of activities are engaged in to achieve an end or outcome which the learner considers worth while and wishes to achieve. Activities and subject matter are selected with this end in view. The entire course of the unit is planned to achieve the desired outcome. Activities are intimately related to each other, not because one suggests another, but because each takes a place in contributing to a common end. As pointed out in Chapter VIII, interest is the condition out of which purposes arise. In this type of unit there is an inevitable point of culmination when the children have achieved their purpose to their present satisfaction. The unit may be long or short, depending upon the willingness of the children to work for deferred values.

Purpose as a basis for instructional organization was emphasized by Kilpatrick in his *Foundations of Method.* It was made one of the determining characteristics of the project. As developed in this connection the concept of purpose was sometime limiting in nature. Emphasis was frequently placed on objective evidences or outcomes of purposes. The tendency thus was to eliminate intellectual curiosity and creative impulses from the category of purposes. Frequently also no distinction was made as to quality of purposes ; for example, in connection with clarity of perception of desired ends, variety and complexity of activities required, and persistency of effort necessitated.

The result of this tendency was a rather general association of purpose with the project method and, as the popularity of projects waned, purpose received less considera- tion. Gradually, however, as units of work (unit based on centers of interest) have developed it has been emphasized by various students of instructional organization that some force other than interest alone must be found to provide the essential unity for an instructional unit. Purpose, as a result, has again received emphasis, this time in connection with experience units.

The utility and soundness of purpose as the basis for unit organization is determined by the care with which the concept is defined. If it is conceived merely as a general term to which a variety of meanings can be ascribed, no common basis for unit organization is provided. Furthermore, if distinctions are not made as to quality of purposes, anything may be permitted to find its way into the curriculum. But with recognition of purpose as an integral part of the process of all conscious behavior, and as such, interpreted in this broad relationship rather than as a mere aspect of a method, purpose takes on real meaning as a basis of unit organization. When so conceived its peculiar characteristics must be outlined in order that a basis may be established for judging what purposes provide a suitable basis for developing units. In a preceding chapter, the nature of purpose was discussed and criteria for evaluating purposes were defined. It was concluded that the type of purpose that may be described by the term *dominating* provides a suitable basis for developing the major experimental phase of the instructional program. Instruction so developed by considered an experience unit based on purpose.

Obviously, units of this type differ with different groups of children and under varying conditions. What may be a significant purpose for one group of fourth-grade children will not necessarily be significant for another group. This point of view is sometimes interpreted to mean that units based on pupil purpose can be developed without regard to any limitations. This, however, is not the case. If the scope of the curriculum is outlined with due regard to pupil interest on the various levels, there will be no difficulty in developing such units within the limitations thus provided. For example, the limitation for the work of the seventh grade in the Virginia state curriculum is Social Provision for Co-operative Living. The environmental conditions of certain schools in the tidewater area might make a unit on Coast Guards suitable, while in the mountain region a unit on the Forest Ranger Service would be appropriate. Yet the same generalizations concerning organized provision for protection of life and property would be involved in the two units.

Illustrations of units of this type must, be course, be taken from specific situations and must be reports of the units as developed. Units reported by Mapes and Harap are illustrations of this type.

UNIT BASED ON PUPIL NEEDS

Need has been emphasized by some students of instructional organization as a sound basis for unit development. As in the case of emphasis on purpose, stress on need has been in part a reaction from units based on centers of interest. For example, Melvin, who is perhaps the leading exponent of need as the basis of unit organization, says :

> Several objections which may be levelled at these longer units make one suspect that they are really little more than a fad of organization, a device or scheme which provides a logical basis for the organization of ideas.

Finding the center of interest an inadequate source of unity, vital life situations were examined to discover what element in them is accountable for the vitality and unity. Melvin concludes that this element is the need of the individual or group engaged in the activity. He developed on this basis the concept of the "unit of conduct" or "unit of life." He describes the basis of this development as follows :

> I have suggested that the root and origin of the unit of life is not to be found in the *purpose*, but rather in the *need*. Consequently, the unit of conduct is to be regarded as an act which may be analyzed into the five processes of needing, purposing, planning, executing, and using or evaluating. More important than this analysis, however,

is the fact that each of these processes throughout the progress of the whole unit is dominated, directed, and governed by the original need. It is the need which is the unifying principle within the unit of conduct. It is the binding force which is analogous to the force of cohesion in the granite unit of the stone wall. Thus when an individual feels the need of a window box to brighten up the front of his house, he plans for it, goes through the necessary steps to secure it, puts it in place on the house, and passes judgment upon it, all in terms of his original need. It is the original need which is the rise and the cohesive principle of a unit of living. So when the child in school feels the need of a window box for the school, he may carry out in school a unit of conduct which is analogous to a unit of conduct in the world outside the school, an act which it a real unit of living because it is unified by a fundamental need.

Conduct units are classified into various types. The diagram reproduced below indicates the important types.

Types of Conduct Units :

	Constructive	*Play*	*Work*
Physical—	Making a Table	Swimming	Sawing Wood
Mental—	Writing a Poem	Reading a Story	Balancing Accounts

Wynne also emphasizes need as the sound basis for unit organization. He suggests that the usual concept of purpose is too limited and that "experienced need" provides for essential expansion of the concept. He does state, however, that the enlarged interpretation currently given to the concept of purpose makes it sufficiently broad to provide a basis for unit organization.

The organism whose life processes continue of function normally makes no change in his way of behaving, But whenever any disturbance occurs from within or from without, he moves in consequence of the lack which thus appears. He tends to move in the direction of restoring the normalcy that has been lost. This movement toward the restoration of a lost equilibrium is now called a purpose. But of course this is not the same thing as the conception of conscious purpose. It may reach the level of consciousness but it does not have to be conscious.

This condition of lack or loss of balance may be designated as experienced need. In point of time, this precedes the purpose even in this new sense. It is sometimes called felt need, but feeling implies consciousness and the mere loss of balance is not always conscious in the ordinary sense. It seems better designated as experienced need when experience signifies all the behavior of the organism. This seems to be the only sense in which experienced need is commonly employed. The principle of purpose referring to the movement toward a progressive balance or the experienced need preceding such purposeful activity thus seems to be the principle of method that is now required. Either the new conception of purpose or the conception of experienced need may be employed ; either is scientifically sound. But it must be admitted without question that the principle here defined is a different conception. This new meaning of purpose is different from the older conception. The two meanings of purpose would doubtless cause considerable confusion. We should put new wine into new bottles if we wish to save either the wine or the bottles. For us, experienced need is the new bottle. However, the main consideration is not the word, but the meaning attached to it. Any expression may be used in logical discussion if we are careful to define our terms. But the use of the word purpose to express the new meaning will not likely avoid the confusion that will result from a misinterpretation that such a double meaning makes probable.

The question as to the relative merits of purpose and need as a basis for unit organization is then one which involves highly theoretical distinctions. It seems clear that in both concepts emphasis is given to the initial phase of a particular aspect of behavior. Adequate description and illustration of this phase of behavior is unquestionably much more important than the term employed to designate the phase. In all probability a unit considered good by those who hold purpose as the unifying element of learning would also be considered good by those who emphasize need. The opposite would likewise be the case.

SUMMARY OF TYPES OF UNITS

Contrast between the various types of units are presented in brief form in Chart VIII. Five points are given consideration ;

(1) source of unity,
(2) illustrative sources for units,
(3) provision for planning,
(4) sequence, and
(5) length.

It will be observed that major differences in the first two items are found between all types of units, whereas in the last three items subject matter units differ little and experience units differ although the two large classifications differ radically.

GIVEN UNITS MAY MEET THE REQUIREMENTS OF MORE THAN ONE TYPE OF UNIT

It should have become clear from preceding chapters that unity or wholeness, considered philosophically or psychologically, is a particular characteristic of experience. Whether or not a given experience possesses this quality depends upon the dominance of a particular element. It was further shown that this element is *purpose*. Consequently, the fundamental basis of instructional organization appears to be *pupil purpose*. We might conclude that instructional units will possess unity only as it is provided by the purpose of the learner or learners. Thus the type of instructional organization described in the preceding chapter as the major experiential phase is based upon experience units which assume purpose to be the source of unity.

It should be noted, however, that additional controls of instructional organization are provided by other aspects of curriculum making. For example, in defining the scope of the curriculum by the social functions approach, the work for the respective grades is limited to areas in which pupils find many objects and activities of interest. Thus, the limitation of the "center of interest" is imposed also on instructional organization. It will be further noted that only areas are selected for centers of interest which are significant aspects of the environment or of culture. Thus, a further limitation is imposed. Consequently, although purpose appears to be the sound basis of unity for a unit of work, a good unit wlll be required by the method of defining scope to fall within an area which represents a center of interest of the pupils and to be of general social significance. Other requirements for Effective units, it will be recalled, are presented in Chart VI.

CRITERIA FOR EVALUATING UNITS

Criteria for evaluating experience units based on purpose are suggested in the chart just mentioned and are discussed in the preceding chapter. Criteria for evaluating other types of units obviously will be different as the basic concepts of unit organization vary. Consequently, in selecting criteria for evaluating units, care should be exercised to see that the criteria are for the type of unit it is desired to develop. Criteria are presented which have been proposed by various authorities and curriculum committees. Study of these will help to clarify concepts of various types of units.

Morrison's definition suggests two criteria for a "learning unit" : 1. The unit is comprehensive. 2. The unit is significant. He explains these terms as follows ;

CHART VIII

Characteristics of Units of Various Types

Type of Unit	*Source of Unity*	*Illustrative Sources for Units*	*Provision for Planning*	*Sequence*	*Length*
1	2	3	4	5	6
I. Subject Matter :					
A. Topical	**A. Sequential relationship between items of subject matter.**	**A. American Revolution, Colonial Period, invertebrates, fractions.**	**A. Planning consists largely of assigning parts of the topic to be studied or pages in the text to be read. The text provides the basic organization.**	**A. A given sequence of units and material within each unit essential.**	**A. Longer than the individual assignment but otherwise may be any length. May be predetermined and uniform if desired.**

1	2	3	4	5	6
B. Generalization	B. Relationship of all materials to one generalization, principle, or law.	B. All bodies of the universe move in as orderly manner; the sun is the source of all energy; man's conception of truth changes; man tends to move from place to place is search of better ways of living; the volume of a gas at constant temperature varies inversely with the pressure.	B. May be planned in detail in advance. The extent to which the teacher must plan the organization is determined largely by the subject. Much more basic planning is required in social studies than in science because of the way in which texts in these fields are organized.	B. Sequence of units may be arranged in advance but may vary somewhat from time to time. Sequence within a unit may be varied.	B. Length will vary. May be approximated in advance.
C. Significant aspect of	C. Relationship of aspect of culture or	C. Industrial Revolution, immigration,	C. May be planned in detail in ad-	C. Sequence of units and with-	C. Assigned proportionate

(*Contd.*)

1	2	3	4	5	6
culture or environment.	environment to race development or contemporary life.	education, crime, machine production.	vance. Use of a great variety of sources is required. Consequently, effectiveness is conditioned very materially by teacher plans.	in units may be planned in advance but variation is possible.	time in coarse importance appears to merit. May be approximated in advance.
II. Experience :					
A. Center of Interest	A. Interest of children in activities and objects that may be classified under one heading.	A. Objects and activities in which children are interested; such as Indians, Eskimos, boats, trains, airplanes, games, and fire departments.	A. Continuous planning is required. Day by day developments are highly significant.	A. Sequence cannot be planned in advance.	A. Tend to extend over long periods. Sometimes an entire school year is devoted to one unit.

1	2	3	4	5	6
B. Pupil Purpose	B. The purpose or interest of the pupils to achieve a given end.	B. Purposes arise from interests. Interest in a fire may lead to the purpose of finding out how the fire department operates, interest in sickness to the purpose of eliminating sources of contagion, interest in new types of goods to finding out how they are made and how they may best be used.	B. Continuous planning is required. The teacher must be thoroughly familiar with all limitations on the curriculum and the interests and abilities of the children. Plans must be highly flexible within these limits.	B. Sequence cannot be planned in advance, although general areas may be indicated for work in various grades and points of emphasis suggested for work in a grade.	B. Tend to be short for immature pupils and increase in length as maturity approaches. The time required to realize the purpose determines length. Different units may vary greatly in leagth.
C. Pupil Need	C. A need which the pupil recognizes.	C. Need to make purchases, to select food, to read, to keep personal accounts.	C. Continuous planning is required. Students must be studied carefully.	C. Sequence cannot be planned in advance, although it may be anticipated if a group of children is well known.	C. Tend to be comparatively short.

"COMPREHENSIVE."—The term "comprehensive" means that the unit must have wide connotations in order that it may be an economical feature in the program. For example, the *Westward Movement* as a unit in American history is comprehensive because it explains so much *The Banking Policy of Jackson* would satisfy the requirements of a unit, since it suggests an understanding or insight, but it would not serve as a feasible unit in the secondary school for the reason that it explains relatively little of our history.

It is this test of comprehensiveness which explains why it is that a unit in the early secondary school may become a full course at the end of that period, and a broad field of professional study in the university.

"SIGNIFICANT."—The unit must be not only comprehensive but significant, that is, it must be important in the field of general education. *Indirect discourse* is comprehensive but it shrinks to the immaterial in educational significance compared with *reading ability*, because it contributes little or nothing to fundamental adjustment.

Melvin's discussion suggests nine criteria for a "unit of living or conduct."

1. The circumstances from which the unit of conduct arises must be a real life situation.

2. The unit of conduct must ... be one which contributes to the growth and development of habits, skills, knowledges, procedures, and ideals which will with a high degree of probability be used by the children in the important activities of life.

3. Units of conduct ... should be of a length which makes possible the children's unified comprehension of them, and should be of a duration which is carefully planned in relation to the other work of the class.

4. Units of conduct ... should not be based on occasional child interest, but on more deeply rooted and firm interest.

5. Units of conduct must provided activities which are appropriate to the children's level of growth, and which are of suitable difficulty.

6. Suitable units of conduct should lead in the direction of curriculum goals.

7. Units of conduct should be related to the other work of the class and to that of the school in general. ...

8. In theie progress and development, units of conduct should proceed within the limits of available and established knowledge, and in accordance with sound standards of scholarship.

9. The balanced use of all types of conduct units should be provided.

In 1926 the Lincoln School staff gave eight criteria for a unit of work :

I. The unit of work must be selected from real life situations and must be considered worth while by the child because he feels that he has helped select in and because he finds in it many opportunities to satisfy his needs.

II. The unit of work must afford many opportunities for real purposing and real projects, and it will be something which the child can carry into his normal activity.

III. The unit of work must stimulate many kinds of activities and so provide for individual differences.

IV. *a.* The units of work must make individual growth possible.

b. The succession of units of work must provide for continuous group growth from one level to the next.

V. Each unit of work must furnish leads into other related units of work and must stimulate in the child the desire for a continued widening of his interests and understanding.

VI. Each unit of work must help meet the demands of society and must help clarify social meanings.

VII. Each unit of work must be accompanied by progress in the use of such tool subjects as contribute to that unit.

VIII. Each unit of work must lead to the development of desirable habits.

Barnes and Young reporting a unit of work on architecture give the following criteria as the basis of evaluating the unit :

I. Does the material come near enough to the child for it to be real to him ?

II. Does the unit give opportunities for real intellectual pursuit on the child's present mental level ?

III. Does the unit stimulate many kinds of activities, thus providing for individual differences ?

IV. Does the unit bring about growth from the present growth level to the next step ?

V. Does the unit stimulate a desire on the part of the individual to proceed on his own initiative ?

VI. Does the unit furnish a real intellectual content, thus aiding in building a cultural background ?

The Teachers' Guide to Child Development sets forth the following criteria for evaluating an activity. Acitivity is given the same meaning as unit of work.

1. Is the activity closely related to the child's life so as to lead him to want to carry it through ?

2. Is it sufficiently within the range of accomplishment of the learner to insure a satisfactory degree of success ?

3. It is so varied from the previous activity as to permit the child's all-round development ?

4. Does it furnish opportunities for many kinds of endeavour ?

5. Does the subject matter involved present major fields of human achievement ?

6. Does the activity involve an extension of present insight and abilities ?

7. Does it provide an opportunity for social contacts ?

8. Will it lead into other profitable activities ?

Harap gives the following criteria :

1. It should involve a variety of direct sensory experiences.

2. It should provide for some free, informal association of the pupils.

3. It should provide an opportunity for manipulative or bodily activity.

4. The parts of the unit should make a coherent whole.

5. It should provide a considerable amount of pupil activity.

6. It should be satisfying or the anticipation of the outcome should be satisfying.

7. It should provide sufficient concrete and illustrative material.

8. The unit of work should have a useful purpose in the present or future life of the pupil.

9. It should reproduce actual life situations, as far as possible.

10. It should utilize materials as they occur in life.

11. It should contain accurate information.

12. It should provide an opportunity for the pupil to originate, plan, and direct the activity, as far as possible.

13. It should provide opportunities to judge, choose, and evaluate.

14. It should be within the available time for the unit.

15. The exposition should be clear enough to make it possible for a new teacher to put the unit in practice, if she so desires.

16. It should state clearly where materials may be obtained.

17. When references are given, they should be complete and exact.

Hopkins presents the following criteria as a partial list to serve as a means of evaluating units of work in connection with a project of the Society for Curriculum Study :

1. *Are there experiences under way that promote growth in habits of critical inquiry* ?

Is there experimental living and investigation—tentative choice of hypotheses—study of all pertinent issues, selection of most promising leads ?

Are there needed skills for experimentation ?

Are conclusions made in terms of consideration of all available issues and evidence ?

Is there growth in questioning and answering questions ?
Is there critical use of experts and sources ?

Is there sensitivity to important issues ?

Is there concern for the welfare of the larger group ?

Is there willingness and effort to relinquish disproved convictions ?

Are there attitudes of openmindedness, fearlessness and sincerity ?

Is there proper regard for pertinent issues from the past ?

Are conclusions held tentatively ?

2. *Do the activities under way offer opportunity for experience in many kinds of meaningful endeavor through physical and social media* ?

Do the activities offer fullness of experience ?

Do the members of the group use materials to best advantage according to their growing standards ?

Is there opportunity for experience in leading an following ?

Is there appropriate use of relevant tool subjects when the need and opportunity for use arises ?

Is the curriculum such that formal lines are dispensed with in order to permit expression to the full ?

Is there experimentation, exploration, investigation, and evaluation in various fields ?

Is there co-operative group living ?

Is full use made of individuals' observations as media of experience and expression ?

3. *Are the activities under way such that the individual may discover his interests or tendencies* ?

Is there sensitivity to problems and suggestions in the environment ?

Are there some experiences which tend to identify individuals with special interests—hobbies ?

Is there interchange of thought ?

Are the ideas, opinions and suggestions of others considered ?

Is there respect for the purposes, ideals, wishes, dreams and capacities of individuals and groups ?

Is there co-operative group living ?

Do individuals possess adequate skills for discovering their interests and tendencies ?

Is there leadership by individuals with the ability to identify with the purposes, ideals and wishes of the individual and the group to carry these forward ?

Is there adequate and timely use of experts and sources ?

Is there the experimental mode of living ?

4. *Do the experiences under way impel the members of the group on into increasingly challenging endeavor* ?

Are learnings an intrinsic outgrowth of the learner's experience ?

Are present experiences suggestive of next steps ?

Are leads to further activities vigorously prosecuted ?

Are previous experiences used as sources of data ?

Is there experimental living ?—are new leads pursued tentatively, are pertinent and comprehensive data considered, are unworthy leads thus rejected ?

Does the learner choose ways and means of work within his control ?

Are the learners acquiring adequate tools to pursue increasingly challenginly and demanding endeavors ?

5. *Are there experiences under way that promote sharing of experiences through social participation* ?

Is there appreciation of the opinions and ideas of others ?

Is there co-operative group living ?

Is there diversity of experiences ?

Is there recognition of responsibility in the group for leading and following ?

Is the group developing standards of social control ?

Do members of the group share in planning the life of their social group ?

Do members of the group share their imaginative and play lives ?

Is there sensitivity to group interests and needs ?

Is there experimental living—planning, trying out leads, evaluating ?

Do individuals seek assistance from the social group and give assistance when needed ?

6. *Will the learners acquire increasing freedom to order there own experiences through effective assumption of responsibilities* ?

Is the assistance of experts and sources sought and used ?

Are more adequate tools and meanings sought and acquired ?

Is there increasing ability and disposition to use controls ?

Is there a desire for richer living ?

Are individuals developing a perspective sufficient for awareness of significant successes and failures and facing squarely and impersonally situations and their implications ?

Is there relevant use of past experience ?

Is there due regard for personality values and individual abilities by all members of group ?

The Raleigh, North Carolina, curriculum committees set up criteria as follows :

1. The unit of work must be selected from *real life situations*; that is, it must be related to the *present living* experience of the *children*, not of *adults*.

The activity should appeal to children's interests and should not only satisfy *present* needs, but should contribute to some of the larger needs of life, as health, citizenship, group relationship, pride in school conduct, the wise use of leisure time.

2. A unit that is worth while should be hard enough to challenge and at the same time easy enough to ensure some degree of success.

Good questions to ask in this connection are, Does the activity present too many difficulties ? Is it beyond the abilities of the children ? An activity should be suited to the state of development of the child. To be really worth while it should require real effort on the part of the children and should call for thinking as well as for manual effort.

3. The unit of work must stimulate many kinds of activities so as to provide for individual differences.

In order to do this, the unit must have some easier possibilities than others. The teacher should so guide the work that each child will get something to do that will bring him satisfaction. It is the doing of a thing *successfully* that brings satisfaction, although *failure* for some individuals may mean *growth.*

The unit should challenge initiative and resourcefulness; should give opportunity for growth in leadership, and in independence. in ability to assume responsibility; it should stimulate the exercise of judgment on the part of the children, and the ability to plan things for themselves; it should tend to real investigation, to perseverance. An activity should have holding power.

4. A unit should lead on to other worth-while activities —make the child want to do something bigger; tend to increase appreciation of worth-while things.

A unit is not very big that does not cause the group to ask questions; it should foster an inquiring, investigating attitude. It shold lead to other related units. When we leave a unit it should be with the feeling that here is a field that is interesting enough for further reading and study.

5. Is the unit practicable under school conditions ? A unit should not be undertaken unless materials and helps are available for carrying it out.

6. Will the unit contribute to the child's efficiency ? Will it develop good habits, desirable attitude, efficiency in some of the tool subjects, or provide opportunity for exercise of specific ethical habits, as thrift, promptness, obedience, courtesy, honesty ?

The activity should bring about the right attitude of the child to the members of the group and help him to become a contributing member of the group. It should encourage co-operation. It should enrich the child's experience - make him realize the work of others in making his life comfortable and happy and what the past has contributed to his present environment.

ILLUSTRATIVE MATERIALS

As has been shown, some types of unit organization make it impossible to teach the same units again and again or under different environmental conditions. Other types of units, on the other hand, may be essentially the same under any conditions. In either case, however, illustrative units are helpful to teachers and curriculum workers in developing units suitable for their own situations. There are many sources of such materials.

The Morrison "learning units" are illustrated as well as discussed in *The Practice of Teaching in the Secondary School.* This source may be supplemented by a series of bulletins developed at the University of Chicago which contain *Student's Guide Sheets* for the development of certain courses. The University of Virginia Department of Education has emphasized the development of this type of unit with work allocated to three levels of difficulty. A series of illustrative units are given in an issue of the *University of Virginia Record Extension Series.*

There are many illustrations of "units of work," as developed at the Lincoln School. *Curriculum Making in an Elementary School* by the Lincoln School staff includes a number of illustrative units. However, a more recent and adequate source of illustration is the series of Lincoln School Curriculum Studies. One or two units of work are reported per volume. These reports are carefully prepared accounts of units as actually taught in Lincoln School. The following volumes are available : Barnes and Young, *Children and Architecture*; Baxter and Young, *Ships and Navigation*; Eakright and Young, *Adventuring with Toys*; Hughes, *Carrying the Mail*; Keelor and Sweet, *Indian Life and the Dutch Colonial Settlement*; Sweeney and others, *Western Youth Meets Eastern Culture*; Wright, *A First Grade at Work.*

The California *Teachers' Guide to Child Development* includes many illustrative units. Waddell, Seeds, and White report in detail three intermediate grade units of work developed at the Elementary School of the University of California at Los Angeles.

Mapes and Harap report six units of work in arithmetic in a bulletin of the Curriculum Laboratory of Western Reserve University. These are good illustrations of shorter units which emphasize lifelike situations and center largely in one subject field.

McCall and Crabbs edit a series of lesson units that are published by the Bureau of Publications of Teachers College, Columbia University. Units for all grades and subjects, and of all types, are included in the series. The units are reports of work actually done in classrooms. The descriptions are in small paper-backed bulletins varying in size, most of them being from twenty-five to fifty pages in length. The cost is twenty-five cents each. Since all types of units are included it is necessary in using these bulletins to select those which illustrate the type of organization desired.

F.E. Compton & Company publish a series of units under the title, *Compton's Pictured Teaching-Unit Materials.* A booklet and a series of pictures are presented as helps for developing units. The booklet includes "subject matter, generalizations, objectives, approaches, and activities." Units are available on such subjects as *Coal and Iron*, *Switzerland*, *Middle Ages* and *Land Transportation.*

In addition to sources such as the foregoing especially designed to provide illustrative units while others present units worked out in detail. An extensive list of units and sources of units may be secured from the *Catalog* prepared by Carey, Hanna, and Meriam.

PLANNING FOR UNITS

All types of units require more extensive planning than does instruction organized by recitations. In subjcct matter units the planning may be done in advance with considerable precision and plans once developed may be employed with different groups. Consequently, in organizing this type of unit, the initial planning is of primary importance.

In developing experience units, continuous planning is of supreme importance, Careful initial planning is required for each group that is taught, and after a unit is initiated the planning must continue throughout the development of the unit. The achievements or failures of each day's work modify what is to be done the next day. Consequently, planning of experience units has two major aspects. Initial planning involves laying out the general lines along which the unit may develop and suggesting the available resources for development. Continuous planning involves developing the detailed procedures and steps to be employed from day to day, and adjusting these as demanded by the progress of the work. The kind of planning is aided by the use of a form of work sheet such as that reproduced in Chart VII and discussed in Chapter XIV.

As efforts are made to aid teachers in planning units of the experience type, it should be held in mind that flexibility is the absolute requirement of these units, both as to planning and development. Consequently, no fixed method of planning should be required.

REPORTING UNITS

Effective develapment of a program of curriculum making which involves units of work depends to a great extent upon reports of units as they developed in classrooms. It is from such reports that the major portion of instructional materials presented in courses of study should come. Consequently, it is important that attention be given to the method of reporting units. There are a number of items that should be given consideration in such report. The outline that follows provides one basis for reporting.

Suggestive Outline for Reporting a Unit

I. The setting

In order to understand how a unit develops and why certain things are done, the reader needs to know the setting in which the unit is developed. The type of school situation, the physical equipment available, major environmental factors, outstanding abilities, disabilities, and interests of the children, previous work undertaken, and other such items should be described. In so far as possible, the effort should be to lead the reader to see the important aspects of the situation with which the teacher has to work.

II. Initial planning

This section of the report should describe how the teacher undertakes to discover the educational possibilities of the situation. Ways in which pupil interests are canvassed and evaluated should be described, and studies of the educational resources of the community and school should be reported. It should further be shown how the teacher deduced from these studies that a certain unit might be undertaken profitably by the children.

The teacher should then show in the report how preliminary plans for the work were made. This should include objectives which the unit could be expected to achieve, activities that might be employed in developing the unit, references, environmental materials, and construction materials available for use, possible ways of starting the unit, and the general line or lines of development the unit might take.

III. *Starting the unit*

There are many ways of starting a unit. It may result from an unusual or unexpected incident, it may result directly from work the children have done previously at school, it may be stimulated by something that is happening in the community, or it may result from deliberate stage-setting by the teacher. In reporting a unit an effort should be made to describe accurately just how the unit started, and to give an idea of the intensity and extent of interest at that time. Methods employed to develop a general group interest should be described. There should also be given the reason the teacher believed the unit as initiated would rest on a fundamental interest of the children.

IV. *Description of development of the unit*

This section of the report should contain an account of the unit in narrative form. Just how did the unit progress from day to day? What difficulties were encountered? What outstanding successes were achieved? What were the peculiar problems involved in directing the unit? What modifications in initial plans were required? What materials, references, and activities were employed? These represent the type of question that should be answered by the description of the development of the unit.

It is important that such an account be based on a carefully kept diary of the unit and that an effort be made to give an impartial picture of the work. Unless care is exercised in this regard, the description may be distorted by over-emphasis of good points and of points of minor significance.

V. Conclusion of the unit

The conclusion of the unit may be described either as a part of the development of the unit or given emphasts under a a separate heading. Concluding a unit so that it is a well-rounded, complete undertaking is very important. A direct tie-up should be made with the purposes for which the unit was initiated, and the culminating activities should represent the acme of satisfaction upon achievement of these puprposes. However, not only success should be emphasized. A good conclusion of a unit of work will also recognize any failures to achieve desired outcomes, and will emphasize what was learned as a means of doing various activities in most effective ways. In brief, the conclusion should represent the general evaluation of the unit by the children. It should provide the high point of satisfaction, and at the same time give opportunity to detere-mine how the undertaking or similar undertakings might be done more effectively.

This narrative form can be used to best advantage for reporting the conclusion, as is also true the section on development of the unit.

VI. Report of outcomes

It is important that the account of the unit include a list of the outcomcs realized. It is desirable to list the outcomes in as specific terms as possible, and to give the evidence upon which the teacher concludes that the outcome has been achieved. Evidence may be noted from such sources as observation of pupil behavior, informal tests, and standard tests. It may also be desirable to indicate the relationship of the outcomes to the aims set up for the unit and the subject fields in which the outcomes may be classified. A major portion of this section may be presented in outline form although ample description and illustration should be included. The tests, of all types, employed may well be described and illustrated.

An illustrative outline for reporting the outcomes of a unit follows ;

Outcomes of Uunt

Outcome	*Evidence of Achievement*	*Subject to Which Outcome Relates*	*Aim to Which Outcome Relates*
Children Co-operate much more effectively than before.	Records of development of unit show 23 special situations in which outstanding co-operative efforts were present. Only three cases are recorded in which lack of co-operation was pronounced.	**All socieal sciences primarily**	**(6) +ability to work as a group more effectively**
Ability to spell and use correctly the following new words : industrial, research, administration, administrative government, etc.	Ninety per cent of the words were used by the children correctly in papers, bulletins, and pamphlets which they prepared. A test in spelling	**Spelling**	**(8) *ability to spell and use new words that will be required by this unit, such as government, administration, etc.**

	showed that the children could spell from 95 to 100 per cent of these words correctly.	

(Other outcomes to be listed similarly)
+Coded to aims listed for the unit in initial planning.

VII. Bibliographies and materials

In this section should be given the references and materials used in developing the unit. It will be found helpful to divide the references into 'pupil references' and 'teacher references.' Each of these lists may profitably be divided into two or three parts, *e.g.*, "most valuable, valuable, not satisfactory."

VIII. Leads to other units

Finally, it will be found valuable to indicate in brief form interests that have been developed through the unit that promise to lead on to other work. Only interests that are really promising leads should be noted.

PLACE OF THE UNIT IN CURRICULUM DEVELOPMENT

We have devoted a great deal of space to the organization of instruction, types of units, and steps in planning and reporting units. This has been done because instructional organization is the crux of curriculum development. It is at this point more than any other that programs fail to achieve the purposes for which curriculum work is undertaken. Frequently, good statements of aims are given, long lists of principles are set forth, elaborate discussion of the need for "education for a new social order" is presented, but when instructional materials are finally presented and organized, tradition rules rather than the introductory statements and considerations. Consequently, it is highly important in curriculum development that the type of instructional organization adopted be compatible with the avowed philosophy of the program. It is in this stage of curriculum development, being closest to the classroom, that philosophy or point of view may really become operative,